returning
frankie's
rocks

returning frankie's rocks

*How a Son's Journey
into the Heart of
Compulsive Collecting
Led Him Back to His Mother*

dana hornig

Jeremy P. Tarcher/Penguin
a member of Penguin Group (USA) Inc.
New York

JEREMY P. TARCHER/PENGUIN
Published by the Penguin Group
Penguin Group (USA) Inc., 375 Hudson Street, New York, New York 10014, USA · Penguin
Group (Canada), 10 Alcorn Avenue, Toronto, Ontario M4V 3B2, Canada (a division of Pearson
Penguin Canada Inc.) · Penguin Books Ltd, 80 Strand, London WC2R 0RL, England · Penguin
Ireland, 25 St Stephen's Green, Dublin 2, Ireland (a division of Penguin Books Ltd) · Penguin
Group (Australia), 250 Camberwell Road, Camberwell, Victoria 3124, Australia (a division of
Pearson Australia Group Pty Ltd) · Penguin Books India Pvt Ltd, 11 Community Centre,
Panchsheel Park, New Delhi–110 017, India · Penguin Group (NZ), Cnr Airborne and Rosedale
Roads, Albany, Auckland 1310, New Zealand (a division of Pearson New Zealand Ltd) · Penguin
Books (South Africa) (Pty) Ltd, 24 Sturdee Avenue, Rosebank, Johannesburg 2196, South Africa

Penguin Books Ltd, Registered Offices: 80 Strand, London WC2R 0RL, England

An application has been submitted to register
this book with the Library of Congress.

ISBN 1-58542-416-1

Printed in the United States of America
10   9   8   7   6   5   4   3   2   1

Book design by Meighan Cavanaugh

Most Tarcher/Penguin books are available at special quantity discounts for bulk
purchase for sales promotions, premiums, fund-raising, and educational needs. Special
books or book excerpts also can be created to fit specific needs. For details, write
Penguin Group (USA) Inc. Special Markets, 375 Hudson Street, New York, NY 10014.

For Frankie

Fa-yen, a Chinese Zen teacher, overheard four monks arguing about subjectivity and objectivity. He joined them and said, "There is a big stone. Do you consider it to be inside or outside your mind?" One monk replied, "From the Buddhist viewpoint everything is an objectification of mind, so I would say that the stone is inside my mind." Replied Fa-yen, "Your head must feel very heavy if you are carrying around a stone like that in your mind."

—TRADITIONAL ZEN STORY

contents

returning
frankie's
rocks

prologue: jewels

 One summer, I discovered my mother's remarkable rock collection. Not the ordinary one. She had one of those, too. This was the other one. Her clandestine collection.

I found it in the loft over the cottage garage, behind a steamer trunk loaded with lace and fabric remnants and a pedal-powered Singer sewing machine covered with mouse droppings, next to twine-tied bundles of *Life* and *Look* magazines covering the Kennedy years, and *National Geographics* going back to before my birth. In black Magic Marker, the box was labeled "Rock Collection."

I was engrossed in one of the unenviable duties of children, deciding what to do with a lifetime's accumulation of possessions after the death of a parent. In this case the possessions of my mother, Frankie. Frankie had surely accumulated her share of stuff, and then some. Enough for a dozen normal humans. Sorting through it all had yielded little. The rock collection that I had found days before in the basement of the main house was your standard collection of shales and schist, garnets and feldspars, adamite and dolomite. Nothing special.

At first glance, the second rock collection seemed more of the same. Inside the carton were a bunch of seemingly nondescript stones. Unremarkable, until I picked one up and turned it over. I felt my face blanch, like when you witness a bad accident, or see a ghost. This wasn't more junk, or even more mineral samples. I had found something unique. Something special. Something secret.

Hand-lettered on the stone in fading ink was the notation *Tintagel Castle.*

Frankie had been obsessive with her record-keeping. She had carefully catalogued her multitude of collections, affixing a label to everything. This wasn't just another rock. This was a piece of that ancient place. I was holding a stone from Tintagel Castle in Cornwall, England, a coastal redoubt built in the twelfth century that Tennyson's poems connected to the Arthurian legend.

I reached back into the cardboard box, afraid that all the rocks inside would be labeled. And, somehow, sure they would be.

Glastonbury Abbey, another read. *Hadrian's Wall, Tintern Abbey, Avebury. Stonehenge.*

I stared silently at the little stone from Stonehenge in my palm. The small tan piece, about the size of a cashew, was almost shaped like one of the giant sarsen stones. It was rounded smooth along its edges like a sea brick. I tried to set it on its end. It wobbled, but stood. I imagined Stonehenge's mysterious creators in 1400 B.C. setting a forty-five-ton piece of this same stone on its end.

The big share of this same stone . . .

I'd been to Stonehenge. In the 1960s, the monument stood unenclosed, in an open field. You could walk up to it, stay as long as you liked, probably sleep there for all anyone cared. I had spent time among the magnificent monoliths, with hardly another soul around to disturb the reveries they encouraged, and with never a voice telling the visitor to move on.

Over the years, though, Stonehenge changed. I had seen photographs of what it had become. The images made me sad. The great Bronze Age stone circle was itself completely encircled with chain-link fence. Entry was gated and guarded. You walked around the perimeter of the stones on a designated path and weren't allowed to move inside among the giant forms. You could look but you could not touch. Not anymore. And the reason was vandalism. People writing on the stones, or chipping off pieces and carrying them away.

One of those people was my mother. A thief? Crimes take opportunity and motive. The opportunity to steal stones in Great Britain came in 1966 when my dad, Douglas, was posted in London to keep an eye on European naval defense developments on behalf of the U.S. Naval Ordnance Lab in Maryland. Frankie and he lived in London until 1969. Frankie had plenty of opportunity. This was before the fence enclosure. But what of motive?

Frankie was eccentric. But a thief? It didn't seem possible. She was always scrupulously honest in her dealings with people. She had taught her sons to be honest and honorable. It was a shock to consider Frankie in this new light. Yet the evidence was irrefutable.

She didn't buy these rocks, I thought, sadly. She just went to the sites and helped herself to little pieces of history. She had no right. The stones weren't hers to take. They belonged to the people of England. Or to the whole world, for that matter. But now they were here. With me. Sitting in a box. What should I do with them? I stared up at the bare, dirty beams along the garage loft's ceiling. What on earth should I do with this collection?

On the one hand, it was merely a selection of rocks—and small ones to boot—that nobody missed. On the other hand, they almost breathed their history at me, almost cried out that this cardboard carton was not where they belonged. Nor did they belong in the yard sale being planned for disposal of much of Frankie's stuff, sold to some stranger or merely given away. And the prospect of schlepping them to the dump filled me with horror.

I turned over in my hand a two-inch piece of chalk upon which Frankie had written, *Dover Castle 40 AD.* I shook my head.

Then I smiled. A notion came to me.

It was a crazy idea. But unlike lots of nutty notions this one didn't race out of my head as naturally as it had entered. It sat there, begging consideration. Think about it, the idea seemed to demand.

I could give them back. Take the rocks back to the sites where they belong. Take a road trip. Undertake this odd effort to right Frankie's wrong, retrace her steps, do my little bit of repair, and talk to people there about what Frankie did.

And talk to people about Frankie.

Actually, that last piece—talking to strangers about my mother and learning about her—didn't enter my mind that day, in front of the cardboard carton in my family's cottage loft. But it gradually became everything. It wasn't until the following winter that I realized opening that box was the beginning of opening my eyes, my head, and my heart to who my mother was. Because I never truly knew her.

I found Frankie's rocks in August. The following February I was still carrying the thought of them around in my head. I hadn't yet done anything with the rocks. I was wavering on my decision to return them. Knowledge of the box had become a burden, custody of it a source of anxiety, and while returning the rocks made some weird sense, I was nagged by the impracticality of taking them back—the effort, time, expense. And I questioned the point. Why not just throw the rocks away? No one would be the wiser. No one has been looking at an empty space at Glastonbury Abbey and noticing something missing. Why bother returning them? The question rolled around my mind, and went south with me that winter to the Caribbean.

I went to Charlotteville, a small fishing village on Man O' War Bay at the far northeastern end of Tobago. I'd been spending a month or two there each winter, in a little house nestled on the steep escarpment that rings and rises up from the huge scenic bay. It's a place of great beauty, peace, and solitude. I try to do a lot of meditating there, try to empty my mind and practice simple awareness. But that winter Frankie's box of rocks kept coming to mind. Get outta here! I'd toss the thought out, but relentlessly the rocks kept coming back.

When in Tobago I love to hike to Cambleton Beach, my favorite spot on the planet. The secluded beach is at the bottom of a deep ravine cut by a mountain stream. The narrow, steep path down follows an overgrown dirt road built in the eighteenth century to reach a sugar mill, which is now in ruins in jungle behind the beach. The hillsides along the way are planted with cocoa and banana, gone wild now, remnants of a nineteenth-century plantation. At different points along the hike overarching immortelle trees drop their brilliant orange blossoms. Jacamars, striking little blue-gold birds with sharp, straight, stiletto beaks, nest in holes in the exposed earthen embankments. Pairs of green parrots squawk in midflight overhead. Along the path is a towering stand of green bamboo, forty feet tall and more, clustered into scabbards of spars. When it's windy the stalks sway and vibrate wooden notes.

Would Frankie have even noticed the music? Or would she have been too occupied collecting immortelle blossoms, trying to photograph the jacamars, cutting a piece of bamboo, or removing a stone from the crumbling old sugar mill? These were my thoughts as I made my pilgrimage down to Cambleton Beach.

The sea was rough. Strong waves were crashing into the beach. Long surges of foam were sent diagonally across the sand, lifting and moving it to expose small black rocks against a tan background. The rocks were worn smooth by sea and weather. I picked them up as they appealed to me. With steady regularity, layers of the beach were swept, revealed, flipped like pages of a book in the wind. A perfect day for adding to my rock collection.

My rock collection? At that moment it dawned on me. Since I'd arrived in Tobago I'd been gathering these small black rocks. Each day I'd idly spent time perusing the sand, collecting, and I'd assembled a pile of black rocks back in my house above the village. In my struggle not to think about Frankie and rocks and collecting, I'd been forming my own rock collection without thinking about it at all and not fully experiencing these precious moments on my favorite beach. And I'd been oblivious to the irony.

I shook my head. I stood awhile ankle-deep in the sea, watching the water pass over the sand. Black stones appeared, disappeared. I found myself grinning. Like mother, like son? Had the Tao, the Zen been going in one ear and out the other? I had a handful of black stones in my hand. My attention had gone there. And it had gone to making the stones mine.

The surf rushed over my feet. As it receded, it sucked sand out from under my heels and I sank. But it also began to paint a picture for me. The sand at this spot on the beach was mostly light-colored, but with a few dark streaks woven through. As the departing water slowed and finished its retreat, the dark streaks had composed the drawing of a woman, head and torso in profile, legs slightly angled, arms hanging relaxed. I stood still, admiring the picture. It was striking. It was the sketch of a modern master, graceful, museum-quality work. It was exotic and erotic.

I stared at the image, captivated by it. And then my brain kicked in. No one will believe this, I thought. How can I get proof? The beach was deserted; there were no witnesses. Can I get a photo of it? No, I've got no camera. The impulse was powerful: to capture this image that had so magically appeared. Preserve it, keep it, make it mine.

And then the next big wave came in and the drawing was entirely erased.

A blank bank of sand. The drawing was gone forever.

It had existed for precisely the interval between two Caribbean waves. It had existed for my eyes alone. But it could not become mine. It was transient and couldn't be fixed. Yet I had seen it, admired it, and it lives in me.

Hadrian's Wall is just as transient. Only the return to dust has a slightly longer time line. All those rocks in Frankie's cardboard box are just as subjective, unfixed, and insignificant as a wave sketch in Cambleton's sand. Removed from the handiwork and imagination of the Romans or Normans or Beaker people, Frankie's rocks were just a pile of so much gravel.

Why bother to take them back?

I got an answer a few nights later at Gail's Restaurant. Gail Caesar is a forty-something West Indian woman. Her restaurant in Charlotteville is a twenty-two-seat, open-air gathering spot protected from Man O' War Bay by a low seawall. She serves curried goat, fresh grilled wahoo, callaloo soup, dasheen, and a routine menu of refreshing humor, friendly counseling, and folk philosophy. Gail listened to me question why I should go to the trouble to take back Frankie's rocks. Then she reminded me, it isn't about the rocks.

"As ragged as they might be, look at them as jewels. Even from that time your mother was taking them," said Gail, "she was making a path. She was spreading a carpet there in stones for you to walk upon. The path leads back to where the stones came from because it leads you back to her."

1.

a time to keep,
a time to cast away

London

There are people like Senhor José everywhere, who fill their time, or what they believe to be their spare time, by collecting stamps, coins, medals, vases, postcards, matchboxes, books, clocks, sport shirts, autographs, stones, clay figurines, empty beverage cans, little angels, cacti, opera programmes, lighters, pens, owls, music boxes, bottles, bonsai trees, paintings, mugs, pipes, glass obelisks, ceramic ducks, old toys, carnival masks, and they probably do so out of something that we might call metaphysical angst, perhaps because they cannot bear the idea of chaos being the one ruler of the universe, which is why, using their limited powers and with no divine help, they attempt to impose some order on the world, and for a short while they manage it, but only as long as they are there to defend their collection, because when the day comes when it must be dispersed, and that day always comes, either with their death or when the collector grows weary, everything goes back to its beginnings, everything returns to chaos.

—FROM THE NOVEL *All the Names,* BY JOSÉ SARAMAGO

Sometimes you realize quite unexpectedly that you don't know a person. You think you do, until one day they tell you they collect sand.

I thought I knew my bank teller pretty well. I'd seen her for years when I went in to cash my paychecks, and we chatted about all sorts of stuff. She was very nice and seemed perfectly normal. Then one payday I mentioned I wouldn't be around for a few weeks because I was going to the South

Pacific on vacation. She lit up as though I'd thrown up a switch. What islands? she wanted to know. There was hopeful anticipation in her voice. I couldn't imagine why; she wasn't going with me. I mentioned several islands, including Savai'i in Western Samoa and Rarotonga, the main island in the Cook Islands group. Her eyes became incandescent. "Please, please!" she intoned. Her voice was pleading. "Would you, do you think you possibly could, bring me back some sand?"

She belonged to a national sand collectors' group.

This is what I mean. You think you know people, but you don't. A financial transaction in the bank each week left no hint of obsession with sand. The personal ads in the paper never say, "WF, blonde, trim, financially secure professional, passionate about Tuscan holidays, gourmet food, fireside evenings, and sand." Such things don't show up on résumés either.

On the Internet there's a site for dirt collectors. I imagine a WM, financially secure dirt collector might be interested in a WF sand collector. A sort of match made in the gravel pit. I imagine my imaginary WF sand gal might get off on this real guy on the Web who specializes in vanity dirt. He's got dirt from Graceland, Mick Jagger and Jerry Hall's flower bed, Vanna White's backyard, Nicole Brown Simpson's front walkway, the Little Bighorn battlefield, and lots more. This guy even solicits dirt samples. (Not always successfully. Disneyland sent him back a very nice letter of rejection: "Thank you for your interest in pursuing 'dirt' from the Walt Disney Company," they wrote. "We appreciate your including us in your world wide 'soil sampling.' We are constantly looking for opportunities that fit with our company's entertainment initiatives. Unfortunately, at this time we do not feel that there is an obvious tie with your exhibit and a Disney contribution.")

This dirt guy isn't the only guy doing dirt. When former New York Yankee (née Boston Red Sox) pitcher Roger Clemens during the 2003 season reached two baseball career milestones in one night, three hundred wins and four thousand strikeouts, two of Roger's sons ran to the mound in Yankee Stadium and scooped up some of its dirt and put it in a bag. Clemens, we all learned later, has been collecting dirt from his career's memorable mounds for quite some time. He even brings different dirt to games—for luck, presumably. Mound dirt from the diamonds where he pitched his two 20-strikeout games are his most prized.

And that Web dirt guy doesn't just do dirt, it turns out. In his vanity collection are peanut shells collected from beside Dick Clark's parking space at the NBC studios in Burbank, California; rocks from Barry Manilow's driveway; Red Auerbach's cigar ashes; splinters of wood from Dyke Bridge, Chappaquiddick Island, on Martha's Vineyard; Dave Barry's lint (and if I may borrow a popular Dave Barry line, I'm not making any of this up); pebbles and concrete from Princess Diana's automobile crash site in Paris; a piece of the Berlin Wall; and tons of other interesting stuff.

My mother would have liked this guy. I think. But what do I know?

I never really knew Frankie. I never knew my own mother. As the realization gradually seeped into me, it rocked me. So to speak. Finding the box of rocks triggered this realization. I was fifty-three years old and understood my mother about as well as I understood quantum mechanics. Bendable time. Black holes. Parallel universes. I grew up unobserved by my mother. I traveled along in some sort of space parallel to hers, not connecting. I never knew her. And in truth, she didn't know me either.

Frankie was wacky. I knew that. She was anxiety-racked, a perpetual-motion machine with an erratic attention span. She showered her Siamese cat Kim with countless kisses, but gave my older brother Doug and me none. She could get passionately involved in issues that moved her, and work tirelessly on them. She organized elaborate community help and recognition for a little girl with leukemia and her widowed mother who lived on our street, and she took under her wing the young adopted son of another single mom she came to know. Yet she showed no apparent interest in the growing-up issues of her own sons. No wing of Frankie's was spread protectively over me or my brother. She never once came to any of my track meets to watch me high-jump (poorly, I admit). I have not one memory of her ever talking to me about me, what I was doing, how I was feeling.

She was a healer for others, a caregiver by profession. She worked as a nurse at Babies' Hospital and then at the Neurological Institute in New York. For most of her nursing life while I was a growing kid, Frankie worked the three-to-eleven evening shift at Suburban Hospital in Bethesda, Maryland. It was clear to me that her bedside skills and professional judgments were admired by her colleagues. She made many fast friends among Suburban's doctors, nurses, interns, and supervisors. Occasionally patients kept up with Frankie after their release from the hospital. They so appreciated the way she had tended to them that for years afterward they'd send her Christmas gifts or cards. Yet Frankie was a distracted caregiver to me. In fact, these many years later, I believe I probably gave her as much care growing up as she gave me. Frankie suffered severe migraine headaches all her life, and many times a month we tiptoed around the house and past her darkened room, delivered tiny paper cups of ginger ale and plates of dry toast tips to her bedside, and brought freezer coldpacks and re-wetted face cloths for her forehead.

I learned cooking out of cans and, yes, Frankie taught me that. She was among the first of the 1950s mothers to discover TV dinners. Turkey, more often than not, with mashed potatoes and sorrowfully soggy peas in the other aluminum indentations. They were gifts from the Better Living Through Chemistry food gods, those TV dinners, liberating Frankie from what she considered a colossal waste of time, cooking. Later, naturally, she was among the first to get a microwave oven.

She was beautiful and generous, and committed to others. She had many close friends who adored her. She was artistic, creative. She was naturally musical—played violin and piano, and sang. I knew all these things. And I knew Frankie was addicted to drugs—painkillers, sedatives, tranquilizers, all sorts of pills and needles prescribed to her apparently without much regard for the overall mix, back when doctors did that, medicated emotional, harried housewives to keep them quiet.

She was a first-generation American, born in New York City on February 5, 1914, to a father raised in London by his French parents and a mother who was Algerian French. Frankie spoke French like a native because it was the language of her home and the New York City immigrant neighborhood where she grew up. Their last name was Franco, the derivation of Frankie's nickname. Her given name was Yvonne.

Her father, Maurice, was a chauffeur. Her mother, Berthe, was a battle-ax. Her older sister, Marcelle, was jealous of Yvonne's beauty, popularity, and musical talents and routinely treated Yvonne with suspicion, superiority, and sometimes outright animosity. The lack of warmth between them pained Yvonne her whole life, and came to a bitter conclusion. In the mid-1970s,

Marcelle flat-out disowned Yvonne and never spoke to her again. My mother took it very hard.

Yvonne's younger brother, also named Maurice, was spoiled, doted upon as the family's baby boy. He became a U.S. Naval Air petty officer, and as a middle-aged man, committed suicide. He had been diagnosed with colon cancer and was said to be ashamed of this. The story is that he took all his money out of the bank and then drove his car into a moving train. Tens and twenties, it's said, were fluttering in the air after the dramatic crash. Frankie's father committed suicide, too. Being with Berthe for over fifty years finally got to him, Frankie believed, but her father had also heard he had cancer. He considered cancer a shameful thing. A few weeks after the diagnosis in 1967 he jumped into the Hudson River and was spotted floating the next morning by a New York Central conductor as the train pulled its load of commuters into Riverside Station. Frankie loved her father probably more than she loved anyone else. I knew these things from her past dramatically affected her, made her who she was.

But I didn't really know Frankie. I had no idea what made her tick, what was going on inside her head, or deep in her heart. I never paid attention, growing up. I never invested in my mother. I didn't pay in because there was scant payout. Today I look at pictures of my mother holding me, in the Massachusetts towns of Fitchburg in the late forties when I was a baby, in Holden during preschool, and in Osterville when I was a little kid in the early fifties, and in the photos I look like a prop. Aren't mothers showing off their little darlings supposed to beam with maternal pride, holding the youngster adoringly? Frankie poses like Greta Garbo holding a bouquet of flowers. I'm an adornment. Frankie is the subject, the focus, the star. What she's holding isn't particularly important. What matters is how she looks. That's the way it seems to me, anyway.

Opening my eyes, seventeen years after my mother's death, I have been left only small clues like these. Clues that the silver screen, the larger-than-life images of Hollywood's magic, were a part of who Frankie was. She idolized Rudolph Valentino as a girl. She said this often. She named me after the actor Dana Andrews, a later screen swoon. In 1937, her father was taken on a long European tour driving for the wealthy New York family that employed him. He sent home postcards. Frankie saved these. One shows a large, grand building on a crowded square. "This is the largest movie house in Oslo, Norway," Maurice writes to Yvonne. "Altho it is large, I was unable to get a seat when I went to see the 'Jungle Princess' with Jean Harlow starring." He knew his daughter would care about that. Frankie actually bears a resemblance to Jean Harlow in individual snapshots taken of her on Cape Cod and Martha's Vineyard beaches in the 1940s, her legs folded under her, glamorous. In a condolence note after my mother's death in 1983, her closest high school friend said, "In describing her through all the years, my mind always conjured up Claudette Colbert."

Frankie cared about stars. And, I think, she cared desperately about starring—about acceptance, and about attention. Which is perhaps why Frankie gave so little attention to me. She was as much the needy child as I was. She sought as an adult what she'd been deprived of as a child—nurturing, love, a sense of security, reassurance that she was important—and I was in no position to provide these things. But she was in another universe. And now, as a middle-aged man, unmarried, childless, with a history of important loving relationships with women breaking down because I'm not all there, not connected, too selfish—those are the raps—I have finally been getting glimpses of who my mother was. And of who I am. I'm finally looking. At her, and in reflection, at myself.

Frankie couldn't become Claudette Colbert or Jean Harlow. But she could become a collector. Little unusual in that. It's estimated that one out of every three Americans collects something. Some collect things quite weird. In the *Boston Globe* I once spotted an announcement that 165 hobbyists were gathering at the Crowne Plaza Nashua (New Hampshire) Hotel for the twenty-sixth annual convention of the National Toothpick Holder Collectors Society. This is a group seven hundred members strong. The article quotes Tom Jiamachello of Essex Junction, Vermont. "When people hear I'm the past president of the National Toothpick Holder Collectors Society, they just go, 'Oh,' " he says. "They don't know what to say."

Get a life. You could say that.

A California man collects hotel soaps. He has 350 little bars. He's proudest of his hotel soaps with transportation logos, like Cunard or C&O RR. "Is this a weird collection?" he wonders. "At least it's a clean one."

A Florida man has collected over three thousand casino match covers. His prize possession: The Northern Club & Bar, Las Vegas, the first licensed casino in Nevada (1931). There's a Web site for Swizzle Sticks International, where collectors of swizzle sticks can stay connected, post messages, stir things up. An avid collector of tissue box covers also has a Web site, where she proudly displays pictures of those fabric things used to hide (or is it enhance?) Kleenex boxes. She likes to say her collection may be obsessive but it's not to be sneezed at. Ka-boom.

Barb in Pittsburgh collects Belgian movie posters. Finnegan in Buffalo collects Dew or Do or Du Drop Inn items of any sort. Gus from New York City collects toy Spideys. Frankie isn't alone. It's a human tendency to gather together objects of fascination, whim, oddity, history, or natural beauty and keep them, and show them off. In the more upscale universe, the beginnings of most museums can be traced to collectors. More than 80 percent of the works in New York's Metropolitan Museum came from collectors. Individuals' collections have made huge contributions to knowledge, enlightenment, culture, and generally to the enriching of civilizations. Which is why Karl Meyer, in his book *The Plundered Past,* observed, "The collector is a friend of the past."

Yet Meyer adds in his very next sentence, "But he can be a difficult friend." The difficulty comes with obsession.

Frankie did not just collect pieces of English castles and Roman walls. This was only the collection we didn't know about. She had many more collections, a dizzying array of others, up front, out front for all to see: Seashells. Foreign stamps. American plate blocks. English coins. Roman coins. Old dolls. Hummels. Wedgwood. Commemorative cup plates. Monumental brass rubbings. New England gravestone rubbings. African Makonde wood carvings. Ancient Asian artifacts. Rocks and minerals. Lace. Antique fans. Phonograph records. Unicorns. First-day covers. Stuffed animals. Postcards. British chinaware teacups. Beer coasters (she stole that one from me). Polished rocks. Antique bottles. Buttons. Sandwich glass. Art books. Music boxes. As well, she was an obsessive photographer of places she visited, amassing a lifetime collection of thousands of slides and photographs. This led to a collection of old cameras.

She collected guidebooks, too, from everywhere she went. She collected cassette tapes of her violin and voice recitals, and then more cassettes of her practice sessions. If amassing family mementos qualifies as collecting, she did this, too. In photo form, naturally. But also with source material. Ticket stubs, newspaper clippings, old letters, and the like.

Most painful for me were her so-called Brain Books, a collected record of her sons' accomplishments. She kept these scrapbooks, I'm now convinced, not so much out of pride in what her kids had done, but rather, I think Frankie simply couldn't resist another collection. I was clueless to this at the time. I took the Brain Books personally. My brother Doug's, by high school graduation, was bursting at the spine, stuffed with everything from a certificate for winning a Martha's Vineyard baby contest to major scholastic testing awards. Mine was, let's say, thin—like, three gold stars in third grade for coloring inside the lines.

Frankie collected compulsively. But not with single-minded focus. That struck me as important when I realized it. It differentiated her from obsessive art collectors, the J. Paul Gettys of the world ever on the lookout for an available Delacroix or Matisse. It separated her, too, from your average dedicated seashell collector who simply can't sleep at night until he finds a rose-branch murex to complete his Indo-Pacific set. For that matter, it separated her from loony closet collectors like Imelda Marcos and her six thousand pairs of shoes. Frankie never assembled truly large collections, nor did she ever complete a collection. She never came close. She didn't really try. Hers was a manifold collecting sensibility, which she pursued with mania. Hers were eyes drawn this way and that, impulsively, compulsively, without specialization. Generally she would start with a passion and gradually, or sometimes quite quickly, lose interest, drawn to something else.

Her obsession, I think, was with the act of collecting, not with the collecting of particular things. In every case but one, the collected items were harmless, and in most cases not especially remarkable. Her shotgun approach to it all could easily be dismissed as eccentricity. But the one exception—her secret collection—nagged at me from the moment I realized what I'd found inside that cardboard carton. Recognition of the ancient rocks toppled a delicately balanced image I had constructed of my mother. Her mania in this case had crossed over a line—a line that in parenting she had drawn clearly for her sons.

At least it seemed to me that it had. Stealing and vandalism were serious transgressions in her espoused worldview. And she raised two sons who became fervent preservationists, neither of whom would litter outside Salisbury Cathedral, much less steal its stone.

I didn't understand. I knew my mother was a good woman, a moral woman, a person of principle. I needed to understand.

Traveling back to Britain, taking back the rocks, I hoped, would help me.

monday, march 3, 2003

Two young American Airlines gatekeepers in Boston's Logan International Airport terminal listen with interest to my short explanation of why I'm soon to board their flight to London. "Now, I ask you," I ask them, "is there a better reason to give a guy a courtesy upgrade to first class than this selfless journey to return these precious, pilfered rocks?"

I get for the first time that look on people's faces that I'll become quite accustomed to over the next month. A look somewhere between suppressed hilarity and serious concern that it must be a full moon and somebody forgot to lock the door to the padded rooms.

The head gatekeeper shakes his head, giving his best Bill Clinton scrunched lips look. "I'm sorry, American Airlines doesn't give upgrades anymore."

"But I need to understand my mother. That's what's really at stake here, and I'll be away for a full month," I say.

"I'm sorry," he says, as his companion now nervously nods, and no doubt moves her finger to the antiterrorism security button under the counter.

So much for corporate sponsorship of a uniquely worthy journey. So much for American Airlines' much vaunted "American Way" slogan, which you'd think would include honoring motherhood and soothing lost sons.

And so the journey to return Frankie's rocks begins, in cramped and crowded economy class, Seat 30G. Which happens to be on the end of the inside aisle of that little open area on airliners just aft of the loo where people stand around and wait their turn to pee.

It has never been my ideal in air travel to spend virtually an entire trip in intimate proximity to a parade of people shifting from foot to foot, idling in response to messages from their bladders, while they try not to seem preoccupied with an "Occupied" message glowing on a small door. Does this signify some personal shortcoming we can trace back to my infant-stage toilet training? If so, I figure, blame it on my mother. Matters of controlling weewee were crucial chapters in the perverse, bringing-up-baby book Frankie followed in the days before reasonable Dr. Spock became de rigueur. Frankie's being-a-mom mentor was almost certainly a guy named Watson (Dr. Watson, I presume), whose advice to 1940s parents on toilet training was force 'em to do it beginning at six months. His suggestion for dealing with thumb sucking was to tie a child's arm behind his back. The guy today would be considered a sadist, and probably jailed.

To make matters even more interesting, in the four Boeing 777 seats to my left are not one, not two, but three preschool children returning with their clearly frazzled mum to visit Granny in Leeds.

In June 1966 it was different. My parents had flown over to England a few months earlier and I was going to join them, and do a year of college in London. In '66 the Boeing 707 was lean and mean and passengers dressed up to fly. Nothing like this fat air bus and its motley assortment of humanity. Thirty-seven years ago, not long after takeoff the aircraft was a stand-up cocktail party, people smiling, laughing, interacting. Now little video screens in front of every passenger have them locked in with pixel narcotic, alone, zombie-like. In '66 passengers radiated a unique awareness that they were making a vast geographic and cross-cultural crossing that had taken America's colonists months of fearful unknowing and given America's waves of immigrants weeks of nervous uncertainty, leaving the familiar for the strange, the Old World for the New. Now everyone is in mindless steerage, aware only of video images. Back in '66, it felt nothing if not first-class. The cabin rocked. We were flying over an ocean. It felt super special.

As it must have felt back then to Frankie. But what more? Her parents, Berthe and Maurice, had both been immigrants. Both had made the east-to-west crossing. Returning to England, where her father had been raised, was Frankie thinking of her European roots when her airliner made its trip? Did she think of those roots with pride? Or did she see her roots as poisoned, compromised, maybe even rotten? Did she feel trepidation, sadness, excitement? I'm guessing she felt a sort of sublime satisfaction. She was going back in high style, nothing like what her parents had experienced steaming into New York Harbor on immigrant ships at the turn of the century. Frankie's was a return almost triumphant—a good, totally American man at her side, headed toward a three-year government appointment, a posh Sussex Place apartment, and considerable diplomatic perks. Her trip was a luxury, round-trip ticket in hand, crossing over to witness European life out of curiosity, privilege, and opportunity rather than her parents' one-way voyage of desperation and need.

Yes, it would have mattered to Frankie that she was doing something out of choice that her mother—and this part would have been about her mother, I think—had done out of desperation. Yet her mother left everything behind in coming west, and would struggle to start over from scratch. Frankie took east to Europe her pride and hurt, and came back with rocks.

tuesday, march 4

The woman at Heathrow passport control is a slim, lovely, black-haired East Indian.

"What's the purpose of your visit to London?" she asks, glancing over my visitor's card.

Well, I say, it's sort of complicated. Then I tell her about Frankie, the rocks, my mission.

Her eyes sparkle and her mouth falls slightly open. "That's the first time I've heard that one, and I see thousands of visitors a day," she says.

Returning to my documents, she says, "So it's a . . . business trip, is it?"

"Well, yes, I suppose so." Unfinished business.

Sussex Lodge has aged, less gracefully than grittily. The yellow façade up to the third floor is smeared mustard-dirty. Rust is visible on many of the iron balconies. The apartment building is where my parents stayed during their three years in London, just a couple of blocks from Victoria Gate along the north side of Hyde Park. It was a very upscale address in 1966.

Peering into the lobby, I notice there is no longer an elevator operator or doorman. There were two covering two shifts when Frankie lived here. Frankie, I remember, loved this little amenity. Her father had been a chauffeur, opening car doors for the privileged people. Her mother had had to carry her groceries up five flights of monotonous marble steps in their Bronx graystone. To this day I can hear Berthe's dreary complaining and huffing breath and her shuffling flats rasping against the stone as she plodded up. In London, Frankie was the lady, doors held open for her, elevators operated for her, and she basked in the servants' attentions. Now, it seems, this is history at Sussex Lodge.

Times have changed. Like the whole area flowing south from nearby Paddington Station, the New Commonwealth Members' influence in the neighborhood is visible. That's what immigrants from former outposts of the British Empire were called in '66, though none had set up shop around Sussex Lodge. Now an Indian restaurant is on the corner across the street, and across from that is a place advertising Persian cuisine.

From Sussex Square, I wander over to Hyde Park and gaze awhile at the still waters of the long Serpentine. Frankie loved to feed the waterfowl here. Slowly I walk up Bayswater Road to Speaker's Corner. These were my old stomping grounds, that school year I spent here. It was Swinging London then. With the Beatles, Carnaby Street, mods, and rockers, it was a magical year for a twenty-year-old. It was a magical time for Frankie, too. She had been reluctant to come, according to my dad. Her immediate reaction to the idea of moving to London was "That gloomy place?" Within a month, she was crazy about England.

I remember regularly coming to Speaker's Corner to yell out answers to the shouted trivia questions from the czar of the Hyde Park Quiz Club standing on his soapbox. Frankie enjoyed that, too. Occasionally she got the right answers. It was a side of her I'd never seen, and I was impressed. I remember Frankie here, listening to Allen Ginsberg speak at an antiwar rally. Frankie was opposed to the war, the Vietnam War, which was heating up, and the dispute between the antiwar movement and the rest of the population was threatening to engulf America.

Walking, I pass the Selfridges and Marks & Spencer department stores on Oxford Street. A frequent sight, I remember, was Frankie returning to our apartment carrying bags from one or the other. She was a regular shopper.

I get these little glimpses of her here. But the sensations are ephemeral and unfeeling and fade into nothing as quickly as they arise. For the first time I ask myself, Will anything meaningful happen to me on this trip?

I have a month to find out.

wednesday, march 5

It's a good thing Frankie didn't steal the Rosetta Stone. It would never have fit in my luggage. This was not a consideration for the British when they stole the stone in Egypt.

My first full day on this trip, I spend six hours in the British Museum, which is where they store and show off the considerable hoard of stones the British have stolen from around the world. The Rosetta is perhaps the most famous.

Most of the stolen stones on display in the British Museum bear some considerable resemblance to things carved or chiseled, be it a granite ram of Amun, limestone falcon, quartzite baboon, or marble pig or bull. Or the rocks are identifiable as obelisks or stelae, friezes or false doors, columns or sarcophagi, Assyrian, Babylonian, Egyptian, Greek, Lykian. But some pieces are a real stretch to see. As with Frankie's telling us that a rock in her possession is from Hadrian's Wall, you have to take it on faith that, say, the limestone fragment of the beard of the Sphinx on display was actually found in Giza between the great figure's paws during an Italian excavation in 1817, and that this hunk of formless rock in front of you is just that, a bit of beard.

I must say, the gall of these cheeky British antiquities robbers! Some exhibits in the museum actually have photos next to them showing the statues or remnants in situ. See, they say, here is how we found them. Now they're here. The huge granite head and one arm of the colossal statue of the king of Thebes is

on display. We're informed on the little placard that the torso of the magnificent sculpture is still standing where it was found in Thebes.

The obvious question is, Wouldn't the statue be better off if all the body
parts were together? It's the kind of question somebody returning stolen rocks
just naturally asks.

I'm not the only one asking. The pressure is intense on the British to return some of these treasures to the places they came from. Meanwhile, other
colonial countries with looted items have been giving in to demands to return
them, increasing the pressure on Britain. No call for rock returning, however,
is more vocal, or public, and no parliamentary debate more intense, both locally and internationally, than Greece's demand that England return the Elgin
Marbles to their rightful place on the Acropolis. The Greeks have been grip-
ing for nearly forty years. And who can blame them? The fifth-century B.C.
Parthenon from which the stone art was stolen is arguably the world's most
famous edifice, and it still stands there majestically on the mesa above Athens.
What the British Museum possesses is no small part of what has survived of
the Parthenon's original adornment. It would take a modern container ship
to ship it all back. The Brits have seventeen carved figures, roughly one-half
of the total from perches on the temple's pediments, along with fifty-six frieze
slabs totaling over five hundred feet of classical gods and heroes and action
scenes, all of which once ringed the Parthenon. They also have fifteen metopes,
four pieces of the Temple of Victory, thirteen marble heads, an assortment of
carved fragments, painted vases, sepulchral pillars, inscribed albas, and a magnificent caryatid column carved in the likeness of a woman.

It's quite a stash. Thomas Bruce is the rock-collecting equivalent of Frankie
in this case. He's better known as the seventh Earl of Elgin, or Lord Elgin. He
was British ambassador to Constantinople during the Ottoman reign, and
the Ottomans at the time were ruling Greece. Elgin visited Athens in 1800 and
decided he ought to take some of the Parthenon marbles back to London. He
probably shouldn't be judged too harshly, because while nationalism and simple profit weren't too far from his mind, he also could see what the Turks
thought of the ancient temples. They considered them infidel relics. They'd
done a goodly amount of explosives testing on the Acropolis, and for small
bribes were allowing anyone with a hammer to take home Parthenon fragments. Lord Elgin just took the sultan's souvenir-collecting offer to a higher

level. He struck a deal, and proceeded to direct over three hundred workmen over several years to chisel and saw away and ship off to England what became known as the Elgin Marbles. Did he save them? Or steal them?

As I leave the British Museum and begin a long walk back to my hotel, I think of the passage in the Bible (Ecclesiastes 3:1–6) which says, "To everything there is a season . . . a time to cast away stones, and a time to gather stones together . . . A time to get, and a time to lose; a time to keep, and a time to cast away." The season to lose had come for the Parthenon in 1800. Perhaps the passing into the next season, the season for returning rocks, is now in front of England. It's in front of me, I think, walking along Russell Street.

I've come to England to right a wrong. But now, on just my second day, I'm not sure what is right or wrong. If Lord Elgin is a hero, could Frankie be a villain? If England can defend its right to Greece's marvelous marbles, might not Frankie have a right to the rocks in my luggage? Does it really matter where the rocks reside, if getting them and losing them, keeping them and casting them away are all just inevitable parts of a timeless whole?

In the morning I begin my fourteen site visits. Tonight I am more unsure than ever of what understanding is out there awaiting me.

2.

a surreptitious collection: clues of guilt

Stonehenge and Stourhead

Collecting can be a rewarding and stimulating pastime. Or it can be pathological.

—*Forbes* MAGAZINE, "THEY'VE GOTTA HAVE IT," DECEMBER 25, 2000

To understand my mother, I knew, I had to try to understand collecting. Collecting is what she did with a passion. It's what she did to excess. And of most importance to me, it's where she focused her attention instead of paying attention to me.

Compulsive or obsessive collecting is a little-studied area of psychology. Early inquiry seems to have been more or less satisfied with the bland conclusion of a Frenchman, Henri Codet, who after consideration in 1921 categorized the four underlying motives of collecting as (1) need for possession, (2) need for spontaneous activity, (3) impulse to self-advancement, and (4) tendency to classify things. Yawn. So what else is new?

Today, in the rare research being done, preoccupation with collecting is becoming recognized as far more complex. It is seen as a deeply embedded, psychological yearning that can have the same sort of powerful hold over someone as alcohol, drugs, or gambling. And like these, it has the potential to be addictive. "Addiction to collecting is as hard to break as addiction to drugs, and I have been addicted," admitted John Walker, the former director of the

National Gallery of Art in Washington, D.C., in an article entitled "Secrets of a Museum Director."

Stories are emerging of marriages destroyed by collecting mania, and of people who have gone bankrupt in the pursuit of amassing ever bigger and better collections of Bakelite costume jewelry, Chinese bronzes, or nineteenth-century European clocks. Just like compulsive bettors at blackjack tables when they're dealt twenty-one, studies show a collector's heart rate and blood pressure spike when he or she finds a desired object, and there's an accompanying release of those delightful feel-good neurotransmitters in the brain, norepinephrine and serotonin.

In pursuit of such a brain chemistry rush, a collector's obsessive collecting can turn nasty or even illegal. It can create for some "a clandestine atmosphere of intrigue and deceit, rather as if they were having an illicit love affair," in the words of Paris auctioneer Maurice Rheims, from his book *The Strange Life of Objects*. A leading researcher in this area, New York psychoanalyst Werner Muensterberger, noted, "We know of numerous cases in which moral standards, legal considerations, and societal taboos have been disregarded in the passion to collect."

I'd never given Frankie's collecting much thought before I found the box of rocks. But the rocks were a red flag. The first thing I thought was that Frankie had disregarded a very big taboo. It was my first hint that there might be something wrong with her collecting habits. I found myself anxious to know whether she also felt it was wrong to take the rocks but just couldn't help herself.

One simple fact suggested Frankie believed she had broken a taboo. Unlike all the other stuff she collected, the rocks were never put on display. But art dealers have noted the lack of guilt, or lack of conscience, on the part of obsessive collectors who have acquired stolen or smuggled antiquities. And in these cases the collections are usually highly private, the items reserved for the collector's eyes only. What had Frankie's conscience told her?

She was dead. I couldn't ask her. So I did all I could. I combed carefully over things left behind for clues. I've come to believe she felt some guilt. I found the tiniest clues. The strongest, perhaps, in her own voice on tape.

During my odyssey of disposing of her numerous collections after her death, it took a long time for me to tackle the hundreds of cassette tapes

Frankie had made. They were all recorded after her retirement to Cape Cod in 1977. Listening to all of them felt like an impossible task, and was sure to be horribly boring. Her writings on the plastic cassette containers were helpful, but often cryptic—notations like "5-30-79 Creation w/ Mr. Pat," or "3-28 con't work on Mon Coeur Souvre." Not much help. Which to listen to? It seemed a huge job, but I decided to undertake a labor of love. I decided to pull together one ninety-minute recording of Frankie's extraordinary talent out of all the practice fragments and rough recordings done on a state-of-no-art Superscope portable tape recorder, often inside echoing churches. I felt a need to preserve her magnificent soprano voice, which when she was in her sixties teachers called the voice of a woman in her twenties, and which routinely brought tears to all eyes in Osterville Community Church during her choir solos. And I needed to save samples of her violin playing, her fingers by this time bent with arthritis but her fingering and bowing still full of feeling.

I wanted, especially, to hear and preserve her singing of two signature songs, "O Holy Night" and "Ave Maria." Her friends often mentioned Frankie's performances of these songs with awe and admiration. I'd seldom heard them. In fact, I'd seldom heard her sing. She never sang when I was a child. Neither did she play the violin, although she had learned the instrument as a young girl. Frankie substantially let go of these immense talents in midlife and only returned to them in retirement. For some reason collecting had replaced performing for this exceptionally talented singer and violinist.

As I tediously picked my way through all the music cassettes, one day I found a tape labeled "11-16-78, Interview WOCB on Hobbies & Collections & Interests." It is the recording of an interview with a radio talk-show host on Cape Cod named Nan Daniels who had heard about this woman Frankie and her inordinate interest in collecting.

The tape begins with Daniels asking, "People become interested in many things for many reasons. Let's take one of the first interests you ever had in terms of collecting things. What would that have been?"

"I started my collections about the time my sons did," Frankie answers. "About the age of eight, children start collecting things. And in my day, it was always stamps. And the children collected stamps, and they traded stamps, and I suddenly became very interested in stamps and started a collection of my own."

Hold it. That's not true. Frankie began her stamp collection about the time of her marriage in 1941. My father recalls Frankie being noticeably intrigued when she was shown Uncle Byron's stamp collection on a newlywed visit to my dad's hometown of North Attleboro, Massachusetts, and that she started her own stamp collection right after that. Byron Carpenter was my dad's uncle. Byron had in-laws working at the local post office. Family lore has it that Byron, in his stamp collection, had one of those 1918 Curtiss Jenny twenty-four-cent airmail stamps, the one where the picture of the little biplane is upside down. So few were printed before the postal service caught the error that the stamp is among the rarest of all American stamps. It's worth hundreds of thousands of dollars. Frankie claimed Byron showed his Curtiss Jenny to her.

After Frankie's death, my brother Doug and I sifted carefully through her voluminous stamp collection to see if she somehow (I won't suggest how) ended up with it. Alas, we came up empty-handed and no richer. For Doug it was double disappointment. He had hoped he might find his childhood baseball card collection buried among Frankie's belongings. In it, he claims, was a Mickey Mantle rookie card, also worth a considerable amount of money today. We suspect the baseball cards were probably sold in the same yard sale my mother held around 1970, when, horrified, I found my Dinky Toy collection and my Flexible Flyer sled on the front lawn offered for sale. I yanked them and heartily admonished Frankie. But my brother wasn't around. Maybe his baseball cards were there and were sold. I don't know. Frankie may have revered her own collections, but she didn't seem to hold much respect for her sons'.

Speaking of stamps and upside-down airplanes, among the many postcards Frankie's father sent her during that 1937 European chauffeuring trip was a card showing Alp Grum mailed from St. Moritz, Switzerland. Maurice posted it with three Helvetia air-mail stamps affixed. But there are only yellowed glue splotches now where the stamps were. The reason, probably, is revealed in the first sentence Maurice writes to Frankie on the card. "Keep these postage stamps (aviation)," he wrote, "especially those whose former value like the first on this postcard has been erased as there are only a few and they may be very valuable some day." Frankie surely removed the two stamps. Where are they today? Are they as valuable as the Curtiss Jenny stamp?

Frankie probably held such a hope. But the point is Frankie developed interest in stamp collecting long before Doug was born, not as a consequence of her children's hobby. Back to the WOCB radio interview:

Frankie goes on, "The second thing usually is shells, and they [children] go to the beach on vacation and collect shells and they mount them on little sheets of cardboard, and I became interested in their collection of shells and started one of my own. Most of the shells we collected was in Florida, and it was very interesting."

Daniels: "The boys went on to other things? But you didn't?"

Frankie: "Although we still had to go through stones and rocks. And the young boy had to have a regular rock pick, and we went to collecting rocks, and I suddenly became fascinated with rocks and I began a collection of my own."

Hold it. I need to interrupt again. Frankie isn't going to blame me for her interest in rocks. I'm the "young boy," and yes, I had long forgotten this but now remember, I did want a rock pick hammer, and my parents gave me one. But I wasn't interested in rock collecting. I was interested in smashing things with the pointed end of the hammer because that's what prospectors did in TV westerns. My brother Doug was the one interested in collecting rocks. He was the one with good grades in science (fully featured in the Brain Book) who did school science fair projects illustrating, with examples, the differences between sedimentary, igneous, and metamorphic rocks. I thought igneous rocks were just stupid rocks. Doug's the one who in 1954 had his picture in the local newspaper showing a white-haired woman handing him a rock. "Uranium Changes Hands" was the headline. The caption stated, "Probably the only uranium on the Cape is changing hands here. Mrs. H.W. York of East Bay Road, Osterville, gives it to Douglas Hornig, also of Osterville, Cape Cod Standard Times newspaperboy who formerly delivered newspapers on her street. He is a rock collector. The ore was given Mrs. York by a geologist when she visited the West."

Doug is ten years old and looks delighted. I remember being envious at the time. This was during America's innocent and ignorant fascination with the mysteries of atomic energy. Open-air atomic bomb tests were still being conducted in the American Southwest. Ordinary people played with fluoroscopes and radiation the way today some nose around with magnetometers hunting for coins in the sand at the beach. And here Doug was being handed a radioactive rock. Up and down Cape Cod, I'm sure, kids saw that newspaper picture and were jealous of him. Little did we know at the time that a hot rock like this would become something no one would ever want around the house. Radiation in the family room is mostly frowned upon today. Frankie, as she points out in her radio interview, blithely inherited Mrs. York's uranium ore along with the rest of Doug's collection.

Anyway, this should set the record straight. My mother can't blame me. Given the turn Frankie's rock collection took during her years in England, I want it known it was not this "young one" who set her on her way. Back to the WOCB interview:

Frankie: "Unfortunately at about the age of twelve or thirteen, many of the young people lose interest in their collections and the shells go on to younger children, and the stamps stay in the attic, or get passed on, and the rocks just disappear. So I took all the collections and added to them and became more selective. And instead of collecting just stamps as such, I began to specialize mostly in plate blocks and American stamps. And the shells I began to make arrangements with; and the rocks, I began to collect rocks from Europe, and collected from Rome . . ."

Her voice trails off dramatically at this point.

Frankie gets awkwardly quiet.

The tone of her voice shifts.

It's clear Frankie is struggling with her thoughts. She isn't quite sure what to say about her European rock collecting. Radio interviewer Nan Daniels breaks in and asks, "You mean you brought rocks back in your suitcase?"

"Yes," Frankie answers, suddenly back to her breezy, enthusiastic voice. "In fact, when we came back here I had a big box. Of course when we came back we were moved by the government, because at that time my husband was with the Office of Naval Research in London. And the mover said, 'What on earth do you have in here? Rocks?' And I said, 'Yes!' And I thought, probably, he thought I was a bit strange. All sorts of rocks came back. . . . Pre-Roman bricks, that they made there, uhhmm . . ."

And there it is again. The halting, lowered voice, as Frankie enters an area of uncertainty, nervous about what to say. She is clearly uncomfortable. She stammers.

". . . The Walls . . . [pause] . . . They were all handmade . . . [pause] . . . hand-fired."

And then she's bailed out again by the interviewer, and we learn no more. "Let's take lace. It sort of fell into your lap. Tell us about that," says Nan Daniels, and the interview turns to lace, found in old attic trunks.

Frankie's stumbling, not once but twice, in the same halting way when the subject came to the same thing—the actual nature of her English rocks and how she'd obtained them—is a powerful clue that she knew she had disregarded a taboo and that it was wrong to take these stones. Her conscience won't allow her any pride in this collection of pieces of ancient sites.

The rocks never got pulled out with pride. She never mentioned them. She never displayed them. She knew, I think, the rocks could not be shown. Because I'm sure, in retrospect, Frankie felt she should not have taken them.

The radio interview was a strong clue. Yet Frankie's very nature suggests she'd consider it wrong to deface important, precious places. More than any other issue, Frankie became furious about vandalism in her community. She wrote letters to newspapers, and to court judges, venting outrage over news accounts of vandalism to public schools or cemeteries on Cape Cod, for example. At the end of the WOCB radio interview she even makes a weird connection in her own mind between the negative of destroying things and the positive of collecting. She's asked what advice she would give to beginners in collecting.

"I think the most important thing," Frankie responds, "is to develop a curiosity and interest in something. I think today with television and all this other stuff young people have, they're getting away from creativity and many of their ways turn to kicks, to vandalism and this sort of thing, and it's too bad. My advice is to acquire a desire to build, to construct, rather than destruct."

She believed this sincerely. I know she did. Yet she didn't add to English sites, she took from them. She took rocks, their building blocks, knowing she shouldn't. In that small way, she vandalized world heritage sites with no intention of showing off the rocks, or bragging to a radio audience about her piece of Avebury, or even hinting to her own sons that she had such a collection. Why did she take the rocks? What drove my mother to do the very thing she rants about—detracting from something meaningful—causing her son these many years later to react, return, restore, resolve?

thursday, march 6

"Well, it's quite a coincidence, this," remarks Peter Carson, the new head of Stonehenge. That's what they call him. Not managing director or executive supervisor. Just "head." Carson is holding in his hands the two small pieces of Stonehenge Frankie took from the site back in '67 or '68.

"Just a couple of weeks ago," Carson says, "a colleague in the London office received a small velvet bag and inside were a couple of small rocks and a note saying they had been taken at Stonehenge. It was an American family, apparently, who'd been here fairly recently, and they were feeling guilty they'd taken the stones. So they mailed them back. With great and gentle dignity, I'd say, cushioned in velvet."

The stones went to the London office of English Heritage, the nonprofit that owns and administers some four hundred ancient British properties, including Stonehenge. "I'm pretty new," says Carson, "but several people at Heritage said that had never happened before, stones coming back. Now you're here with your mother's pieces. It's very reassuring."

Preservation hasn't always been the watchword. A famous British collector of medieval antiquities, William Stukeley, for example, noted in his diary in 1751 that his library collection included "some of the [Stonehenge] stone, the common sort, polished, the granite of the lesser obeliscs." And if you think Frankie was just the odd Ugly American, consider this: Founding Father John Adams on an English tour with Thomas Jefferson in 1786 noted in his diary that at Stonehenge "we cutt off a Chip according to Custom." Even into the twentieth century it was possible to rent a hand pick or hammer in the closest village to Stonehenge, Amesbury, to use for chipping off a memento. Frankie, I could see, was just one in a long line of people who have desired a piece of this wonderful place.

I've decided to return my first rock at Stonehenge on the eastern edge of the Salisbury Plain because it's one of the best-known attractions in Great Britain, and none of the rocks I found disturbed me more. If I was going to make any amends, it seemed important to start here. After settling into a B&B in Amesbury, I've tracked down Peter Carson.

With a million people a year visiting the national treasure, Peter tells me, it was imperative on English Heritage to rein in people, just as it was inevitable that some would take home souvenirs. Vandalism and wear and tear led in 1978 to limited access and twenty-four-hour security.

"But now with all the stones coming back," says Carson, "if you've started something, perhaps we could build another Stonehenge."

Stonehenge looks different than it did when I visited, and when my mother visited, in the 1960s. Then there was no visitors' center, no surrounding retaining fence, no full-time security guards in Plexiglas guard booths, and no footpaths on which visitors must stay. Tourists could roam at will between the monoliths, touch them, hug them. Or deface them.

The sheer numbers, as well, made crowd control and controlled access essential. Most were just tourists, tromping around day in and day out. But some came dressed in robes, bedecked with rings, ready to dance and chant, and as high as the field hawks riding thermals over Salisbury Plain on any number of mixtures of pagan religion, numerology, mythology, mysticism, UFO belief, Wiccan worship, Druid devotion, or hallucinogenic drugs. The 1970s and 1980s soon saw thousands of these "user groups," as Peter Carson politely calls them, flocking to Stonehenge, and these visitors tended to want to camp out and stay awhile.

The central attraction for many of these groups is the site's suspected Stone Age use as an astronomical computer, with key megaliths aligning with the rising or setting sun on key dates. "Around the solstice and equinox, I'm afraid, things built up into a festival, rather than a quiet spiritual or religious experience," says Carson. "It was having quite an impact on the local community, and on the stones." In 1985 access at these solar periods was curtailed.

Carson is young and new and is trying to build up a new relationship with the, ah, user groups. He's into new ways of presenting history, "stimulating all the senses," he says, not just the eyes. He likes for people to interact with what they're seeing. And he likes it that in the year 2000, with Stonehenge controls in place, managed open access was permitted again at the solstice for a twelve-hour period of sunrise rites. In 2001 over six thousand pagans participated. By 2002 the number had swelled to twenty-five thousand.

Frankie was no sixties hippie. She was one of the thousands in the most ordinary user group: gawking sightseers. But she was one of those sheer numbers of people whose actions led to the need to strictly police the place. At least that's the way it looked at first.

In fact, taking a closer look at the stones I'm carrying, Peter and I come to the conclusion it's very unlikely that Frankie should be blamed for anything here. I find myself a little disappointed. I have started at Stonehenge because it's such a major historic site. But the first rock return is turning out, dramatically speaking, to be a real dud. I should be relieved, I guess. But I'm feeling gypped.

First off, Peter decides, the two Stonehenge stones Frankie took hadn't been chipped off larger stones. They are too smoothly formed. Best guess is that they were rounded off by mechanical action, not water. Water rounds the ends of stones, taking them toward balls or lima beans, but Frankie's rocks are smoothed in a way that would eventually yield cylinders. Rolling on the ground, it appears, wore them down.

Second, the pieces aren't the right kind of stone. They are fine-grained limestone, of which there is plenty in Britain, and in the general area, but not in the actual prehistoric monument's important pieces. Stonehenge's biggest standing stone blocks, its lintels, the station stones, slaughter stone, and heel stone, are all of sarsen, a particular type of sandstone that occurs as huge boulders on the land surface of Marlborough Downs, about twenty miles away. The stone circle's builders dragged the rocks that distance before tipping them upright. The smaller stones in the two other circles in the monument, known as bluestones, are of several types of blue-colored rock that came from the Preseli Mountains in southwest Wales. It's thought they were brought by raft the two hundred miles to Stonehenge, hugging the Bristol Channel coast and then up the River Avon to Salisbury Plain.

The recent security changes have meant a return to a more natural setting for the monoliths. The circle's off-limits central area has been resodded and is now grass, as it was in 1400 B.C. It looks a lot better for that. But when Frankie visited over thirty years ago the ground between the standing stones, where she would have walked, was gravel—gravel worn by the mechanical action of countless visiting human feet into shapes like the stones I have brought back.

The conclusion seems clear. Frankie's rocks weren't ever handled by Stonehenge's builders. Most likely they were handled by no one more romantic than one of the site's maintenance crew members sometime in the twentieth century.

Peter Carson asks that I leave the stones with him. He wants to give them to English Heritage's archaeologist to take a look. But foreign, modern gravel brought in to the site is Carson's best guess. And so, mine.

Rather unceremoniously I hand him the little rocks. I thought I'd feel plenty of emotion giving back pieces of Stonehenge, one of the world's true wonders. But I don't feel much. A piece of walkway gravel. What could be more anticlimactic?

Will all Frankie's rocks turn out to be so mundane?

No way.

friday, march 7

Cloudy, rain threatening, and then rain starting as I drive the 20 or so miles west with a two-inch-long piece of chert in my pocket, clearly marked "Stourhead."

I'd never heard of Stourhead. Frankie had, though, and she'd been there, and she'd taken one of its white, chalky stones. But from where? It's a big place.

Stourhead House is a 1720s Palladian mansion, one of those three-story, yellowish palaces with wide crushed-stone skirts in front, a place that looks like a set for any Merchant Ivory movie needing a residence for a duke or a prince. It's in lovely shape. The rock couldn't have come from there.

Behind the house is a huge, sprawling, world-famous garden. It's full of exotic shrubs and trees like hanging beechwoods, and a three-mile walking path weaves around a picturesque lake designed to reflect temples imitating classical Italian models, stylistic structures named Pantheon, Temple of Apollo, and Temple of Flora. There are tunnels and bridges, obelisks and water cascades. Yet Stourhead Estate is even bigger than this. It is spread over 2,650 acres, and encompasses woodlands, open countryside, and striking chalk downs. The whole thing is owned and operated by the National Trust.

The Gardens is the place for me to start. Sheelagh Duly, a Trust employee at the entry building, has never heard of anyone taking Stourhead's stones. Or of anyone returning them. She does offer, though, that "now and again we see visitors leaving with very stiff arms, held right tight and out straight." When she sees by the look on my face I haven't got a clue what she's talking about, Sheelagh says, "They're carrying cuttings. Pieces of the shrubs or trees. They've put them up their sleeve." That's what you take from gardens. That or seed heads, not stones, she figures. But I ought to talk to the head gardener, she says. He's in charge of the entire one-hundred-acre garden grounds.

Head Gardener Andy Mills is six-foot-four, lanky, clean-shaven, maybe thirty years old, with bushy sideburns and tousled hair. He rides a mountain bike around the garden grounds tending to his duties. He examines Frankie's rock and quickly declares, "It's definitely not part of my gardens. It's not off the temples or statues. Wrong stone." And even stone lying on the ground here wouldn't be this white chert, a form of chalk, silica-based with a core of flint.

He guesses the stone came off Whitesheet Down, probably Whitesheet Hill at the western edge of the chalk downlands of Wiltshire. The hill is at the far eastern edge of the estate. "You'll likely find one exactly the same up there," says Andy.

"Why would my mother go up there?" I wonder aloud.

"For the ancient sites, I'd think," offers Andy.

I take a right at the Red Lion pub and drive about a kilometer down Whitesheet Lane, a narrow dirt road between hedgerows separating fields on the estate. Straight ahead is the down, a half-barrel shaped ridge interrupting the otherwise flat landscape, and running north-south. At its very end, to my right, stands Whitesheet Hill, a natural defensive spot some eight hundred feet above sea level. If you were a stone-tool age, Bronze Age, Iron Age, or nuclear age commander in charge of protecting your interests in this area, this is where you'd put the troops. And if you were interested in putting your dead closer to the sun, this is where you might put their graves. In fact, up on the hill are traces of a range of ancient use: a neolithic, causewayed enclosure dating from 3000 B.C. where prehistoric farmers met for markets, fairs, and religious ceremonies; a Bronze Age burial barrows and several burial mounds, which show up as big grassy humps, plus intriguing cross-ridge dikes from the same period; and out on the commanding plateau, at the very end of the down, an Iron Age hill fort, dating from about 500 B.C. The fort is what most tourists want to see.

Whitesheet Lane ends about a kilometer from the fort, and getting up to it is a hike. In the cold rain the parking lot is empty. A sign says, "Do not leave valuables in vehicles. Thieves operate in this area." An odd message for rural England, I think. Then I think of Frankie. It's time to give back your loot, Mum. I decide this is the area she was operating in, way back when.

I set out with umbrella, rain slicker, and the hunk of white sedimentary rock in my pocket. As soon as the steep, muddy path emerges from a thorn thicket and reaches the ridgeline, the full force of the wind hits me. Forty mph, at least. Frigid rain is drenching me. The brolly is useless. I struggle on. I'm considering turning back when I look west and see blue sky. Within minutes the rain has stopped, the wind has dropped, and other than chalky mud, the way is clear.

Enjoying views of quilted green pastureland parcels spread out below, the Stourhead great house in the distance, the troubled but forgiving sky overhead, I hike to the hill fort. It is a round earthen circle at the end of the downs escarpment. A perimeter trench depression rises to a rounded defensive mound in the central fort area. Rather like a Jell-O mold ring. The floor of the fort is mostly grassy. But true to Andy's word, rougher sections show pieces of exposed chert exactly like the piece in my pocket.

I decide this is where Frankie came, this is where she took the rock, and this is where I ought to replace it.

At 1:37 P.M., Greenwich Mean time, 7 March 2003, I drop Frankie's Stourhead stone into a small hole I've opened upon the turf at this Iron Age fort, gently cover it, and tap down the sod with my boot. Quite spontaneously, before dropping it in, I surprise myself and kiss the stone. I do it without thinking.

"It's been a long, strange journey. But here you are. Back where you began." I say this aloud.

I feel somehow very sad.

I stop at the Red Lion on my way out, to dry out in front of their log fire, and to fortify myself with a bowl of mushroom soup and a pint of Butcombe bitter.

The proprietor, Chris Gibbs, collects cask ale pump clips, those small, usually oval cards that affix to the ale pump handles, facing outward toward the customer to identify the brew available to be pulled.

All over Chris Gibbs's wall are cask ale pump clips. "I guess that's about all I have in common with your mum," he says of his one collecting passion. Blindman Brewery's Mine Beer Bitter, Cortleigh Brewery's Barn Owl and their Golden Eagle, Hopback Brewery's Summer Lightning, Moor Beer Company's Merlin's Magic, Coach House Brewing's Dick Turpin, and on and on. "I've got boxes more in the back," says Chris.

Joan Shepherd comes up to the bar and begins chatting with Chris, and I begin talking with her. She has come to the Red Lion to show the place to a lady friend who is with her. "I was born upstairs here," says Joan, a bespectacled, full-figured woman with a florid face. She is also back in the area to research some of her roots.

At her request, Chris opens an old wooden door behind the bar so Joan can show her friend the eighteenth-century spiral staircase going upstairs. "There, see," she says. "I told my friend that when I was a little girl I had to go through the pub to go to bed."

I look at the pint of ale in my hand. "Sounds familiar to me," I say. "I, too, often go through pubs on my way to bed."

I tell Joan about Frankie. She doesn't seem much concerned about the loss of stones. She has a sister in Ohio. On one visit to America Joan went to Oregon. "I took a rock from up a river there," she says.

"Just a rock at a river, that's okay," I say.

"Well, they said it was near where the red Indians had settled," she says.

Joan needs to leave to go put flowers on her mother's grave.

"It must be a day for remembering mums," I say to her, as she's going out. "I just did the same thing. Sort of."

My B&B is only a few miles from Stonehenge, so that evening, near sunset, I return for a final visit. I stare at these stones, so associated with the sun, with the sun now setting behind them. I had been here with Frankie. I remember standing in front of a sarsen stone while she took my picture. Thirty-six years ago. Her hair was going gray. Arthritis had begun to twist her hands.

It's my hair graying now, my left thumb feeling the first pains of arthritis. Did Frankie pick up her stone that day? She wouldn't have thought anything of it, taking pebbles from the path.

The big gray Stonehenge stones are ghostly in the fading light, backlit, square geometric shapes in such a familiar pattern. Depth perception is lost with the loss of overhead light, and I'm staring through the perimeter fence at darker and darker gray, irregular squares, upright, leaning, balanced horizontal hunks—stone giants outlined against a dull silver horizon the color of a ten-pence coin.

I feel very, very lonely.

3.

alienated, anxious
child extraordinaire

Salisbury Cathedral

Irrespective of individual idiosyncrasies of collectors, and no matter what or how they collect, one issue is paramount: the objects in their possession are all ultimate, often unconscious assurances against despair and loneliness. They function as defenses in the service of self-assertion. They are magic remedies to ward off existential doubt and, most of all, they are witnesses of credibility.

—Dr. Werner Muensterberger, psychoanalyst

Dr. Werner Muensterberger has done probably the most thorough, modern psychoanalytic study of obsessive collectors. He writes it up in a 1994 book entitled *Collecting: An Unruly Passion.* He concludes that the roots of pathological collecting go deep into a person's childhood and represent a coping substitution for childhood loss, lack of nurturing, trauma, vulnerability, deprivation, or inner longing. The pursuit and accumulation of objects, he believes, are a way for these people to control anxiety and uncertainty.

Or as one of his patients succinctly summed it up, "It's a hedge against nothingness."

Most children in some way turn to objects to help them cope, Dr. Muensterberger points out. Even children who get plenty of love and understanding in their earliest years will often turn to tangible things like stuffed animals, toy dump trucks, or security blankets as they anxiously try to figure out how to deal with feelings of vulnerability or of being left alone. I remember mine growing up. I still have him. Dr. Pick, a small stuffed gray rabbit, now on about his sixth set of sewn-on button eyes.

Dr. Pick was also a real person. He was my pediatrician when I was an infant in Fitchburg, Massachusetts. Frankie told me I began calling my rabbit Dr. Pick when I first began to talk. Why would any kid name his stuffed rabbit after his pediatrician? It seems unlikely I would have if the experience with my first doctor was tied to hypodermic needles and long waits in the waiting room. Was it, instead, because Dr. Pick (the real person) held me, tickled me, spoke soothingly to me in the otherwise strange, scary setting of the doctor's office? Was it because my mother didn't? Was it because Dr. Pick simply showed interest in me, and in my earliest years that felt uniquely welcome? Did the stuffed rabbit become Dr. Pick because I yearned for something missing, something I wasn't getting from my mother, something I wanted to take home with me and keep close to me?

Who knows? Not me. I probably never will. What I do know is that I'm the only two-year-old I've ever heard about who named his stuffed animal after his doctor.

The more traumatized a youngster is, or the more he or she feels alone, in doubt, frightened, or anxious, the more desperately the child turns to inanimate objects for solace. This is Dr. Muensterberger's conclusion. A child who comes to learn people can't be trusted to meet his or her emotional needs will find in a teddy bear a rock-steady, dependable friend, ever patient, a tireless listener who can be hugged and hugged without ever asking to be let go. "By discovering that he can improvise companionship," Dr. Muensterberger writes, "the baby can, at least for a while, push aside the menace of the real world."

Dr. Pick, frayed and faded and restitched so many times along his seams that he has a Frankensteinesque appearance now, shows just such signs of a needy child's desperate clinging.

Dr. Muensterberger applies his premise back into ancient times, too. He suggests that many early cultures, with whole populations of grown-ups who didn't get very sensitive nurturing in childhood, came to imbue all sorts of objects with mystical, magical, or life-force powers. Whole religions became structured around representations, relics, and icons. Powerful persons in the society, in turn, collected as many amulets, holy relics, or talismans as they could buy or plunder. Objects represented power. But equally important, they represented ... well ... hedges against nothingness, or at least against the unknown.

Modern obsessive collectors often show attitudes similar to the ancients. They attribute to certain objects magical significance, or at least dynamism, revering them, and sometimes even naming them. But principally, Dr. Muensterberger's research suggests, collecting is a symbolic substitution for some individuals, and to the extent these people "can touch and hold and possess and, most importantly, replenish, these surrogates constitute a guarantee of emotional support."

"What else," he asks, "are collectibles but toys grown-ups take seriously? They are signposts in the struggle to overcome the reappearance of the notion of old feelings of abandonment, or separation anxiety."

Dr. Muensterberger, meet Yvonne Franco "Frankie" Hornig, emotionally fragile, anxious, alienated child extraordinaire.

Berthe Attard brought an attitude to America. Frankie's mother had suffered a miserable, lonely, abusive childhood growing up in Algeria and she brought little tenderness or tolerance to the raising of her own children in a poor French-immigrant neighborhood of turn-of-the-century New York City. She had been unloved as a little girl, and what love she was able to find for her three kids was reserved mostly for her last-born, her only son, Maurice Jr. Any love left over went to her firstborn, Marcelle. Middle child Yvonne was the black lamb, the shy and sensitive one, the most beautiful and talented of the children, but also the most vulnerable.

Berthe was born in 1889 in Bone, Algeria, a city today called Annaba, at the far east of the country on the Mediterranean coast close to the Tunisian border. Her father, Charles Attard, was Maltese, a metalsmith by trade, and had come to Algeria as part of the flow of non-Arab immigrants encouraged to settle there after the French annexation of the country. The Attards had played a role in that bit of North African colonial expansionism. Although from Malta, Charles's father had spent considerable time in Tunis and spoke Arabic like a native. After the French conquest of Algeria began in 1830, the elder Attard offered his services to the French as a spy, traveling through Arab territory and passing for one of them. He was rewarded with a homestead stake in the new French Algeria in the 1880s. Berthe's mother's family had also come to North Africa as part of this European Mediterranean immigrant-settling effort. Her mother, Justine Carbuccia, had been born in Bastia—on Corsica, a French island off the west coast of Italy.

Justine and Charles Attard had two sons, Jerome and Paul, before Berthe's birth. Their first daughter was their last child; Justine died in childbirth. The tragedy immediately became Berthe's. Charles had loved Justine intensely. Her death crushed his spirit, and his reason. He blamed his baby daughter for taking his wife away. From her first moments of life, Berthe was loathed by her father. Charles wanted no part of the child.

My grandmother was sent as an infant to live with an evil aunt who, she told us, burned her with an iron, beat her, and locked her in a closet as punishments. By school age, Berthe was placed in an Algiers orphanage, growing up without a father or mother or true home. Her years there were lonely and full of fright. Rules were rigid, punishments harsh. Berthe had few possessions, no luxuries, few friends, and no one to nurture her. She kept in contact with her brothers, however; Paul had married and lived nearby in Algiers, Jerome was in Tunis about three hundred miles away. She saw them when she could. Yet they couldn't do a lot for her. She was mostly on her own, her personality shaped by the hardships of growing up an unwanted child in the care of uncaring strangers in the dusty heat and spartan surroundings of a turn-of-the-century North African orphanage.

In 1909 everything changed. In the spring, Paul Attard, then twenty-nine years old, and his wife Maria, boarded a German-flagged steamship, the *Cincinnati*, and sailed to America. They arrived in New York City June 7 and found an apartment on West Thirty-ninth Street. Late that autumn, younger brother Jerome, twenty-four years old, gathered up his sister, Berthe, and the two of them took steerage berths aboard the 1,370-passenger, 554-foot American Line vessel *Saint Paul* and made their own passage to America. They arrived in New York Harbor the day before Christmas, with $41 and Paul's address in Jerome's pocket.

All at once the Attard children became American immigrants. Life had changed. But for Berthe, at least, one thing forged by her unloving past crossed the Atlantic with her. At age twenty, my mother's mother disembarked at Ellis Island a bitter, emotionally scarred young woman with a permanent scowl on her face and a chip on her shoulder larger than Lady Liberty's torch.

This same year, 1909, was life change for my grandfather, too. Maurice Franco arrived in America two months before Berthe. He came over on the *Louisiane* out of Le Havre, a French Line steamship that docked in New York Harbor on October 30, 1909. Maurice was just eighteen. His father had paid for his passage. Maurice settled on West Twenty-third Street.

Both Maurice and Berthe first took up residence in French-immigrant neighborhoods on the west side of Midtown Manhattan. But how they met, I never knew. However it happened, within a year they did meet and in October 1911 they were married in St. Columbia Church.

It will always be unknown to me, this fact of how they met. It's ancient history now. Like so many American kids, it never occurred to me while they were still alive to ask Pepère, as we called my grandfather, or Bah, as my grandmother was nicknamed. They were always old in my eyes. And always so foreign. An even bigger mystery is what on earth soft-spoken, gentle Maurice Franco saw in the way of a match with this short, stout, agitated young woman. But he fell in love with Berthe, married her, and stuck it out for fifty-six years—over half a century living in a household dominated by Berthe's shrill caviling and carping, criticizing and complaining. I never once saw my grandmother smile or laugh. I rarely saw her out of her housecoat and slippers. She resisted speaking English or adopting American ways to her dying day, giving their small, fifth-floor walk-up apartment in the Bronx a very Old World feel. Her verbal assaults on her husband and children were constant and endless. She was a victim and needed everyone to know it. Caring and emotional support for her children was not something Berthe Attard Franco had a clue how to provide. She'd gotten no tenderness, love, or support growing up and, in motherhood herself, had none to pass on.

Yvonne, perhaps more than either of her siblings, needed a healthy dose of emotional support. Marcelle was smart, shrewd. Little Maurice was precocious, arrogant. In between, Yvonne was timid, nervous, and withdrawn, and suffered regular, excruciating migraine headaches. She was the feeling child who showed early abilities in art, singing, and music. But in the Franco home, art was out of the question, a pointless pastime in a poor family making its way in America. Singing by the children was not encouraged. It was an annoyance to Bah, although she frequently sang French songs herself as she shuffled bullishly around their apartment. Frankie's father might have praised his daughter's talents in art or song if Bah hadn't dominated the tone of their home. But Berthe was in her husband's face as much as in the others'. Her husband, a gentle and timid man, chose most often to withdraw. By nature Pepère was not a confrontational person. He kept his own sanity by taking a fishing pole out to the banks of the Hudson and sitting for hours, with a line in the water, alone.

Little Yvonne was allowed no such escape. Berthe's bullying was something the children simply had to endure. Especially Yvonne, the child Berthe liked least. Yvonne had little social life, little freedom. She had no chance to be a collector as a youngster even if the inclination had been there; if she had tried to collect things, Berthe would have thrown them away. Berthe threw away clippings of movie stars that Yvonne had saved, so my mother eventually took to hiding these. She was punished routinely, unjustly, cruelly, as Berthe played out her own history of trauma upon the next generation. Yvonne was chastised even for speaking English, so that she went to her first day of school, at St. Patrick's Cathedral School in the city, semi-illiterate in the language of her family's chosen land. The result was that Yvonne felt even more like an outcast. Her confidence was hammered. She was reluctant to speak up and participate in classroom work, which thrust her into the firing line of the teacher-nuns, who concluded she was lazy, uncooperative, slow, or all three. She was openly humiliated, and sometimes even physically struck by the nuns. The language difficulties kept her a year behind her classmates.

The memories of all this remained with Frankie for a lifetime. Raised a Catholic, my mother had nothing to do with the Catholic Church after she left childhood. In later life, in Protestant churches, her beautiful voice would soar in emotion singing religious songs and hymns. But Frankie left childhood deeply alienated from the Church of Rome, and she sang not out of churchly faith but, I believe, because the sound of such songs was just plain uplifting to her spirit, and hers was a spirit in serious need of lifting.

In church, during her child-rearing years, music was Frankie's sole interest, never sermons, devotion, or ecclesiastical matters. But by the time she moved to London, Frankie showed one new interest in religious edifices: their rocks.

saturday, march 8

Salisbury Cathedral's visitors' services manager isn't in, it being Saturday. But Leslie Burton, who works in the visitors' services department, is in, catching up on some work. Leslie suggests I snag one of the volunteer guides inside the cathedral. They're talkative and knowledgeable, she says, and clearly identifiable. Just look for anyone with a blue sash across his chest.

The color is closer to teal, actually. And snag a guide I do. The perfect guide. Ken de V. Lorrain, a round, white-haired gentleman with sleepy eyes drooping down to a long nose and puffy jowls, has worked as a volunteer in Salisbury Cathedral for forty years. I show him Frankie's rock pieces labeled *Salisbury Cathedral.*

I have two pieces. One is fine-grained limestone/chalk. The cathedral is made of the same stuff. The other piece is actually a tile—brick red with a yellow inlay diamond-pattern design. Frankie had noted on the back that it was a hundred years old. That's far younger than the Gothic cathedral, which dates from 1220. Did she mean a thousand years old? That would be too old.

As it happens, I saw very similar tiles on display in the British Museum several days ago. One that looked almost identical except for a different design was labeled *Medieval tile with stars in quatrefoil. Late 13th C., from Salisbury Cathedral.* Other designs were in oak leaves and fleurs-de-lis, two birds back-to-back, a dragon in a circle, and stars in quatrefoil. Yet another plaque in the British Museum led me to believe Frankie was right about the hundred years, and that she hadn't actually removed an original tile. In 1852, the museum plaque said, William and Henry Godwin founded a company to make Gothic revival tiles of the same style and color as Salisbury's originals, and they were used in restorations.

Ken Lorrain pretty much agrees with my thinking Frankie's tile piece isn't original. Still, he takes me to view the two floors in the church where tile is laid. They look much older, much more faded than Frankie's tile. The design on the tile I'm carrying doesn't match. Ken says there used to be boxes of tiles and tile fragments above the north porch, but he doesn't think they are still there.

The stone piece Frankie took is of much more interest to both of us. Ken cuts it with a knife. "Piece of sand silica limestone with flint interruptions, from Chilmark or Tisbury, which are quarries there, adjoining," he declares. "There's sixty thousand tons of this in the cathedral. All the light stone. The ceilings are tufa, which comes from the Mendip Hills in Somerset. The pillars are Purbeck marble, which isn't a true marble. It was formed millions of years ago when the sea covered Dorset. Quarrying there is still going on," he says, his head swinging slowly, his eyes fixing on things in familiar succession. Ken has been guiding visitors through Salisbury so long that mention of one thing automatically leads to the next thing, and the next, a practiced audio text unfolding like a triptych. Deviations are only possible if you interrupt. Ken walks along with short, slow, accustomed steps, as he would with a group of twenty tourists, even though he's alone with me.

"Let's try to figure out where my mother might have taken this from in the cathedral," I say. The man is invaluable to me, but the guide will need a little guiding.

"Maybe she picked it up in the workshops," he suggests. "They used to let visitors see the workshops. But I doubt they're open today. We'll see." And off he glides. I follow along. He veers off—he can't help it, I decide—to show me the Magna Carta on display in the Chapter House; then again to show me the tomb that had broken open during a moving, at which time they found a rat inside the skull of the interred bishop.

"A rat in his skull?" I say.

"It sort of confirmed suspicions the bishop had been poisoned," says Ken, "seeing as the rat died in his head."

"How did the rat get in the tomb?"

"Don't know, but the rat picked the wrong one, didn't he?"

When we get to the workshop it's locked, as Ken suspected.

As we glide back toward the central nave of the cathedral, we pass along the side of the open cloister. I notice stones sort of like Frankie's lying in dirt around the shrubs. But I don't say anything.

When we're back inside the cathedral, I ask Ken, "What should I do with the stone?"

"I would be inclined to keep it," he says. "As a memento, a souvenir."

"Ken, I can't go home with the rock. I've come all the way here to give it back."

"To us it would be of no consequence," he says.

I am struck hearing him say that. I am even a little offended. But as I think about it, it makes sense. Repeatedly during our walk through the chilly, stone chambers of the massive cathedral he has made reference to repairs, stone scraps, breakage. It becomes clear to me that for Ken (and perhaps for any-body who works in an edifice of stone as overwhelming as Salisbury Cathe-dral) the fact is that stone comes and goes and that pieces like the small piece I have in my hand accrue naturally from the life cycles of stone and rep-resent the great building's vitality. It may take a volunteer who has spent much of his life in such a place, like Ken, to see it. But the cathedral is not an immutable thing. It is dynamic. The pieces are not what matters. What matters is the whole. For Ken de V. Lorrain, what matters is the majesty of this cathedral, and nothing Frankie did, in his eyes at least, has affected that one whit.

"Take it home," he says, as he moves back to the volunteer guides' staging area. "To most people it would be a very prized thing."

It's home now, I think silently. I've brought it home.

After leaving Ken, I find my way back to the cloister, the old meditative square inside the cathedral, canopied around its sides but with its center open to the sky and seeded with grass. Tourists exit the cathedral along the clois-ter's east side. I walk around to the opposite side, where there's no foot traf-fic, it's quiet, and there's privacy.

I press Frankie's stone into the soft earth in the shrub and flower garden surrounding the cloister. It vanishes in the brown soil. And there I leave it, on the west side of the cloister, closest to America. A little bit of Salisbury Cathedral Frankie had taken away to be with her, now returned, and a little bit of my mother now a part of Salisbury Cathedral.

I stop by the visitors' services building on my way out of the Salisbury Close. Leslie Burton is still there. I leave the small floor tile with her. She lights up, genuinely pleased, I think.

"It would make quite the proper paperweight," she says, placing it on a stack of papers. It does look pretty good on her desk, medieval in style and all. And if the 45 mph winds howling through the close today are any indication, a paperweight will be a useful item on days Leslie might want the window open.

4.

a different kind of
musical rock star

Corfe Castle

 Music in childhood was Frankie's salvation. Despite the insensitive, repressive household policed by her mother, Berthe, Frankie was somehow allowed to take up the violin.

She took violin lessons, beginning at least as early as 1926, when she was twelve; that year Russian-born musician and painter Michael Baxte gave her a photo of himself signed "to my dear little pupil Yvonne Franco." I found it among her things. Later she studied with Zareh Tate, and the bond between them lasted the rest of their lives.

In a condolence note after Frankie's death, Zareh recalled that when he began giving young Frankie lessons, he realized right away her special talent. Frankie never learned to sight-read music but she had the gift of ear. Zareh and later teachers found that after one listening Frankie could play back pieces from memory. Her father, Maurice, came to take great pride in this talent, and it even gained grudging respect from Berthe. In turn the violin became Frankie's refuge, setting her apart from Marcelle and her small brother, bonding her to her gentle, beloved father, and providing her a place of relative isolation and safety away from her domineering mother.

And it gave Frankie a place to star, a way to get the attention for which she yearned.

In 1930 this starring role reached a height Yvonne could barely have imagined. The young chauffeur's daughter was invited to the late President Theodore Roosevelt's Victorian-style summer estate, Sagamore Hill, in Oyster Bay on Long Island, to play the violin for an assortment of family members of the former president's grown children, Theodore Jr., Kermit, Ethel, and Archibald.

She didn't normally run in these circles. Not socially. The younger Roosevelts had become aware of Frankie through talk and connection among the groundskeepers, gardeners, house servants, cooks, and chauffeurs attending to the wealthy families of posh Oyster Bay. In 1929 Frankie's father had taken a job in Oyster Bay driving for the Perrine family, and the job included housing and the requirement the Francos live there.

The move was an enormously liberating one for Yvonne. The Franco family was able to leave the hardscrabble immigrant canyonlands of New York City, where Frankie's life had little exposure to the privilege of her father's employers, and settle into the pastoral chic of coastal Long Island, where my mother discovered long gravel driveways and lush lawns, flower gardens and garden parties. The Franco family members were still hired help, for sure, and they hardly had the run of the neighborhood's estates. Yet overnight, it must have felt to Frankie as if she had moved into a scene from *The Great Gatsby*. My mother read that book soon after moving to Long Island, and it became a favorite of hers for life. When I was a boy—about thirteen, I think—she made sure I read it. I wasn't sure why, because Frankie almost never recommended books to me. In fact, she didn't read much herself, other than books connected to her collections and hobbies.

The move to Oyster Bay dramatically changed my mother's early life. It was a ticket out of hated St. Patrick's Cathedral School, where Frankie never forgot the corporal punishment and emotional severity of the nuns. She enrolled in Oyster Bay High School, quickly became a popular newcomer, and blossomed into a seemingly confident, outgoing girl. Frankie took up acting. In going through stuff she saved, I found old playbills. In *Tulip Time*, a romantic operetta put on by Oyster Bay High Glee Clubs in 1930,

"Christina, charming Dutch girl" was played by Yvonne Franco. Frankie was just sixteen and probably enticed by the chance to sing. Along with the musical numbers sung by the entire cast, Frankie sang several duets. In 1932, Frankie was one of just two actors in a one-act play, *The Baggage.* In 1933 she played Minnie Belle Carter in *The Love Expert.* The same spring that year, she starred in another romantic operetta, *The Wishing Well,* singing two solos and two duets.

Meanwhile she had not forgotten the violin. Playbills show Frankie was a featured violinist at two community programs when she was fresh out of high school, playing solos in Beethoven, Kreisler, Wieniawski, and Dvořák pieces.

The Roosevelts' first attraction to Frankie, however, wasn't to her music. It was to her humility, her soft-spoken personality, and her fluency in French. Some of the ex-president's young grandchildren, it was felt, could use regular exposure to such traits during summer vacation at Oyster Bay, and so Frankie at age sixteen was hired to be a companion to the kids and to speak regularly to them in French. Eventually the Roosevelts came to know of her violin talent. They invited her to play for them one day, unexpectedly.

My mother never spoke to me about her Roosevelt violin recital. But it must have been the stuff out of which youthful dreams are born—an affirmation that life held grand possibilities. This teenage daughter of immigrant hired help, one foot still clamped by an overbearing mother in Old World sensibilities, was striding into the summer home of the former First Family of the Free World, the New World her parents had chosen, as a personally invited guest and star attraction. If such a thing was possible, if such a thing was happening, anything was possible, anything could happen.

Frankie was not a collector of things at this early age. Yet she must have walked wide-eyed through Sagamore Hill's ground-floor rooms so full of things—its walls covered with the antlers of wildebeest and impala, and ivory tusks of elephants and black rhino shot by Teddy Sr. on African safari, lion pelts taken on the Kapiti Plains now spread on the opulent North Room's floor, display cases and shelves filled with exhibits, specimens, trophies, and memorabilia collected by the twenty-sixth president and self-described American hunter-naturalist during his celebrated world travels.

What did happen to Frankie, later in her life, was considerably more mundane than what must have been imaginable there that day at Sagamore Hill, among the rich and famous, surrounded by the ex-president's curio cabinets and the many strange, fantastic things from faraway lands Teddy had collected and put on display. There was no subsequent makeover into a Daisy Buchanan for Frankie and no Gatsby from new money who came to pine for her. Frankie would ultimately marry and settle into the middle class. Yet for one brief, shining moment she came face-to-face with a kind of Camelot. And it held things. Magical things. Objects.

Is it possible that one slender root of Frankie's eventual passion for collecting goes way back there to Sagamore Hill? Did she carry out of the Victorian mansion, and into her later life, an association between collections and achievement, or between collections and personal worth? And as her life evolved into American normalcy and she moved into modest, ordinary homes on ordinary streets, is it possible she carried with her the memory of the magic of displayed things, and of the grand feelings collected things can produce? Things from a far wider world than her own, a world she could only dream of but had once walked through?

Who knows. There's no one to ask. No way to know. No one left. Only clues. Like the rocks.

Yet even if this experience influenced her, it was no more than a brush stroke on a canvas already full of discordant, emotional color coming out of childhood. Frankie left her childhood home for nursing school a prime candidate for psychiatrist Muensterberger's couch. People who lack nurturing and love in their earliest years often turn to a range of perceived equivalents in adulthood. Common ones are religion, drugs, or careers in caregiving. To this Dr. Muensterberger would add collecting. Frankie rejected the church but found much solace in religious music. She relied heavily on drugs, and arguably became addicted. Her profession became the most classic caregiver job, nursing. Her most all-consuming pastime became collecting. Frankie could be a starring case study for the New York psychoanalyst.

There must have been a great sense of liberation and psychic comfort for Frankie to leave the onerous orbit of her mother, Berthe, begin nursing people, marry a solid, good man, make many loyal friends, get her own home, and give birth to two bright, healthy boys. But as so many people later learn, and which today drives an industry of therapists, analysts, and counselors, leaving childhood doesn't necessarily mean leaving childhood behind.

sunday, march 9

Talk about taking coal to Newcastle. Taking stones to the Isle of Purbeck, Dorset, where Corfe Castle is located, is close to insanity. At least in Newcastle the coal is underground, out of sight. The sedimentary rocks of south-coastal Dorset, though, expose themselves as shamelessly as burlesque strippers, in dramatic, naked cliffs and outcroppings of sandstone, limestone, and chalk. On Purbeck, rocks are in your face.

While twenty million years ago the area was a muddy swamp with dinosaurs lounging around, the slow, grinding collision of the European and African geologic plates gradually buckled the rich sedimentary rock layers, forcing them up in some cases ninety degrees, and revealing ancient fossils and a practical source of livelihoods. Major quarries have been located here for hundreds of years, and before that, more ancient peoples found it a convenient area to take stone. Quarried stone has gone northeast to London for centuries to build the great buildings and streets of the capital. Old rail lines crisscross the landscape, remnants of the mechanical horsepower once used to haul stone out of old tunnels that crisscross the same landscape underground. Quarry owners were the aristocracy in these parts, and the villages grew up to serve mining and stonecutting labor. By late Victorian times, men in the area were more likely to be quarrymen than fishermen or farmers. There isn't a house of timber in all of Corfe, best I can see, and few buildings across the region made of anything else but stone. Everywhere your eye turns it sees stone walls, sheds, churches, gateposts. Everywhere you look is stone.

And I'm bringing back a small piece of stone.

Hearing I have a stone from Corfe Castle, Ozzie in the Red Lion pub in the nearby seaside town of Swanage lifts his Irish sweater to reveal his T-shirt: "Far Corfe," it says below a black silhouette of the castle. You have to say the words aloud with an English accent to get the pun. He makes a living that way, Ozzie does, designing T-shirts with clever, if off-color, messages.

Of the taking of the rock, Ozzie says, "That's not the problem. Everybody does that. The problem is when they start bringing them back."

Ozzie's friend, Roz, a sad-eyed, big burly man with a full white beard, is a stonecutter. Roz takes a look at my Corfe piece and declares, with authority, "It's cliff stone. Came from round about Cannon Cove."

"Would it have been used in building Corfe Castle?" I ask.

"Couldn't say," he says.

Later, in the Castle Inn pub in Corfe village itself, several other men weigh in with thoughts.

"I've got a considerable bigger piece than that in my mantel," says one man.

"It's because of your mum, is it, that I'm having such a time putting a new bleedin' roof on the castle?" says a workman.

Another guy notes that taking castle stone is nothing new. The whole back of the Greyhound pub at the foot of the castle is built with Corfe Castle stone, he says. And everyone nods.

monday, march 10

James Parsons, a short-haired, young guy with a penetrating but friendly stare, is Corfe Castle's visitors' services manager. He just happens to be in, filling in for the fee taker at the National Trust gate on this quiet off-season Monday morning. He is delighted with my rock, my journey, my story.

"I doubt you'll find where to fit it in," he says, "but you're welcome to try." But please don't leave it in the castle, he asks of me. "I'd love to have it. I'll write something up. Or maybe it could be put in the visitors' center, in one of the glass cases, with some sort of write-up about where it came from."

People picking away at the site is a chronic problem, Parsons admits, because so much of Corfe is in ruins, its stone ragged, exposed, and crumbling in places. It's not its age that has ravaged the castle. Corfe was arguably the most sturdily built fortress in the country's history, its buhrstone walls and towers as much as 3 feet thick and built on solid limestone bedrock. It was the favorite of several kings, including William the Conqueror and King John, precisely because of its massive, impregnable, indestructible construction. They felt safe there—no small matter to them, because the actuarial table for the life expectancies of medieval English rulers was not a pretty thing. No, Corfe isn't easy pickings for stone stealers because of decay. The castle is broken up because it was deliberately blown up in 1646 during the English Civil War, by order of Parliament. Oliver Cromwell and his meathead Roundheads felt Corfe Castle was just too tempting a place for royalists to hunker down.

It's a crime to do anything destructive to Corfe. Yet Parsons admits that people who just pick up a piece from the ground are rarely challenged. "If anyone was found chiseling off a piece, that's another matter." He says, "Last weekend, we could hardly believe it, two children were going around with a rock hammer hammering away at the walls. Their parents were just chatting away and admiring the views. They had brought a hammer into Corfe Castle. I guess they had been down along the coastal cliffs earlier. There are lots of fossils in the Jurassic rock in the cliffs, and people do dig them out. But obviously, if that's what they had been doing, when they got here the hammer should have stayed in the car."

Parsons takes me outdoors into the village and points to the edge of a private building across the street from the visitors' center. It has a carved piece of rock set in among the stone blocks. "That came from Corfe," says Parsons. His arm makes a sweep of the village. "So did lots of all of this," he says. The 1700s, 1800s, even into the 1900s, were not times of historic preservation. Cut stone close at hand was a gift to a builder. It wasn't seen as historic artifact or precious legacy. Stone was stone, and with Corfe Castle in ruins, who cared about the castle?

I have brought a 1967 picture of Frankie along with me as I walk the castle grounds alone. I glance at it, then gaze down at the village of Corfe spread below—a sea of rock houses, all a nearly uniform, mottled mix of browns and grays. Then I glance at Frankie's face again. It's a picture of her sitting outside on the balcony at the Sussex Lodge apartment in London. She's got some sort of picture book open on her lap and is looking at it. She's wearing a pink-and-white patterned dress. Her legs are crossed. She's showing the slightest of smiles. I look away again, this time at Corfe's rugged remains, and try to place Frankie here, try to transport and transpose her image, freshened by the photo, into where I am, where she once was. I want her to be with me here today. To help me. To talk to me about taking rocks. Or about anything. To laugh with me about how silly it was to take rocks, or about how silly it is to return them. I glance back and forth between her frozen image, serene on the balcony, and the bleak, gray stone surrounding me, a low, flat, gray sky overhead, and I can't do it. I can't bring her back. I'm the one here. She's there, a pale-green tree leafed behind her.

I wander slowly around the castle, and try to fit Frankie's souvenir into places; the choices are endless. It is, of course, ludicrous to try. But still I do. Frankie's rock is a rough, sharp-edged, shallow wedge shape with the top side very flat, as if it had been the facing side. It fits in exposed slots in the Horseshoe Tower, the leaning South-west Gatehouse, the Butavant Tower, the King's Tower in the Keep, the Gloriette.

It fits in wherever I want to fit it.

Back in the visitors' center, I speak with Nancy Grace, a hefty, pretty lady with an easy laugh and gentle manner. She is a Trust archaeologist and has been working on the Corfe site off and on for seventeen years. She examines the stone carefully.

"It's a bit suspect," she says. "I don't think it's Purbeck buhrstone, which makes up the castle's walls and buildings, which is quite coarse and shelly." She shows me the ancient shell deposits in the ruin's limestone walls. "That was what was brought here from the cliffs and used in construction. This piece is very fine-grained for what the castle is built of."

"But what about the flat side?" I say. "Isn't that a cut face, from the smooth side of a building block?"

Nancy shakes her head. "It's a natural flat face. It tends to break that way. And there's no sign of chisel or working marks, and no minute fossils. No, I think this is the same stone as the hill the castle sits upon. I think it's a bedrock piece."

"It wasn't brought here?"

"No, I think it was already here."

"It wasn't a piece of gravel from the path?" I'm thinking of Stonehenge.

"Again, I don't think so. The stone on the paths now isn't gravel, it's slats. And that only was put in in 1987. Your mother was here in the late sixties, right? At that time the paths were grass. Or in some areas it was gravelly, but that was material from the actual walls which had eroded and washed onto the paths. And this isn't that kind of rock. It's just the wrong grain.

"I think it's bedrock from this hill the castle occupies. When Corfe was built and they excavated, they hit bedrock in several locations. Some of this rock became exposed, some was used in other ways at the site. I think, somehow, your mum found herself a piece of the hill."

"Cool," I say.

Nancy is now studying the flat side again. "Or maybe, not," she replies, and gives me a smile. The flat side has a dark smudge to it, which she can't identify. It isn't flint, found in area limestone. It isn't part of the horizontal bedding plane of the limestone. It is curious.

"Could this be from gunpowder?" she wonders. "Now wouldn't that be something? We'd have to put it under a microscope to decide. But could this black be the result of being blown up?" Could Frankie have inadvertently taken away evidence of Cromwell's destruction?

"Way cool!" I say.

A visitor has been eavesdropping. "Or maybe someone was having a picnic roast," the visitor says.

"That's not allowed, surely," I say. I am getting defensive. I won't allow Frankie's find to be from some caravan camper's outdoor sausage and mash.

"It wouldn't be allowed now," says Nancy. "But three hundred years ago? A hundred? Or maybe even on the outer bailey when the castle was occupied a thousand years ago."

"Okay, that I can accept," I say. "A queen's cookout."

The Square and Compass pub in Worth Matravers is in the heart of quarrying country, about three miles south of Corfe. It is an authentic antique pub, a seventeenth-century place where ales are drawn directly out of kegs lined on their sides horizontally on racks and pints are served through a window. There is no bar. The two rooms are all wood and dust, the tables thick wood and the seating communal. The ceilings are low, the doorways narrow. Two dogs lie on the stone floor, and a fire burns warmly.

Attached to the pub is a museum. It's a forty-by-fifteen-foot space and it's crammed with collected things. Raymond Newman, it seems, the previous proprietor of the pub, became an avid collector of fossils and artifacts along the Purbeck peninsula heights and sites. He inspired his son, Charlie, who runs the pub today. Charlie set up the museum and dedicated it to his dad.

It's the oddest little museum. Pine display cases line the walls of the narrow space, and what doesn't fit in them is piled along the floor, hung from racks or pegs on the wall, or simply set on top of other things. It's a *wunderkammer* of collectibles. There is much stone: Roman stone roof tiles, Iron Age floor stones, whetstones, grain rubbers, a rotary quern, hand axes, hammer stones, convex scrapers, flat flint axes. There are many fossils: cephalopods, echinoids, ammonite whorls, assorted dinosaur footprints, and bones of iguanodons, plesiosaurs, and pliosaurs. And much more.

Next to a newspaper article from June 2002 reporting the Tate Gallery's exhibition of a load of human excrement called "Canned Feces" is the Square and Compass Museum's response, a display entitled "Turbeck Turds," consisting of fossilized prehistoric turtle turds, fish turds, and crocodile turds.

And finally, there is a jumbled assortment of human relics: eighteenth-century beer barrel keys and taps, bronze cauldron legs, a fourteenth-century buckle, love tokens (coins popular in the 1600s), a spur rowel from the 1300s, a seventeenth-century copper alloy bridle boss, a wavy-rim ninth-century Saxon horseshoe, penny pipes and clay pipes, Roman finger rings, brooches, and coins.

Weary from trying to absorb all these collectibles, I take a pint in the pub. It's been raining today, and the March wind over the peninsula highlands here has been brutal, icy, stinging. The fire in the Square and Compass common room feels good. As I sip a cask ale, life feels good. The present feels good.

A young woman with a walking stick under her arm comes and sits on the bench beside me. We get talking. Her name is Melissa Viney. She's a freelance radio reporter in her mid-thirties. She is in Wellington mud boots and wool, and is hiking a piece of the coastal Purbeck Way walk. She's stopped briefly for refreshment. She gets intrigued with my story.

We exchange e-mail addresses, and I promise to try to keep in contact and keep her informed of my progress as I loop around England. She hopes to sell the story and interview me toward the trip's end. Perhaps at Avebury.

After Melissa leaves, I lean back against the wall and again let in the sensation of warmth and well-being.

I'm lonely. But life is feeling good.

I think a little about Melissa. She's intruding into my future. I think some about what I'm doing, intruding into the past. I think about a quote I have somewhere in one of my notebooks, a thought that Nathaniel Hawthorne had entered in one of his English notebooks in 1856 after viewing the Elgin Marbles and other artifacts in the British Museum. "The present is burthened too much with the past. We have not time . . . to appreciate what is warm with life, and immediately around us."

I have been thinking about the impulses and attention Frankie spent on taking these rocks. Too much focus on the past sacrifices being in the present. This energy she spent on the old, it must have cut into the time and energy she had for the new—for creativity, discovery, creation. Frankie was a very creative person. Her music, her most awesome talent, could have been a tremendous creative outlet for her. But it wasn't. She had played violin for the Roosevelts as a girl but then almost completely set aside her music as she entered adulthood. Singing and making music took a back seat to other things— to being a wife, a nurse, and a mother, naturally, but as far as her spare time went, music was replaced particularly by collecting. What warmed her heart in Frankie's early life—one of the very few things of warmth she then had— gave way to the cold, meaningless collecting of old rocks.

Before coming to England I read an enlightening book by David Lowenthal, *The Past Is a Foreign Country.* Lowenthal believes, "A past too much esteemed or closely embraced saps present purposes, much as neurotic attachment to childish behaviour precludes mature involvement in the present." Collecting is a child's pastime, really, and psychologists believe its roots may burrow deeply into troubled childhoods. But sitting in the Square and Compass, I'm hit by a sudden insight. Perhaps Frankie's rocks are evidence of her inability to carry on a mature, mothering involvement, one of feeling in the moment, with her son—with me—when I was growing up.

It feels to me like a Eureka! moment.

For most of my childhood I felt invisible. I felt lonely. I didn't know my mother, and she didn't know me. But I didn't know anything was wrong with that picture. It was just the way things were.

The past has a hold of me right now, I see. It speaks to present purposes. But I decide I won't let the past sap this present moment here in the Square and Compass. I concentrate on my glass of ale. I savor its nutty taste. I feel the warmth from the fire. I push out of mind the dizzying array of old artifacts and fossils I've just seen in the pub's museum. A couple comes in with a shaggy brown dog. Three dogs are now slumped around the room. The moment is getting crowded with dogs, and I'm a cat person. So was Frankie.

I can't ignore it. Frankie is the present for me here. And letting Frankie into my thoughts is why I'm here in England. I'm not here to meditate.

Another thing Lowenthal wrote comes to mind. He believes obsession with ancient things is a symptom of self-contempt.

Did Frankie like herself? She certainly showed a strong need to be liked, and worked at that. Outside the family anyway. But did she like herself?

I drain my pint, and get up, pondering this. I'd never considered it. But it sounds plausible. There's a strong bit of evidence to back it up. They say drug addicts participate in self-destructive behavior because they hate themselves. And Frankie was addicted to drugs.

5.

stew of drugs,
lifetime of pain

Bodiam Castle

Frankie and my father moved to England for his three-year posting there in late spring 1966. In leaving her comfortable Maryland home, nursing job, old friends, and collecting routines, Frankie had to leave behind a slew of her security blankets. But at age fifty-two, Frankie had well-practiced, transportable coping systems in place to deal with the emotional injuries, psychic pains, and reparative needs she had carried out of childhood into middle life, and now was taking overseas. Keeping constantly busy was one coping system. Collecting was another.

Another was drugs.

Even today migraine headaches are poorly understood and extremely difficult for doctors to deal with. But at least today they are recognized as separate from simple headaches. When Frankie was a child, migraines were just bad headaches. Everybody got headaches and got over them. The discomfort was understood but the uniquely disorienting, nauseating, debilitating agony of migraines wasn't. For Frankie's primary caregivers—bullheaded Berthe and St. Patrick's severe nuns—her pain was either all in her head (well, yes it was) or at most exaggerated. So her complaints were routinely dismissed, with disdain, and she was often forced to be on her feet, at school, or doing chores when she ought to have been in quiet, in the dark, in bed. She got a little aspirin but little sympathy, and less comforting care.

Her sister and brother only added to her misery, treating Yvonne like a wimp when she was hurting. Only her father would comfort her, and only when he could. He alone seemed to understand that the knives in young Yvonne's temples were real. He didn't understand migraines any better than anyone else. But he seemed to understand that even if his daughter's headaches were simply bad headaches, there was sufficient cause in their home, overseen by such a mother, for a little girl to hurt badly in the head.

Along with migraines Frankie had high blood pressure, exhibited a variety of anxiety and depressive traits, and suffered from insomnia. When I was growing up she always claimed she only slept two hours a night. We didn't believe her. Then in 1972 the National Institutes of Health (NIH) just down Wisconsin Avenue from where we lived in Bethesda, Maryland, announced a study of insomniacs and Frankie volunteered to be a subject. They were delighted to have her.

No functioning person only sleeps two hours a night, they told her; you only think that's what you do, they said. So she went and slept at NIH from February 28 to March 5. She was wired with brain-activity sensors at midnight and watched until 6 A.M. At the end, NIH reported Frankie's average was two and a half to three hours of sleep per night. My dad remembers the researchers were amazed, and a little spooked, by the consistent storm of Frankie's brain activity going on all night. They tried some new drugs on her, and something called Trans Cerebral Electro Therapy, but these didn't help.

Frankie was wide open to trying drugs, new or old. After suffering migraines with no medication at all during her youth, Frankie in adulthood enthusiastically embraced America's new promise of "Relief Just a Swallow Away." Today a person with Frankie's childhood history, and exhibiting symptoms like hers—depression, anxiety, acting out, impulsiveness—would probably be diagnosed with borderline personality disorder and would be prescribed one of the attitude-enhancing wonder drugs like Prozac. There's some evidence, too, that this family of drugs is helpful in cutting the occurrence and lessening the severity of migraines. But in the 1950s, 1960s, and 1970s doctors treated depression with stimulants, anxiety with tranquilizers, insomnia with sleeping pills, and pain with painkillers. Frankie went for the whole package.

There's no evidence anyone paid any attention to the overall toxic stew being created inside her body. She formed a friendship with a Doctor Feel-Good in Maryland and became his best customer. As a nurse, she was surrounded by doctors and easily able to supplement her supplies at work. Other doctors became family friends. She began gobbling prescription drugs and kept it up for the rest of her life. My brother and I used to joke about how most people had medicine cabinets in their bathrooms while Frankie had a medicine closet.

How desperate was she for relief? Very.

Among Frankie's many life-coping habits was starting and stopping journals or diaries, cataloguing things, and making lists. Like her collecting, the journals or lists usually began and ended with her whims. They were rarely kept up or comprehensively compiled. They just appeared, and then one day disappeared. But a couple of them were reasonably long-running. On September 14, 1971, for example, she began a notebook listing everyone to whom she wrote a letter or sent a package and on what date. Her last entry was April 6, 1983, seven days before she died. In between are short gaps. But there are remarkably few. Month by month Frankie faithfully records a clipping sent to Marian, a thank-you note to Ross, a letter to the editor of the *Cape Cod Standard Times*, a fifty-cent refund coupon sent to Pertussin Cough Syrup, Jefferson City, Mo., and so on. For eleven and a half years. Most often she records just a name and a date.

Another long-running effort was a journal Frankie kept from March 1961 to October 1972 in which she documented all the days she had migraine headaches, their severity, other symptoms she could identify, correlation with her menstrual periods, the drugs she was taking daily, and the drugs she took specifically for relief from the migraine. There are occasional skipped months where Frankie puts in a question mark. But overall it's a shocking record of remarkably routine suffering, faithfully kept in hopes of discovering something, some pattern or clue, anything, to help end the agony.

Not one month in 109 months—almost a decade—is Frankie headache free. The lowest number of days of pain is three, which happened just six times over those years. The average number of days of pain per month over this span is 7.62 days—on average, a week per month, a quarter of her time, she suffers. A few months are monsters. Frankie was in pain twenty-one of the thirty-one days in January 1964. She notes, "Since Jan. 8th have had moderate to severe headaches every day. Becoming depressed, irritable, short tempered. Feel 'all in.' Becoming discouraged." The next month things improve a bit: eleven days of pain out of February's twenty-eight. She had seventeen days of headache in June 1962, thirteen days in October 1963, eighteen days in November 1970, fifteen in April 1971. Month after month the journal records a life lived with, in her words, "terrific shooting pain," "dull ache constant," "acute pain," which by the next day was "getting more and more severe with nausea and vomiting," "no relief with medications," "still excruciating pain, constant," and on and on.

I knew my mother got migraines. And I knew when she had them she was very sick. It would have been impossible growing up in a house with her not to know this. But until this poking into her leftover belongings, I never realized how chronically she endured pain. Now it takes my breath away and brings tears to my eyes.

She embraced drugs. Who could blame her? Anything any doctor suggested she try, she did. Drugs by themselves. In combinations. She made note of many. One tally for just a four-year period listed twenty-seven different drugs. Narcotics, barbiturates, sedatives, tranquilizers. The list is staggering.

Fiorinal, I remember, was Frankie's favorite. She spoke about the drug openly, almost like a friend. She took it over and over when the pain got bad. Fiorinal is a very strong painkiller containing butalbital (a barbiturate), codeine (an addictive painkiller derived from opium), and caffeine, which these days is considered a trigger for migraine headaches. All three drugs are addictive. Often Frankie supplemented her Fiorinal doses with more codeine in prescription Empirin or Tylenol tablets.

She took drugs by mouth. And she injected drugs. In rummaging through her boxes of collections after her death, I found her collected works. And the works I'm talking about here aren't writings. Inside a gray steel lockbox and an orange California Cobbler shoe box I found a stash of 133 individually packaged disposable syringes, sixty separate hypodermic needles, and forty-two other syringes. As a nurse she had opportunity to get syringes. In the years before she retired from nursing, perhaps she felt an urgency to stockpile them.

Like so much with Frankie, she seems to have done this obsessively. And like so much she did, in this, too, can be found her instinct to collect. The vast majority of the 180 or so syringes are fairly modern, unremarkable plastic throwaways. They represent a hoard, not a collection. But inside a crumbling lime-green pouch I found nine vintage syringes. They had dosage measurement lines painted on glass bodies, glass plungers sliding effortlessly into them, thick reusable needles screwed onto their tips. They probably dated back into the early days of Frankie's nursing. Each was a different size, from a baby-sized syringe to one that could be used on a horse. It was, I realized, another collection.

For a doctor today the mix of drugs Frankie ingested and injected through the fifties, sixties, and seventies makes no sense. Especially all the narcotics. Today it's recognized that migraines are not well treated with narcotics because the physical withdrawal that follows use of addictive prescription painkillers causes new headaches and makes migraines worse, leading to more and heavier doses of narcotics. Today, migraine sufferers take over-the-counter painkillers, plus nonnarcotic medicines to treat symptoms such as nausea. "Treatment" for a migraine's emotional components is in the psychotherapy realm.

I asked my family doctor to look over Frankie's record of headaches and drugs. When he was done, he just shook his head. "Probably lots of these weren't migraines at all, or didn't start out as migraines. I'd say her condition, her psychic pain, was made worse by the medical profession." Either one of her favorite painkilling combo, Fiorinal and codeine, let alone the pair together, could lead to addiction and withdrawal and would make depressed people more depressed.

Frankie's migraine journal includes the thirty-one months she was in London, from 1966–1968. It shows she had 203 days of pain over the roughly 930 days she spent in England. Drugs helped her cope. At least she thought they did. More likely the drugs gave only temporary relief, and at the cost of locking Frankie into a cycle of headaches, drugs, depression, withdrawal, new headaches, more drugs, depression, withdrawal—the cycle rolling forward unceasingly, with fearful certainty, ensuring that for Frankie anxiety was built into every day and that every day her sad, desperate attempts for more lasting relief, for some sort of magical help, would go on.

Collecting, I've come to believe, was its own sort of drug for her, another hopeful remedy she added to the pharmaceuticals. Collectors, obsessive ones, it's been observed, lose all sense of the present. "The setting up of a collection itself," said sociologist Jean Baudrillard, "displaces real time." By the time Frankie became a middle-aged woman, the passage of time had become a feared enemy. Real time had come to mean a time certain for the return to her head of excruciating, disorienting, debilitating pain. Displacing time—putting that inevitable hourglass countdown out of her mind—would have helped Frankie cope.

"Collecting represents the perpetual fresh beginning of a controlled cycle," said Baudrillard. Each time Frankie emerged from under her forehead cold-packs, out of her darkened rooms, she must have yearned for a fresh beginning, a new phase in which, finally, she would gain control over her migraines. But the cycle of pain remained out of control, of course, unaffected by Frankie's frantic, neurotic collecting of things each time a new cycle began. Alas, there's no genuine time out of time, no stopping time.

Yet Baudrillard is sympathetic. "To seek refuge within a synchronic haven might be seen as a denial of reality and a form of escapism," the sociologist wrote, but it becomes "the consolation of consolations, an everyday myth capable of absorbing all our anxieties about time and death."

The loss of little rocks from big British sites seems a small price to pay to provide an anguished person a sliver of hope. The rocks gave Frankie a piece of relief time, with peace of mind, from her migraines, and from all those deeper anxieties from a hurtful childhood.

It wasn't right to take the rocks. I'm critical of that. I'll return them. But I'm sympathetic now, too. My mother lived a life of unimaginable, disorienting pain, and somehow, I suspect, taking these rocks helped her cope.

tuesday, march 11

This morning I set off east, on a drive of a couple of hundred miles along England's south coast. I'm heading to Bodiam Castle, about twelve miles north of Hastings. On the way I notice signs to Brighton, the popular, best-known seaside resort city in the British Isles.

Bathers and partyers, from royalty to working-class blokes, have been taking the sun and sea in Brighton since the middle of the eighteenth century. It's the site of perhaps the most bizarre edifice in the country, the Royal Pavilion, a fantastic jumble of neoclassical, Indian, and Elizabethan styles. It's also the site of two immense, cast-iron piers, the Palace Pier and the West Pier, world-famous for their honky-tonk, arcades, junk food, rides, and amusements.

Well, there used to be two piers. The 135-year-old West Pier had been condemned and closed for a number of years, and was scheduled for a costly renovation when a huge section of it collapsed. I remember a news photo I saw in the *Boston Globe* at the end of 2002. West Pier's ornate, domed pavilion was shown sagging into the sea. Wooden rubble littered Brighton Beach. The photo caption said, "Crowds scoured the sea front, taking pieces of wood as souvenirs." It seems Frankie wasn't the only one with a penchant for collecting historical pieces of England.

I don't stop. I'm in the business of returning souvenirs. The one in my pocket this morning is a hunk of Bodiam Castle, another National Trust property. Bodiam was a favorite of Frankie's. It's not difficult to imagine why.

Picture a castle, the storybook type, tall and square, built of solid rock, four-story rounded drum towers at the corners, square towers in between, crenel and merlon sawtoothing along the entire top wall's battlements, defensive arrow loops scattered about, a drop-down iron portcullis at the entrance gate, and surrounded by a moat. Get the picture? Anyone who's ever read about knights in armor and princesses locked away in towers gets the picture. That's Bodiam.

The rock I'm carrying is a couple of inches long, an inch thick at its widest spot, flat on one side, where it's a lighter shade and there are traces of mortar, and rounded along its bottom like the underside of a boat. Approaching the castle, which is set in a bucolic green valley, I see right away the rock is the right rock. It's a much more brilliant orange-brown limestone than the chalkier white and gray stones of Stonehenge, Stourhead, Salisbury, or Corfe I've been handling up to now. Even from a distance Frankie's piece of Bodiam looks like a piece of Bodiam.

George Bailey, the castle's property manager, was going to take the day off, but he agrees to talk to me. George is tall and thin, wears glasses, and is officious and brusque, but friendly enough. Though he's clearly not delighted to be working on a day off. If you can really call this work.

"We hate to lose bits," he says, hearing the Frankie story. "I'm sure we do, bits taken here and there. It's obviously our job to conserve and preserve, but you can't do that a hundred percent of the time because of the nature of the building. It's exposed to the elements. It's old and crumbly in places. Wind and rain do damage. Actually, something that's been of concern to us recently is acid rain. We've been looking into that problem. The mortars in the castle are alkaline and if the rain's too acidic it can render the mortars ineffective. We're investigating how much of a problem this is."

No one has ever brought a stolen stone back to George Bailey. Though sometimes people give him things they've found. "People pick things up, stone or pottery bits or bits of old metal, and they wonder if what they've found is historic. They say, 'Here, you can have it.' It's hard for the Trust to make a determination about things people find," he says. "Somebody could say they found it in the castle, but how do we know where it came from? Even if it was found here, it doesn't necessarily mean it's part of Bodiam's history. The river [River Rother, running close to the castle] overflows regularly. It has carried bits of things along for centuries in its swift flow. What people find could have come from far upriver." An old Roman road also runs through the property and passing traffic could be a source of artifacts, too, he says.

I ask George for permission to replace Frankie's rock inside Bodiam. He thinks a few seconds.

"No," he says. "It would end up being confusing with those markings on it." He means Frankie's handwriting, identifying the stone. "Somebody finds that later, they think, 'Was this a piece marked by the archaeologists? If it is, where's its identifying number? Is it important? Why is it back in the castle?' No, the last thing we want to do is confuse the archaeology we've already done."

This strikes me as a bit overly cautious. "Well, I wouldn't want to confuse British archaeology," I say, careful in my tone to disguise the sarcasm. We square off a second, staring at each other.

"I could throw it in the moat," I suggest. It occurs to me Frankie might especially like that.

"No," George says quickly, "and for the same reason. We dredge the moat periodically, and we always carefully sift through what comes up. Years from now I'd not want people wondering about your mum's stone."

I'm turning the little stone over in my hands as he's talking. I try to imagine some workman in the year 2233, having just dredged Bodiam's moat with a hydrolaser specific gravity–defying liquid levitation device, or some such thing (I mean, I doubt they'll just be sucking muck by then), and coming upon Frankie's rock. I see the workman scratching his head. Then I see him throw it back into the moat.

"We had something happen late last year," George goes on. "Some lads were working on a corner of the moat, and they had a bunch of modern padlocks but no keys, so the locks were worthless. So the lads began lobbing them into the moat. About thirty or forty padlocks were thrown in before I could stop them. Imagine two hundred years from now, you and I are long deceased, and they bring these padlocks up out of the mud."

"Ah . . . yeh?" I say.

"The inference would be there was some sort of padlock-making in the area," he says.

"Or padlock-pitching," I say, "a sort of popular game at the end of the twentieth century." I swear my sarcasm is disguised. It's one of the beauties of Americans talking to Brits. They miss a lot of Yankee sarcasm.

What he will do, says George, is put Frankie's rock in a plastic envelope, catalogue it, and place it in the castle's archives.

I also get the impression this cataloguing is what's promised to hopeful tourists excited they may have found something of value—appreciative filing away as part of the medieval fortress's permanent record.

"Okay," I say, nodding.

But before I fork it over, I ask George for permission to carry my stone through Bodiam. "Just to sort of have it close to me as I get closer to my mother."

George gets up. "Of course. Just bring it back and leave it at the desk when you go." The inference is he will be gone.

"Of course," I lie.

Bodiam Castle was built by Sir Edward Dalyngrigge, of whom not a lot is known. He took part in many knightly military campaigns, apparently, between 1359 and 1387, was a brave and chivalrous soul, and built up for himself solid court connections. This led to a manor house at Bodiam and considerable local influence. But in the Middle Ages a big house was nowhere nearly as prestigious as a castle, so Dalyngrigge petitioned King Richard II in 1385 for permission to "crenellate" his building. That means putting up typical battlements, a real sign of status. Kings only did this for guys they trusted because it was rarely in a king's interest to have a lot of strongholds around the country, where insurgencies might incubate.

Permission was granted, and the castle rebuilt, but what happened after that has mostly been lost to history. It passed through various hands, including the Crown itself after agitators against Richard III took refuge there. See? Those castles can be pesty things. By Cromwell's time, of course, royalist castles were very much on the outs. Paintings of Bodiam in the eighteenth century show it in ruins and overgrown in ivy. Two nineteenth-century owners saved the place, doing the restoration and preservation work that has left the castle in the relatively fine shape it's in today.

Modern archaeological work has revealed one thing, and called into question another. Excavations in 1988 found traces of extensive terraced surrounding pools, which, along with its encircling moat, would have provided an approaching viewer with dramatic, shimmering reflections of the centerpiece castle. Bodiam was designed to be a thing of beauty, that's the conclusion, which wasn't exactly the first thing on the minds of most medieval castle builders. In turn, scholars have begun to doubt whether Bodiam was built to be a true fortress at all. Many believe that from the very start it was makebelieve, and that the turrets, crenel, and merlon wall toppings, arrow loops, drawbridge, and all the rest were just put up to impress folks.

There's no question it works. Bodiam is impressive, romantic, and quite beautiful. Not the least impressed was my mother.

Frankie may have taken a stone, but at the entrance gate I begin to see the more common visitor erosion on the sanctity of Bodiam: graffiti. It's all over the place. The soft, darkish stone is a perfect template for people's propensity to scratch their mark. They leave mostly names, but some comments, some dates. "You can't trust the dates," says a gatekeeper. "Some bloke put 1100 after his name but the castle wasn't built until the late 1300s, so you know that one's a hoax."

Many of the names and symbols are genuinely old, though. "Some writing is so graphic and ornate, it doesn't look like present script," the gatekeeper says. "And it looks like they had lots of time to do it, so those are probably authentic." He shows me a scratched triangle, an arrow, and an X. "We know those are original stonemason marks from when the castle was constructed," he says. "Masons liked to sign their work."

"Canadian troops were billeted here in the war," he says, meaning World War II. "They would have had time, and time on their hands, to scratch their initials here and there."

It's cloudy and threatening rain. Almost no one else is here. I take my time. All four walls and all four round, four-story corner towers are in remarkable shape. Three once held lodging chambers above, the other the water-well chamber below and dovecote above. All four square towers, midway along each wall, are also in good shape, though their floors are gone. The square of living space inside the castle enclosing the central courtyard is mostly in ruins, but the setting is so inspiring that it's not hard to walk through and imagine the great hall, pantry, buttery, kitchen, withdrawing chamber, chapel, and sacristy. As I wander around, Frankie's rock in hand, I idly lift the orange-brown stone up to the ruined rock walls here and there for comparison. It's clear it was taken from somewhere in this castle. This is nothing from a path. It isn't bedrock. It's building stone.

Open to the sky, the courtyard is a thick carpet of chlorophyll-rich grass. In a flash, I remember lying on this same grass, in 1967, with my first girlfriend, Elaine. I was twenty, she was eighteen. She was from Vermont and had come over after high school graduation to see Europe with me. We imagined we were in love, living a fantasy life visiting romantic places like this. Our eyes were on each other, not the old castle around us; our thoughts were about each other, our interests driven by hormones, not history. Obsession can obliterate surroundings. Elaine was mine that day thirty-six years ago. Finding a rock was Frankie's.

It feels like it's time to go. I finish my visit by ascending the narrow, stone steps that spiral up to the top of the castle's Postern Gate, the tower directly opposite the main gate. I'm alone at the top. Looking at the stone one last time,

I think of Frankie, her love for this classic castle, and the odd round-trip this small stone has taken. Then I kiss the rock, and flick it over the wall.

Gravity takes the stone on a final downward journey through the hazy spring air of East Sussex. It makes the tiniest splash and ripple ring on the still waters of the moat as it disappears.

As I'm leaving Bodiam, I pick up a small, nondescript stone from the gravel pathway. I'm outside the castle; the stone is clearly part of the modern landscaping designed to channel Bodiam's 170,000 annual visitors up to the ticket office and gift shop. I walk back to my rental car, take a black marker pen out of my briefcase, and write "Bodiam Castle" on my new rock. I blow on it a few seconds until it's dry. Then I return to the visitors' center.

When I get inside the office, the receptionist puts my rock in a plastic pouch, writes my name and Frankie's name, and the date, and where we came from, and other such information on the outside, and then takes it away.

Frankie's find at Bodiam is back at Bodiam. Not where they think it is, encased in plastic in a file cabinet. But, instead, silently settled into the moat's mud. Where it almost certainly now rests next to carbine shell casings flicked in by bored Canadian soldiers in 1944, and forty-odd padlocks back from when padlock tossing was a national fad.

6.

collecting facsimiles, history's real deal

Dover Castle

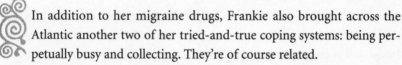 In addition to her migraine drugs, Frankie also brought across the Atlantic another two of her tried-and-true coping systems: being perpetually busy and collecting. They're of course related.

As soon as she stepped off the 707 Pan Am airliner in London in late spring 1966, Frankie got busy. It was crucial that she be busy, so she furiously threw herself into friendships, meeting and endearing herself to a brand-new batch of people. She threw herself into the cultural life and social functions that came with my father's diplomatic position in London. She took adult education courses. She shopped. She volunteered. She visited galleries, museums, and historic sites of interest. She became a regular visitor to Regents Park and Whipsnade zoos. She went to concerts and plays. She made lists, organized things, and turned on a torrent of correspondence with everyone back home.

And, of course, she kept busy collecting. All the new friendships were a sort of collecting people. All the museum and site visits resulted in growing collections of guidebooks and pamphlets and photographs. She started collections of English coins and stamps. And within months of arriving Frankie became passionate about one activity in particular: brass rubbing.

A much more elegant Old England cousin to New England gravestone rubbing, which Frankie had done back home in Massachusetts, brass rubbing involves transferring onto paper the images of ancient monumental brasses. Dating back to the 1200s, the slightly raised brasses are found on floor-level tombs in English churches. The engraved plate brass memorials usually show images of the people interred under them. Often they include inscriptions, shields, and animals. Many of the figures of the medieval men and women represented in brass are life-sized or nearly so.

It is painstaking, time-consuming, numbing work to rub brasses. Yet for her entire stay in England Frankie regularly traveled to churches in Dorset, Oxfordshire, Surrey, Denbighshire, Kent—all over Great Britain—as well as to several sites in Belgium, where she carefully covered floor brasses with special rag paper and spent countless hours on her hands and knees, rubbing and rubbing with special black crayons. By the time she returned to America she had rubbed more than 150 brasses and had joined memorial brass societies, taken courses on brasses, lectured on the art form, subscribed to several publications, and meticulously noted and catalogued her collection.

The rubbings she did were of exceptional quality, in the judgment of her brass society peers. Frankie never rough-rubbed. Less careful, more impatient rubbers fixed smudged, over-the-edges mistakes by cutting out a completed image and pasting it onto a clean piece of paper. Frankie never did this. She considered it cheating, and to brass-rubbing purists it is. She was meticulous in respecting the fine line of the brass edges so that the black impressions on paper were complete and true. She also never took another bogus shortcut: rubbing the biggest brasses in separate sessions on separate pieces of paper and then joining together the blocks when all were done. Doing this reduced fatigue—the biggest brasses could take six hours to rub—but they were clearly inferior efforts.

For Frankie, the only way to rub was the right way, the respected way, the exhausting way. It was the way Frankie did many things: with compulsive, consuming energy.

Keeping busy.

For Frankie, rubbing brasses in England began before taking rocks. But in retrospect, it's hardly surprising that the old rocks followed. The real deal is often, for collectors, a logical progression from facsimiles. In this case, in

England Frankie found something her compulsive collecting hadn't encountered in America, ancient history, and she got hooked. And history, I think, came to represent a powerful new and soothing magic for her hurting side.

Frankie had never been a historian or showed any particular interest in history. Not at home in the U.S.A. But moving to England put her in touch with antiquity, literally and figuratively. Very old things clearly impressed her. "She got caught up in it," my father once said. She raced around to museums and sites. One day early in their stay a Queen Victoria penny showed up in her change. At that time it wasn't really rare for big pennies from the mid- to late 1880s to show up in ordinary transactions. Soon Frankie was pulling old English pennies out of circulation and collecting them. "It wasn't academic or book history that turned her on," said my father. "It was history in your face, history you could feel, touch. She hadn't experienced anything like that in America. She was charmed by history that could be counted in the thousands of years." And, clearly, with history you could touch. And possess.

Monumental brasses on the floors of churches were something ancient that Frankie could literally feel and rub and then take home. As well, brass rubbing provided something else significant, which is found in a whole category of things people collect: faces and names. The collectors of baseball cards, portrait paintings, dolls and stuffed animals, stamps, autographs, masks, and much more are drawn to this. Faces and names, identities, help simple lifeless items serve more intimately as substitutes for interpersonal relationships. It's not uncommon for collectors of everything from antique automobiles to firearms to give names to individual objects in their collections in an effort to create a personal intimacy—Sally the '57 T-Bird, say, or Gus the Colt .45.

In collecting brass rubbings, Frankie assembled around her a sort of community of historic people whom she could see, name, and learn about and whom she could make a part of her life. I heard her on occasion address them as if they had life. She was "introduced to" Adam de Compton (1360), she would say, on the Isle of Wight; Sir John de Foxle and Lady Maud Foxle (1378) "joined me" from Bray, Berkshire; the Earl of Essex (1483) was naturally found and brought back from Essex to Frankie's home, and she was "proud to have him." Over her English stay, Frankie relentlessly drew into her rubbed family more and more ancient personages, many of the men in chain mail and medieval armor or tight-fitting jupons, the women in simple kirtles or more elegant, long-flowing cotehardies, some shown with dogs or elephants or lions wrapped around their feet.

She loved brass rubbing; it became a new passion. She was impressed with the history behind her rubbed friends. Mostly, though, she welcomed their willingness to become a part of her life.

It wasn't book history that interested Frankie, it was history she could hold, take home, own. Real things, like her vintage coins, or representations, like the postcards and guidebooks. Or like her photography. She took thousands of photographs. In going through her things long after her death, I spent hours looking at her slide collection. I was searching for family faces from different times in our family history. But the vast majority of Frankie's photos held no interest for me. Picture after picture showed buildings, sites, things. The same things the postcards and guidebooks showed. All were just attempts to capture and keep the places Frankie visited and the old things she saw.

As I dropped slide after slide into an industrial-size garbage bag, I thought what an enormous amount of energy it represented. I envisioned my mother, ever busy, rummaging in her camera bag at all these sites in England, deciding on lenses, aperture settings, where to stand, and then shooting a picture. Repositioning herself and shooting another and another. I can count on one hand the times I remember Frankie returning to these collections and projecting the slides for friends or for our family to view.

Frankie was incapable of visiting a historic site or a place of beauty and leaving with it only in her memory. There is a passage in *Gift from the Sea*, by Anne Morrow Lindbergh, where she ruminates about her days spent on a beautiful island beach: "When I think back to my first days here, I realize how greedily I collected. My pockets bulged with wet shells, the damp sand clinging to their crevices. The beach was covered with beautiful shells, and I could not let one go by unnoticed. I couldn't even walk head up looking out to sea, for fear of missing something precious at my feet. The collector walks with blinders on; he sees nothing but the prize. In fact, the acquisitive instinct is incompatible with true appreciation of beauty."

Tourism photography is driven by its own sort of acquisitive taking-home

instinct. It too cheats experience. In her imperative to photograph every ancient or scenic place, Frankie put herself behind a lens and out of the moment.
When a tourist isn't in the moment, in the sensory presence of what's in front
of him or her, that person sacrifices a huge amount of understanding, appreciation, awe, and a whole range of other reactions that make site visits enriching experiences during travel.

Cameras have a nasty way of transporting people up and out of a moment. A tour bus pulls up to a breathtaking overlook and the doors open. Forty
tourists rush out to a fenced viewing platform while pulling cameras out of
bags. Very few of the tourists simply stand and take in the view. Instead of
using the bus company's five-minute stop to experience the moment, most in
the mob spend their time creating an image of the moment, which serves to
remove them from it. When they get home and show their pictures to friends,
that snapshot will be great proof they were there. But having been there will
be a technicality. They take in the magic of a special place through a lens, in
hopes of capturing it and later reliving it. But in the end they fail to take the
magic into themselves, and thus never truly live it in the first place.

Frankie traveled to terrific places with blinders on. Contemplation in the
presence of a wonder, or meditation in the face of things surprising or fascinating, was for Frankie a contradiction in terms. She couldn't stay still. She
couldn't contemplate or meditate, or even truly admire. In time allotted her
at sites, she focused on gathering guidebooks, examining gift shop souvenirs,
selecting postcards, taking notes, talking to companions, shooting pictures,
and figuring out the next picture to shoot. Thousands of photos. Frankie left
England with massive amounts of reproductions of antiquity. All of them
somehow sterile, without soul, and when her life came to an end, tossed into
black garbage bags and hauled to the landfill.

She also came back to America with that box of rocks.

Was taking the rocks a twisted kind of borrowing of the significance of the
places? Or was it something deeper? In Frankie's case, it nagged at me that
there might be a connection between her parents' European roots and her apparent need to physically possess pieces of European history. Specifically, I
wondered about ways in which her taking the stones might be connected to
her father. She adored Pepère, and in her traumatizing early years he probably looked like the only person who loved her. I wondered if she felt compelled

to gather historic rocks around her, pieces of the old country, pieces of her father's past—and although he was French, he did grow up in England—in order to feel more connected to him. Perhaps she planned to bring the rocks back to him, or at least be able to tell him she had such remarkable pieces.

But in the back of the journal Frankie kept of her migraine headaches, I found a newspaper clipping that reminded me of something important. Maurice took his own life while Frankie was in London. Folded into the headache journal was a New York newspaper article reporting her father's suicide and the discovery of his body. When Maurice stepped off the seawall into the Hudson River in September 1967, Frankie had been in England a year and would stay another two. She had tucked the painful news account of her father's suicide into her own account of agonizing head pain. Which is where it stayed, folded up, for another five years of head pain entries, and where it would have been lost if I hadn't been poking around her things decades later.

I don't know when during her stay in England Frankie began taking rocks. I spent my sophomore year of college in London, August 1966 to June 1967, and I lived with my parents. We visited lots of historic sites. I saw my mother buy guidebooks and take plenty of pictures, but I never saw her take rocks. So probably she didn't start at the very beginning. On the other hand, the start of the rock collecting was certainly not at the end of her stay either. One third of the way through her stay sounds about right. So she almost certainly didn't begin taking rocks to bring them back to impress her father. He died a third of the way through. If anything, the opposite is more likely. Was it a coincidence, the timing, or did the shock of losing her father, especially while she was so far away from him, actually trigger Frankie's taking of historic stones? Did it begin because of that?

She wouldn't be alone if it was. Sigmund Freud started collecting classical antiquities following the death of his father in 1896. He didn't make the connection at first, but later came to see the collecting as a direct response to losing his father. The death triggered sudden self-doubt, a sense of mortality, and musings about immortality, and led to collected objects that, Freud felt, provided him with psychic renewal and comfort. Frankie was collecting things long before Pepère died. She had lifelong self-doubts, I think, and was in routine need of psychic help and comfort. Yet, still, the English rocks were a different collection, an unacknowledged collection, a private and somehow personal one. Was it connected to Pepère's death?

I never saw my mother mourn her father. I suspect she didn't, in any traditional way. It wouldn't have been like her. More likely she would simply have become busier. I was back in Maryland when Pepère died, so I never saw her the first days after Frankie got the news. It was several days before Frankie flew back to New York City. I drove up to be with her and with my grandmother. We met at my grandparents' apartment. By the time I got there, mother and daughter were reeling around the apartment acting the way they always did together: Bah scowling, fatalistic, complaining, accusing; Frankie busying herself, placating, ducking and weaving. There was no warmth or shared sense of sadness between them, no crying, hugging, or shared support. Bah kept pacing around the apartment, repeating that she never knew her husband could do such a thing, and how could he do such a thing? What was she to do now? She had become suspicious that day he took his life, she said over and over, because Maurice had left his wallet and wristwatch behind when he went out, and he had told her only to remember that he loved her.

Frankie was in their cramped kitchen doing dishes at one point as Berthe passed, her slippers rasping against the floor, her self-pitying litany pouring out again. I was drying the dishes. I understood enough French to get most of what my grandmother was repeating. I heard again that Maurice had told Berthe only to remember he loved her.

Frankie muttered softly toward the faucet, "No. He loved me."

Her beloved father had taken his life without saying good-bye. And without telling Frankie in person what a childhood left her hoping was the truth—that he loved her, and that he always would. After visiting her mother, Frankie returned to England to face a new, aching loneliness after a heartbreaking loss. Two years later she returned to America with a box of rocks. If collecting them wasn't directly related to honoring her father or remembering him, taking the Old World's stones was at least an imperative need for new hedges against nothingness, new tangible relics to possess, more powerful than photos, guidebooks, and rubbings.

I'll never know when collecting the stones started, or what started it. But at some point, reproductions of magnificent sites were not enough. Coins and stamps were not enough. Memories were never enough. Frankie had to have actual pieces of the ancient, mystical places. In these rocks, it seems likely, she held deep-seated hope she'd find the most powerful magic of all. Magic to soothe her soul.

wednesday, march 12

I'm in Dover, and after breakfast I hike up to Dover Castle and make my way to the spacious English Heritage offices located in a stone building within the castle walls. Jeannette Cole is the acting site manager. She sees me, but insists I have to speak to Kevin, the site's archaeologist and a curator for EH in the southeast region.

Delightful chap, Kevin Booth, thirty-two years old or so, with steady, brown eyes, extremely close-cropped hair, and ears that stick out a bit far. He's wearing a fleece vest and rumpled pants and shirt, looking very archaeologist-like. He offers me tea in the archaeologists' workroom and offices, a long, warm, stone-walled room with arched windows, and a seemingly endless worktable following along all the walls, every inch of it covered with notebooks, open papers, and boxes of old things. Many items in the boxes are in plastic bags with labels from English Heritage Ancient Monuments Laboratory, saying stuff like, "Site name: Battle Abbey. Context, small find No.: XII 811 FT193. Lab #920041." It feels like the right place to be with the two rocks Frankie took and carefully labeled *Dover Castle 40 AD*.

One rock is about an inch long with five irregular faces, whitish gray with several rusty brown splotches. The other is two inches long and has a convex and a concave side. The latter is very smooth and very white. One end is broken and a dark flint core is visible. I think the pieces are chalk, which doesn't seem like castle building material. Since morning I've also been perplexed by Frankie's *40 AD* (properly written, A.D. 40) notation. The first fortress earthworks and palisade on the Dover Castle site date to King Harold's days, about 1065. The fortification's hefty stuff—curtain walls, keep, and towers—begin to show up with Henry II, about 1168. I hadn't thought twice about Frankie's date until Jeannette Cole mentioned all this. Now I question, as the acting site manager had, how Frankie's piece of Dover Castle could be from A.D. 40 when the castle wasn't even started until 1,100 years later.

Jeannette and her people this morning had also wondered why the purple ink Frankie had used to label the stones thirty-six or thirty-seven years ago was now coming off on my fingers. I didn't do myself any favors when I expressed irritation aloud that I was getting all purple. I imagined myself in their shoes, looking at this unannounced, scruffy-looking middle-aged man who could use a shave, and who suddenly had purple fingertips holding these rocks, and who in almost every respect appeared just a very short cricket shot shy from being a street person. If I had been them, I might have guessed the guy scribbled on stray stones in some local pub and carried them up here for the attention or, in the most charitable explanation, free admittance.

For Kevin Booth this afternoon none of this, clearly, matters. He examines the rocks with enthusiasm. "I don't want to sound insulting," he says, and he pauses.

"Hey, just go for it," I reply.

"Well, the stones are particularly common pieces of flint. You usually think of flint as bluey-gray, and it is in cross section, and I have no doubt these pieces would be if we cut them in half." He points to the broken end of the concave-convex piece. "As you can see it here."

Flint forms in nodules or pockets within chalk, he explains, and can even form into seams the way coal does. In Dover's famous white chalk cliffs there are plenty of discrete bands of flint throughout. The silica-based flint is much harder than the limestone-based chalk. It tends to last longer. He says the stones on Dover's beachfront are mostly weatherworn and waterworn pieces of flint.

"But these pieces are white," I say. "I assumed they were chalk."

No, he says, both are solid pieces of flint. They just have a chalk dusting, which has adhered, hard, to the silica.

I nervously inquire whether flint was used in the castle construction. I thought sandstone was mostly used.

"It absolutely was used. Flint was a major construction material of the castle," Kevin says. "When the medieval builders brought sandstone from the beaches of Folkstone, flint came with it." Most of the blocks of the castle's buildings are sandstone, true, but the defensive walls were built with inner and outer blocks, and the space in between was filled with loose rock. Much of this was the flint—readily available and hard. There are some spots in Dover Castle where flint was actually used in facings. But, he says, there is no sign on Frankie's pieces that they were deliberately cut or worked.

Could Frankie have simply picked up a stray stone?

Of course she could have, says Kevin. "But I think the likelihood is that the pieces did come off a building in the castle. So let's take your mother at her word," he says.

"Meaning?" I knew Kevin couldn't have had secret conversations with my mother. He couldn't have been more than a baby when Frankie was pilfering two pieces from his future employment site.

"Meaning, she gave a date to the rocks." His forefinger gently traces a line under *40 AD*.

"Yeah, I was wondering about that," I say. I feel sheepish, for Frankie and me both. Math was no more Frankie's strong suit than my own. To be off more than a thousand years wasn't making my mission, or my purple fingers, look any better.

"Was she the sort of person who would know what she was taking, and where, and what its age would be?" Kevin asks.

For all Frankie's peculiarities and zany flights between thoughts and things, she was a meticulous cataloguer. And none of the dates on any of the other stolen stones gave cause for question. At least they hadn't yet. Why had I questioned her now? I suddenly feel angry at myself for assuming that Frankie didn't know what she was talking about with this rock. For this sort of thing she had a decent track record.

"Yeah," I say, "I think she'd likely get that right, more or less."

"Well then let's assume she got it right," says Kevin. I flush with a fuzzy feeling, a weird mix of embarrassment and pride, that this young archaeologist is willing to believe my mother where I'd quickly assumed she was wrong.

"There is one building in the Dover fortress from roughly that date," says Kevin.

I feel my spirits lift. "There is?"

"The Roman lighthouse," he says.

"Yah, mahn," I say, reverting to West Indian dialect, as I often do when I'm feeling a sort of warm, organic, sunshine blast of elation.

"Let's go see," says Kevin. Then he adds, with a smile, "And let's go put it back."

Long before radar and satellite global positioning systems, a known point of light could be a crucial point of reference for a navigator. As the Roman Empire marched—and sailed—north two thousand years ago, it took this awareness with it. Its ships of conquest and supply had been crisscrossing the Mediterranean for centuries, and they'd come to know the dangers of approaching distant shorelines from sea. So the Romans built and maintained lighthouses, known as pharoses—tall stone towers on the headlands at key spots, beacons from which signal smoke poured during daylight and bright fires were kept burning at night. They went up all along the coastlines of the expanding Empire.

In A.D. 40, the Romans reached Boulogne in Gaul on the northern French coast, and eyed Britain just twenty miles away. There Emperor Caligula built a pharos. Emperor Claudius did the conquering honors, sailing over and quickly taking over Britannia in A.D. 43.

The closest point between the Continent and England is at Dover, then known as Dubra, a Celtic settlement at the outfall of the little River Dour. The village rested between two high hills either side of the river, each with bright white chalk cliffs facing the straits. The Romans built a fort and supply harbor at Duba, and soon matched their pharos beacon at Boulogne with two lighthouses, one on each promontory.

Only slight traces remain of the western pharos. But the eastern pharos still stands, on a cliff spot 380 feet above sea level, now entirely surrounded by the much more modern Dover Castle. The lighthouse's original height would have been about eighty feet, constructed in a telescopic outline of eight stages with wooden floors, arched windows, and a topping parapet for the signal fire. The beacon, then, would have stood some 460 feet in the air—clearly visible on most nights for ships crossing from Gaul.

As Kevin and I turn a corner by a castle wall, the pharos finally comes into view. I suck in my breath, struck by the sight of it. Though overshadowed by the massive castle keep and defensive ramparts behind it, and set awkwardly next to a small Saxon church that once used it as a bell tower, the classical-age pharos radiates a preeminence—a striking presence, so individual, so antique and unique, that I simply tune out all the more modern castle remains around it and see the pharos shining, defiant, alone with its commanding view over the English Channel. I look on in wonder. It's no wonder this tower is considered one of the most remarkable Roman structures north of the Alps.

The stage walls have crumbled over the centuries into a sloping conical shape. But the pharos is in remarkable shape for a tower that has been so exposed to wind and storms, and enemy guns, for nearly two millennia. And so exposed to those with the responsibility for fortifying the Dover cliff heights against invasions of Vikings, Saxons, French, and Nazis, defenders who were always quick to grab the closest available rock. And, most recently, so exposed to tourists like Frankie, many of whom must find this noble tower a tempting souvenir source. It is easy to take pieces home. The pharos is not smooth and hard-packed; its stone is loose.

Kevin and I compare Frankie's souvenirs against the pharos wall. It's exactly the same rock. Her pieces could easily have once been embedded here. Kevin very gently wiggles a discrete chunk that is protruding out. If he tried, he could yank it out. We look at each other, and nod, wordlessly agreeing this is very likely exactly what Frankie did thirty-six years ago.

I pick a spot on the east side of the pharos, facing the channel, and facing France. Just as it wouldn't be hard to pull a piece off, it isn't difficult to wedge Frankie's two pieces back into the lighthouse. When I'm done, it's impossible to tell they were ever removed.

I'm satisfied. Kevin is smiling.

Frankie's Dover rocks, which once helped hold up a beacon of firelight for Roman ships, are back, facing the sea, and facing the cross-channel shore of her ancestral heritage, France.

7.

from a bronx brownstone to a feud

Balkerne Gate

 To understand someone you have to understand where she came from. Her past. Her story. Her childhood. Her siblings. Her parents. It begins with the parents.

But there's a handicap, I think, when you're trying to understand your own parents' parents. Your own parents are the beginning of your own story. Prior to them, for you there was no such thing as past. Things, figuratively, start there. Looking back at what made someone who made you is not the same as an exercise in biographical scholarship. It's never simply following a family tree backward to examine the early lifetimes and lifelines and ancestral influences that made presidents or rock-and-roll stars or dot-com billionaires into what they became. Objectivity examining background isn't a problem studying strangers.

It's sad, really, because unlike inquiry into other living people's parental influences, when you're looking at your own mom and dad the study can often begin in your own home, with grandparents front and center, present and accounted for, in relationships playing out in their pre-wired ways right smack in front of you. It could be that easy, firsthand. If your grandparents are still alive. If they live close enough and your family spends time with them. If you're mature enough—what, thirteen, fourteen years old or so?—to see subtle things. And if you invest attention and pay attention.

My grandfather Pepère lived until 1967; I was twenty when he ended his life. Bah my grandmother lived until 1975, so I was twenty-eight when she died. In both cases, I was old enough to know these people. Although my grandparents lived in the Bronx while I was growing up, we saw them regularly. I had opportunity. But I'm afraid I never invested attention. In the years Bah and Pepère were alive and part of our lives, I never observed Frankie trying to determine how she fit in. I never tried to assess the nuances of her interactions with her parents. I didn't ask questions. I didn't question what I saw. So it's hindsight here evaluating what I do remember seeing.

I saw a mother, my mother, cowed by her mother.

I saw an emotional edge between Frankie and Bah that was sharp enough to plane petrified wood. I never saw Bah give praise or Frankie become disrespectful.

I saw an unloving arrangement of lives in the Franco apartment on Greystone Avenue in the Bronx. I never saw a loving marriage or a welcoming home.

I saw no battle of wills, only my grandmother's tyranny, my grandfather's resignation, their daughter's deference.

I saw a father, my father, exchange warm pleasantries with his father-in-law, whom he always called Pop, and dutiful words with his mother-in-law, whom he always addressed more formally, with Berthe. I never saw him take charge or take sides.

In the Bronx apartment I smelled stale cooking odors, lilac bathwater, the absence of sunshine and fresh air.

I saw routines—cooking, dining, wine watered down from a crystal pitcher, pots and pans scrubbed—repeated each visit with obligatory hospitality, ways understood, behaviors accepted.

I heard Bah's swishing housecoat, along with groaning plumbing from apartments above.

When I climbed to the roof of my grandparents' apartment building, I saw a chaotic collage of building tops, vents, pigeon coops, clotheslines, and antennas spreading out in all directions. I always felt liberated leaving the old people back in the dark apartment, ascending the remaining stories in the building, and emerging through a dented steel door onto the black tarpaper covering of the flat roof. The air was undoubtedly polluted, but when I got there it always seemed as fresh as the wilderness, the sky as big as all of outer space.

Our visits from Maryland to see my grandparents were often combined with stays in Massapequa, a bedroom community out on Long Island about thirty miles east of the city. That's where Frankie's sister, Marcelle Crisona, lived, with her husband, John, and my cousins Louise and Nancy. We traveled there frequently, it seemed, usually around school holidays.

Marcelle and her family rarely visited us in Maryland. I guess that might have told me something.

The Crisonas' modest ranch tract house in Massapequa was a pleasant destination for my brother Doug and me. Louise and Nancy were nearly parallel in age to the two of us. We liked them, played games, teased, joked around, laughed. I think the girls enjoyed our visits. On the other hand, it never seemed the older sisters, the two mothers, Marcelle and Frankie, enjoyed being together.

There was never any outright fighting. There were arguments between Marcelle and Frankie—in the kitchen, over cooking, sometimes—but the disagreements weren't harsh and never lasted long. Visits were cordial. But it always seemed to me that Frankie was on good behavior in Massapequa. Marcelle asserted her authority. And why shouldn't she? It was her house. Frankie stepped cautiously, yielded ground. Marcelle was often irritable, Frankie frequently fidgety. Marcelle was loud, and while Frankie wasn't exactly quiet, she was much quieter than around our own house, away from her older sister. The brothers-in-law, my dad and uncle John, were secondary characters. They were both strong, smart, sociable men and luminiferous presences in their own family's lives. Yet when the two families got together, they both dimmed into the background. It was the invisible human fission of Marcelle and Frankie, individually and in relationship to each other, that dominated our times together.

The power that pulled focus onto the Franco siblings wasn't their effervescent love or expressively broadcast joy. It wasn't sisterhood. It was underlying tension. I wouldn't, I couldn't have identified it as that at the time. But that's what it now seems. Under one roof, almost always Marcelle's roof, they played out something the two of them were used to: Marcelle, angry and superior; Frankie, a couple of years younger, uncertain and anxious, with an almost awkward desire to please.

Frankie, I believe now, always wanted her older sister to love her. Marcelle, it seemed to me even then, didn't much like Frankie. All this didn't strike me as especially odd. I wanted my brother Doug to like me, while it sure did seem as though he didn't like me. He was three years older than me, but because of his accelerated passage through school he was many grades ahead of me and several years younger than his friends. He was the little guy in his social life. I was the little guy in his life. He picked on me, beat me up when given good opportunity, and routinely put me down. By the time he was a teenager he was calling me Scott, my middle name, which quickly evolved into Squat. Using the name Dana would have been too obvious an admission that I had an identity separate from what right to exist he gave me. I suppose many big and little brothers and sisters share at least some of this hierarchical gamesmanship. Anyway, sibling distance and tension seemed quite ordinary to me. It's probably why I enjoyed seeing my cousins Nancy and Louise so much. As peers, they were my only other close relatives, and they treated me with genuine warmth. I wasn't used to that.

Warmth between Marcelle and Frankie was also missing on Cape Cod, when they came to visit us there summers in the 1950s and early 1960s. And much later, when Marcelle and John retired to Cape Cod, where my parents would also retire a short time later. Warmth was always absent. There was civility, and some shared activity. There was nothing overtly ugly. Nothing until, I guess inevitably, there was.

The Franco sisters' feud started around 1973 or '74, roughly, not too many months before Bah died. Like most feuds, the flashpoint was money. Like many feuds, the amount of money was minuscule, and the true issue was something much more personal, much more complicated, based in feelings from much, much earlier in Marcelle's and Frankie's lives.

I don't really know the feud details. Very early on my cousin Nancy and I decided to distance ourselves from our mothers' fight. So I never probed the issues, and I refrained from taking sides. The feud had something to do with

Bah's switched maternal allegiance in the last years of her life. It seemed like overnight she went from close contact and caring for Marcelle to closeness with Frankie. What a switch this was for Frankie! And what a turnaround for Marcelle, I guess. During their childhoods and the vast sum of their adult lives, Marcelle was the daughter favored by their mother, Frankie the outcast. Now, at the end, Frankie found herself suddenly with the responsibility for their eighty-four-year-old mother, for her affairs and well-being living alone in the Bronx during deteriorating health. Marcelle found that the many years she had kept an eye on Bah while living close by on Long Island were suddenly just history. Interactions between Bah and Marcelle in my grandmother's last years soured Bah. I don't know what went down between them. I do know that Bah made the decision to disinherit Marcelle and turn toward Frankie. And that Marcelle made the decision to disown Frankie, suspicious that her sister had conspired to turn their mother against her. The inherited estate here, the savings of a long-retired, long-deceased chauffeur and his wife who never worked, was negligible.

Despite the fact that they had retired to a house across a common drive-way from our Cape Cod summer home, where my mother and father would retire a couple of years hence, Marcelle and John cut off all communication with Frankie, my dad, and even my brother and me. Cousin Louise bought into it, too; a birthday card I sent to her young son shortly after the feud began was returned to me with a scribbled note from my cousin, "We do not accept cards from Hornigs." Fortunately, cousin Nancy and I remained close, and have to this day, no doubt because of our pact to hold the feud far away from us, our recognition that both sides probably had a perspective that made nei-ther one right or wrong, and our understanding that the feud had nothing in the slightest to do with us.

And so for the Franco sisters and their husbands from then on, it was stony silence; no letters, no calls, no relationship; no recognition whatsoever when the families would be outside on their respective next-door lawns, or later, after Marcelle and John moved a few miles away, when we'd pass in a supermarket or movie theater lobby. The Crisonas' cut was clean, complete, irrevocable. When Frankie died in 1983 she'd gone a decade without a single interaction with her only remaining Franco relative, her only sister, a woman who was liv-ing just a few miles away in the same town.

Marcelle did not come to Frankie's funeral. I just shrugged about it at the time. I'd been written off, so I had written Marcelle off, too. She wasn't missed at the service. The church was packed.

I've wondered a lot since those days how Frankie must have felt. After a lifetime of feeling like the outsider—and worse, unloved by her mother—it must have been a powerful head trip to all of a sudden have her mother reaching out to her and singing her praises. I don't think it's how Frankie wanted things to turn out. I don't think by this time she cared much what her mother thought of her. There had been sixty years of Bah's cold criticism. I don't think Frankie felt any sense of vindication or justice, closure or relief, satisfaction or peace. If anything she seemed hugely confused and disoriented to have her mother now in her camp, and her sister now spurned, rejected by their mother, outside, residing in what was Frankie's familiar place.

I don't think Frankie cared much about what her mother was feeling. I know what she was most emotional about was what Marcelle was feeling, and how Marcelle was acting. After the estrangement, Marcelle would sometimes say to people on Cape Cod, "I never had a sister." My mother heard from friends that this was what Marcelle was saying. It made her very sad. I saw it in her. Frankie knew she had a sister. Frankie wanted a sister, and missed her sister terribly. I think she always had.

thursday, march 13

It's a big half-circle arc drive from Dover to Colchester. A crow flies there nearly due north. But driving my rented Renault I need to get west to a narrowing of the River Thames, pass under the Thames through the Queen Elizabeth Tunnel, then swing back east to Colchester.

I drive into town and check into the George Hotel on High Street almost precisely in the geographic center of this square-walled city.

The Castle Pub tonight has kangaroo on the menu, a special of the day, £6.99. It's just above ostrich on the chalkboard.

"It's from Australia," says the waitress, who's showing some bare belly, and a brassiere under a thin white top.

"I should hope so," I say.

"Well, they're raised on a farm in Kent, too, aren't they?" she says.

"Are they?" I reply.

I decline to tell her about SAVE. In our last year of high school, my friend Vit and I founded Students Against Violent Extermination to save kangaroos from becoming extinct. At the time, as well as today, it would come as a considerable surprise to your average Australian or American on the street to learn that kangaroos were ever in any danger of becoming extinct. And I suppose there never was any real danger of that. But Vit and I had read some off-mainstream article about the wanton kangaroo hunts Down Under, where 'roos are considered pests, and about the growing value of kangaroo hides for lightweight leather goods and 'roo meat for pet food. My memory is (which is not to say my memory can be trusted on this) that the article's author warned that kangaroo populations could not stand such pressure. Vit and I rose to the call. Not that there was any call.

Truth is, I now admit, we hoped SAVE would be a way to meet girls. We printed up buttons that said "Save the Roos." Then we handed them out to handpicked (read, comely) young women. It was, of course, an instant conversation starter. And the kangaroo noncause clearly made us entertaining party guests at a time everyone else was concerned with the more mainstream matters of America's growing involvement in Vietnam and lingering Cold War A-bomb threats.

At one point Vit and I decided to picket the Australian embassy in Washington. This wasn't a major commitment, because we lived in Bethesda, Maryland, just over the D.C. line. When we called the Metropolitan Police to obtain a permit, they were surprised it was the Australian embassy we sought to picket. In fact, I think they laughed. The Russian embassy was much more popular at the time. We were told the regulations required protesters to stay back a thousand feet or something from not only the target embassy but from any embassy. The Australian building was on Embassy Row along Massachusetts Avenue, and to get far enough away to be legal we would have had to march around with our placards a block away, somewhere around the Brazilian embassy or something. So we abandoned the idea.

And anyway, by then we'd found out that saving the 'roos just wasn't impressing girls.

Naturally I pass tonight on the Castle Pub's kangaroo steaks. And on its ostrich, too. I order the lamb. The waitress is not impressed.

That night, back in my room, I'm depressed. And sad. I'm eleven days into this trip, a third finished. I'm frustrated, I think, because I don't think I'm realizing one of the trip goals: discovering my mother here. Experiencing her presence.

Trying to imagine Frankie here, I've found, is like trying to imagine myself in England over thirty years ago. They say a human body, in shedding and renewing its cells, becomes a completely new body about every six years. A new person. I'm five Danas removed from the kid just out of his teens who wandered around the Sussex Lodge apartment in London and spent time with Frankie here in England.

Fully shaped memories of my mother here have been absent. I see just flashes of her:

Frankie with her string sack bringing back to the London apartment bottled milk with cream on top.

Frankie at the London Officers' Club, demure, beaming, made-up.

Frankie with a migraine in her Sussex Lodge bedroom, surrounded by yellow wallpaper.

Frankie cuddling and cooing over her friend Natasha's white poodle when she poodle-sat. Frankie kissing the dog.

Frankie flustered the day she got the call from my brother Doug that he wanted to marry Jenny and needed someone to come back to America to talk to the seventeen-year-old girl's parents.

Frankie skipping with excitement because actor Van Heflin was on the street below our apartment with a film crew shooting a scene for a movie outside the Victorian pub across the street. I watched with her as Heflin drove up in a Rover, pulled to the curb, and got out. Cut. They do it again. Cut. And then again. Frankie taking a roll of photos of Van Heflin doing it over and over.

Frankie desperately trying to count out money for transactions—at Selfridges, or Marks & Spencer, or the corner grocery—always, it seems, desperately trying to make sense out of pounds, shillings, pence, a quid, or a guinea, and always, it seems, confused and resorting to her little-girl voice to express her need for help.

Frankie joking with Sussex Lodge's two cockney doormen, putting on that pouty-lipped expression between little girl and Hollywood actress.

Frankie at Regents Park Zoo, cooing lovingly to the big cats.

Frankie perusing the cheap, formulaic watercolor artwork hung on the Hyde Park fencing along Bayswater Road on Saturdays. And collecting many paintings over her stay.

I've had all these flashes of my mother in England. But eleven days into my journey she hasn't appeared in full form. I'm depressed.

And I'm lonely.

friday, march 14

Stepping out of my hotel in the morning I'm stunned by a bright sunny sky. And by two passing young men sporting purple hair piled into pyramids on their heads.

The two rocks I'm carrying back to Colchester were the only ones in Frankie's "Rock Collection" box that were in a separate plastic Baggie. And they are the only stones I'm taking back without Frankie's handwriting on them.

There were many other rocks in the box that were without identifying marks. Some were quite interesting. The biggest piece of all, bigger than my Hadrian's Wall chunks, looks like a capping stone to a wall. It's sandstone and shows lichen specks, so it almost surely sat in a spot with open exposure to weather. Another piece is limestone breccia, something you find in caves. There is a piece of black tourmaline. And a piece of rose quartz, an igneous rock that would be unlikely building material and so would carry a story all its own. But Frankie never wrote on these, and a bunch of others. Did she forget where she picked them up? Or was her cataloguing of the collection interrupted by some new collection fancy, and she never found the time to continue?

I know the Colchester stones came from here because Frankie wrote a note in pencil, double-folded it, and inserted it in the Baggie. These were the only stones identified in a separate note. "This bit of wall," she wrote, "comes from

Colchester, from the Balkerne Gate. Which was the north entrance to Colchester in Roman time when there was a wall built all around Colchester town."

No mistaking these two rocks. They are identical in coloration, mostly reddish, with orange-gray and some darker splotches. They are rounded, but irregular and angular with several flatish faces. One is about an inch in size, the other about half that. They are very low-grade limestone. The lack of weathering indicates they were broken apart from a larger mass quite recently; and in geologic terms, the late 1960s would be considered very, very recently.

Before going to see the gate, I wander in to see the folks who have responsibility for what survives of the Roman wall, the Colchester Borough Council. In their offices, I meet Tom Hodgson, curator of social history for Colchester Museums, a wing of the council. He's another young man, about mid-thirties, slender, with a trim mustache. He's in a suit and tie and talks very rapidly.

"Well, first off," he says, after reading Frankie's note, "the gate is the west entrance, not north." It faces almost due west, in fact. And for the record, Frankie, the gate is spelled Balkerne, not Balkern. With that squared away, Tom goes on in quick fire to inform me that Balkerne Gate is one of only two surviving Roman arches in England, the other being in Lincoln, and that the earliest mention of Colchester was by Pliny the Elder in A.D. 77, when, in talking about the Druids, he mentioned that these peoples lived two hundred miles from a town called Camulodunum, the mentioning of which makes it Britain's oldest recorded town. King Cunobelin was ruling over much of southern Britain from Camulodunum then, and when the Romans invaded, in A.D. 43, seizing Camulodunum/Colchester was a major objective, at which, as we know, they were quite successful and immediately set up shop.

I try to catch my breath from listening to Tom, as he turns his attention to Frankie's rocks, and examines them.

Tom notes they are very typical of East Anglia. "We have very poor building stone here," he says. Which is why the Romans did a lot of clay brick-making here, and built most things out of brick. The town walls, which date to A.D. 65–80, average eight feet eight inches thick, and about twelve feet high with an additional three-foot parapet. They have a rubble-and-mortar core faced on both sides with squared clay nodules. Frankie's pieces are not brick. So they are probably from the rubble in between Balkerne Gate's facing blocks.

The taking of mementos by tourists, pulling out bits of wall, happens, Tom knows. There's so much Roman wall—enclosing 108 acres, it runs for a length of over three thousand yards—the temptation is great. "I think people feel privileged to be able to handle ancient things," he says. "The taking is mostly to be able to hold, I think, not so much to own." Which is one reason the castle museum has a number of authentic ancient things that people are allowed—even encouraged—to touch. "We have so many Bronze Age ax heads, for example, it was no problem to put some into a handling collection. People like that."

But tourists picking away at the walls is small potatoes compared with either natural erosion or authorized destruction, he says. As recently as the 1980s, one hundred yards of Roman wall was demolished to make way for an underground car park.

We are talking in a conference room in the Borough Council offices next door to Colchester Castle, built by the Normans between 1076 to 1125. Tom has been turning my two rocks over in his hands as he talks. Now he sets them down on the wooden conference table. "You know, this is a classic example that context is everything. Sitting here on the table," he says, gesturing at the two lumps, "the two stones are nothing. Knowing what type of rock they are makes them somewhat interesting. Knowing they came from a Roman wall makes them more interesting. Knowing they were taken out of the wall and put in an American collection makes them more interesting still. Knowing they've been brought back and they are the subject of your story gives them even more interest. The more context, the more interesting they become."

He thinks a few seconds, then says, "But I think they were always most interesting as parts of the Roman wall around Colchester. They've lost that context, I'm afraid. You're giving them new context, but it isn't the same."

Watching him, I can almost see the gears turning in the head of this curator of social history. "We have a place in the museum," says Tom, "where maybe we can give your mother's rocks some context." He stands up abruptly. "I'll show you."

He strides abruptly out of the conference room, and I hustle to follow. In the museum next door Tom takes me up to the second floor, around a couple of corners, to a display case. He points to a big key on display. The placard under it says "Key from Holy Trinity Church, Colchester. The two-hundred-year-old key went missing in the 1940s only to reappear over fifty years later! Gift Mr. E. Dalzell."

"A few years ago," explains Tom, "this elderly gentleman came in and said this key was purloined forty or fifty years before. He was stationed here during the war. It was just in a door of the old church, I guess. So we accessioned it, gave it a catalogue number, and here it is.

"Leave your mother's stones with me when you go," Tom says, as he turns to run to a meeting. "We'll fill out a museum object entry form and see what we can do."

By now twenty-four hours in Colchester and I've still not laid eyes on the famous Balkerne Gate. I set off to do that.

One of the most intact sections of Roman wall separates the upper and lower portions of Castle Park, running parallel to the River Colne along the northern edge of the walled city. I make my way there, planning to reach the wall and then follow its remains counterclockwise until I reach the western gate. I take my time, strolling through the Upper Castle Park, enjoying the springtime sunshine, and photographing seas of bright-yellow daffodils and lavender crocuses in full bloom. The sky is brilliant blue. Young kids are kicking soccer balls; young mothers are pushing baby carriages. There was over a foot of snow on the ground on Cape Cod when I left, with temperatures in the teens and with any hope for flowers still months away. It feels unquestionably as if I've traveled from a northern clime to a place much farther south. I shake my head, realizing that Cape Cod, about halfway between forty-one and forty-two degrees latitude, is a good ten degrees, over seven hundred miles, south of Colchester on the globe. The Cape is on a line with northern Portugal, Barcelona, and Rome. A latitudinal line running west of where I am now in England would pass north of Newfoundland Island.

Thank you, Gulf Stream, thank you. The warmth feels very good.

As Tom Hodgson had hinted, the Roman wall isn't exactly a pretty pile of stones. It's an amalgam of different rock pieces and red brick forced together, and now looking weak and fragile. It was thrown up by the Romans with whatever was around, and the intervening years have not been kind. Of course it has been close to two thousand years. But we're not talking a granite-blocked citadel here. The wall is crumbly, like Dover's pharos. I spot a sign affixed to a section of it: "The public are earnestly requested to assist the owner in protecting the ancient Roman wall by checking children whom they may see climbing upon or otherwise injuring it and by giving notice to the police of any willful damage to it of which they may be witnesses."

I guess this didn't pertain to Frankie. She wasn't a child. Was she?

On my walk to Balkerne Gate, two young women pass me on the sidewalk wearing red plastic noses and floppy, elastic rabbit ears. Then I pass the office of the local newspaper serving the Northeast Essex area, the *Evening Gazette*. "Why not?" I say to myself, and on a whim, I turn into the office.

The receptionist listens seriously as I explain that I'd like to speak with a reporter because I'm here from America and have come across the Atlantic Ocean to Colchester to return a pair of rocks my mother stole from the Balkerne Gate thirty-six years ago. "Uh-huh," she says. "One moment, please."

No flies on the *Gazette* newsroom. Recognizing a good story (or is it a good joke?), a young reporter, Tom Weatherill, promptly appears and takes me into the conference room. He's dressed in a rumpled coat and tie and can't be more than twenty-five years old.

"So what is this again, then?" he asks. I notice his notebook is closed and his mouth is turned up in a discernible smirk. He seems barely able to contain some dammed reservoir of mirth. I'm not sure why I look that humorous, although it has been quite a few days on the road.

"My mother, you see, was this collector, and years after her death I found this box . . . ," I say. And so on.

The notebook in Tom's lap and the grin on his face remain fixed in place.

". . . and I've been to Stonehenge, then Stourhead, and Salisbury Cathedral and Corfe Castle, Bodiam Castle, Dover Castle, and now I'm here," I say, pausing. I then say, "Shouldn't you be taking a few notes? I'm a former newspaper editor myself, and that would be my advice." I'm thinking of those waitresses that never write anything down, and then get your order all wrong.

Ever so slowly, Tom Weatherill folds open his notebook. "You're serious, aren't you," he says, and he shakes his head.

"I suppose it is a bit odd," I respond. "Not your average unsolicited story idea. But, hey, I just thought . . ."

"I assumed you were Comic Relief," he says.

"Well, I suppose I am comic relief," I reply. "What's the normal Friday fare? A multiple lorry mash-up on the motorway? Business-page piece about hoof-and-mouth? Incidentally, is that why the pubs serve kangaroo and ostrich around here? You should know that I was once president of an American student organization established to save kangaroos from becoming extinct."

"Now I'm not sure again," says Tom, a grin spread across his face. "You most certain you aren't Comic Relief?"

"I guess that's for you to decide."

It finally dawns on Tom Weatherill that this middle-aged American rock returner may very well be clueless about Comic Relief. So he fills me in. Every two years, since about the mid-1980s, a project called Comic Relief has been raising money for international relief charities. Across England, people dress up in weird costumes or do wacko things to make people smile or laugh, and to part them from spare pounds and pence. Today is Red Nose Day. But this year's overall theme, Tom thinks, is Mad Hair.

I realize my longish, thinning hair is customarily a mad mess. And that my accumulating total of evening pints of cask ale just might have brightened my nose.

"So I just assumed . . . ," says Tom.

"Well, naturally," I say. Then add, "I do take donations."

Tom summons his staff photographer, Steve Argent, and the three of us hike the remaining couple of blocks to Balkerne Gate. It's a lot smaller than I thought it would be. It's actually two arches next to each other, a mishmash of gray rock, light mortar, and red brick. Steve has me stand in the sun with one of Frankie's rock pieces in my hand, held out against the arch. He snaps off a couple of shots. I feel very stupid. Comic relief, indeed. Then we shake hands and the two news guys go away.

(Tom does, indeed, write up a little story for the *Evening Gazette* a few days after my visit. I don't see it, of course, until a month later when I get home. He's sent me a copy. It's the Tuesday, March 18, paper. I appear on page 7. Pretty prominent placement, for comic relief. The headline is big and bold-face: "Son tours country to return rocks." The story is straightforward and contains no mistakes. With my newspapering background, and the way I've seen the quality of American journalism plummet in recent years, I'm pleased and impressed with Tom's write-up. It even contains an inspiring quote I gave him in an attempt to take the trip beyond me. "We have a common responsibility to protect these sites," I say. "They are world heritage sites and help us understand ourselves, just as this trip is helping me understand my mother." I like that.)

(My only complaint is to Tom's editors. They positioned the story, and its picture of me looking weirdly washed-out and a little too wasted, immediately next to a story headlined "Would-be Flasher Ran Off.")

Balkerne Gate is impressive. It looks very, very old. It looks like a good kick could cause it to crumble to the ground. It looks like a Roman antique, which is hardly surprising, because that's precisely what it is. It has that silent, defiant solemnity to it, like any precious piece of ancient history preserved for many centuries in a setting that has gone way modern all around it. Here, for sure, its stance struggles with its surroundings. At Dover, at least, the crumbly Roman lighthouse shares lofty, open space with a Saxon church immediately next to it, and the medieval fortress surrounding it. Balkerne Gate suffers stark contextual indignities: the Whole in the Wall Pub, built directly over what was once the gate's north carriageway and footway; the modernesque Mercury Theatre abutting its south side; the divided, sunken four-lane A134 highway paralleling its north side, steady traffic whizzing by perhaps fifteen feet below the level of the gate; and across the roadway, a huge banner announcing "Sales Centre Now Open" for anyone interested in buying into the Barratt Balkerne Heights upscale condo complex immediately behind the banner.

With all these dramatic distractions, I find it hard to conjure up Frankie here, or to envision Colonia Claudia Victricensis, the first capital of the new Roman province of Britannia, at this, its main entrance.

Had the pub been here in the first century, any self-respecting Roman centurion would certainly have dropped in for a pint. So I have to go inside.

"Fever" by Kylie Minogue is on the jukebox playing at full volume. The ubiquitous slot machine game here is the Beaver Las Vegas version. A poster says, "Watch Out. Spikers are about!!! Please do not leave your drink unattended." Lounging at the tables are no obvious drink spikers, though it wouldn't surprise me if one of them was suddenly accused. There's a lot of spiked hair and one spike-studded belt. "Metallica," says the printing on the front of one shirt. "Britney Swallows," says another.

The past two thousand years have not been kind to the ambience of Balkerne Gate.

As I leave, a girl comes in with a red plastic nose.

I do as I promised. I take Frankie's Balkerne rocks back to the Museum Resource Centre. No moat here to toss them into. And besides, I'm hopeful they'll end up in the museum case next to Mr. Dalzell's key. The two secretaries at the center are delighted to see me again. They've been charmed by my story, and are quick to help me. I fill out a pink Museum Object Entry Form (#3075, if you're counting), and in the area for description of "when, where or how was it found," one of the ladies politely writes, "Items of brick work from Balkerne Gate which were removed circa 1966–1969." I sign the form, squeeze the two rocks one final time, and hand them over. The two ladies are grinning ear to ear.

I've booked ahead at a farm B&B for tomorrow. It's in rural land, a tiny hamlet called Holdenby, out of the traffic, away from the pierced youth, streaks of spittle on the sidewalks, £2 pints, and crowds. I'm anxious for a slowdown. It's so lonely in the crowds. I'm desiring a more lonely setting, to be surrounded by what I feel. Lonely. Lonely, watching people party, eating alone in city restaurants, trekking along alone site to site with my rocks.

How did Frankie deal with loneliness? Was she lonely in her marriage? Her whole life? Certainly in her childhood, in her family. And certainly in her pain—lying in the dark alone with her agonizing, pounding headaches, under her cool washcloths. Was she alone in sex? At night in bed when she was headache-free? In friendships?

A porky barmaid dressed up as a pig and carrying a plastic bucket passes through the Olde Marquis Pub. She's collecting donations. I drop in a £1 coin.

8.

finding meaning to life in philosophers' stones

Holdenby Interlude

In one sense, Frankie was a twentieth-century successor to sixteenth-and seventeenth-century curio collectors and the curio-cabinet fad. As the Renaissance bloomed and journeys of world discovery brought back to Europe more and more strange or miraculous objects of beauty, antiquity, or *naturalia*, folks who considered themselves to be cultured, or simply aspired to be hip, took to keeping display cases of acquired oddities in their homes. The cases ranged from modest to grand. Into these curio cabinets, also known as *wunderkammern*, people arranged their collections of peculiar things in unique ways for all visitors to see.

Like Frankie, the curio collectors did not attempt to collect complete sets of things. They weren't interested in acquiring as many versions of one thing as they could find either. The basic goal was to have in your *wunderkammer* an intriguing assortment of stuff. Yet the assortment was not supposed to be random. The idea was to create a display of things that could be viewed together as some sort of statement about the multifaceted wonder of the world.

Each curio cabinet was thus each individual's statement, and while any visitor might examine a friend's collection with genuine interest, only its owner could say for sure what message his arranged objects were meant to communicate. The curio cabinets of those days have thus sometimes been called "cabinets of reason," or "world theaters," again indicating that the whole was expected in some way to be more profound than the sum of its parts.

Often, the collection had little value to the owner beyond displaying it. Pride of ownership, a mantle of worldliness, and ego satisfaction came with sharing the sight. Such collections existed for others as much as for the collector. And so, at a superficial level anyway, did some of Frankie's collections. She sought to show them, and possession of curious things for her was closely tied to the feedback of interest and admiration she got from friends, or strangers, who examined her collections.

Before Frankie and my dad moved permanently to Cape Cod from Maryland in 1977, they added a huge, open room to their modest retirement home. Built into one full wall of the room was a floor-to-ceiling curio cabinet. Into its many cubbies and onto its dozens of shelves Frankie arranged pieces of her many collections—a fourteenth-century black polished Chimu clay pottery jug from Peru; a Chinese bronze mirror, Ming Dynasty, with lion-and-grape motif; assorted antique dolls; several Swiss music boxes; turquoise specimens from New Mexico; and much more.

Outside her home Frankie had a second curio cabinet, a more public one: the large display case in the lobby of the Osterville Free Library. Management of this village exhibition space was virtually handed over to Frankie when the library staff came to realize her mania for collections, and for arranging them and showing them. Several times a year Frankie created elaborate displays in the library lobby, enhancing old lace with borrowed antique dresses, or cutting out gravestone rubbings and gluing them to Styrofoam gravestone shapes. Most of what was shown sprang from Frankie's own collections. But if she needed to expand or fill out an idea, she found other collectors. She always provided carefully typed explanations of what was on display.

Frankie took great pride in both her public and private curio cabinets. Newspapers wrote articles and took pictures. The radio station interviewed her. Friends stopped her in supermarkets or at church and gave praise for her latest library display. Visitors to her home admired the specimens on her shelves. She basked in the explaining of the many unusual or lovely things she had to show. Her collections became inseparable parts of her life, constant draws upon her time and attention. Her genuine enthusiasm for her eclectic collections, an enthusiasm cast frenetically one direction one moment and another direction the next, became a defining part of Frankie's charm and character. And she shared all this openly with all.

With one exception.

The stones from the ancient English sites.

Collections tell stories. No less than books or movies, really. They're just open to more interpretation, and take more audience investment.

Written or spoken stories, built on language, have it easy. Verbs, prepositions, adjectives, gerunds (remember those?), adverbs, and all the rest assist people in following a narrative tale constructed around subjects and objects. In standard English grammar, nouns are called objects. Collections are missing the grammar, but they're loaded with objects. Only in this case they're three-dimensional.

Movies have screenplays. Yet the most common mistake a moviemaker makes is believing the screenplay tells the story. Dialogue shapes a movie's story. But movies are stories told with pictures, not words.

Collections are stories told with objects.

A trend at many restaurants is to line the walls with objects having not the slightest thing to do with dining or cuisine—license plates, old wooden skis, traffic signs, airplane propellers, saxophones, vintage movie posters. Yet observing the stuff is often a dead giveaway of what's offered on the menu.

In Culver City, California, there once was (and may still be) a storefront museum known as the Museum of Jurassic Technology. In it one could find a bizarre assortment of man-made and nature-made items that may, or may not, have been real. The museum owner wouldn't say. Which was his way of saying it doesn't matter. Collected, displayed objects are allegories. They create reactions. They make you think. They take you on inner journeys. They tell stories.

Whether in private homes, restaurants, museums, library display cases, or *wunderkammern,* or hidden away in cardboard cartons, wherever someone has assembled a bunch of objects there's an underlying story. The collection's story. The collector's story. And the all-important story of what unites them.

Humans are natural-born storytellers. Cavemen probably sat around fires and grunted out stories. We know they left them painted on cave walls—stories of hunts and heroics. So too were walls of ancient Egyptian or Mayan or Khmer temples adorned with painted or sculpted relief narratives. The Parthenon Marbles—Lord Elgin's famous booty—relate a story in stone. Museums are packed with stories left chiseled into marble, worked in silver or gold, set in mosaic, glazed onto pottery, woven into tapestry, or brushed onto anything that would hold paint. Cultures across the planet created and handed down epics, myths, or legends in all the various story forms—oral, pictorial, physical, printed. Storytelling is universal, and probably instinctual. Is it any wonder collectors would get in on the act?

Screenwriters and book publishers are fond of saying there are only a handful of story lines in life. Finding love. Losing love. Solving a mystery. Overcoming great odds in facing a great challenge. Sacrificing self for someone or something else. These are some. Many of the really big basic story themes go back to antiquity and address the most fundamental questions. Here's three: Is there order in the universe? Is there meaning to life? Is there life after death?

Call it human nature. There's a yearning on the part of people that there be universal order, that things aren't simply arbitrary, random, accidental, chaotic; that there is meaning to life, that existence isn't just an empty exercise; and that there is afterlife, that a life doesn't begin and end with birth and death, that people can achieve immortality. There's been no shortage of attention to these subjects by the pens, points, and palettes of artists. But not everybody is an artist. What to do, for those art-challenged folks, when the angst over life's great questions gets too great?

Collect. It takes no way with words or brushes or chisels to create a collection. It used to take a certain level of affluence. Today in mass consumer cultures it doesn't even take that. Just collect. Select things from among the onrushing, disconnected jet stream of junk racing through life, procure them, organize them, present them in a focused, fixed way. If the anxiety is great enough, collecting will help. It will help in facing up to the fear of chaos and nothingness.

The *wunderkammer* trend was an early attempt by nonartists to make stabs at finding meaning in life. On one level they were, for sure, simply cabinets full of weird stuff meant to intrigue and impress viewers at a time when a world of new wonders was finding its way into fashionable society. But on a deeper level a cabinet's contents were a collector's hope, her attempt, to fashion out of the oddities of creation an insight into the nature of creation. They were arrangements of things that, just possibly, might hold the key to life's meaning. They were objects in individual stories designed by people without artistic outlets, hoping, by linking the profound complexity and diversity of life, to reveal an All Truth whole.

Frankie had artistic talent. She was a superb musician. But she was an interpreter, not a composer. She didn't work out life's imponderables in song or on violin in music she'd written herself. Neither was she an especially good wordsmith or oral storyteller. Yet Frankie was definitely one of those people who are seriously unsettled by the questions of the meaning of life and mortality. And she channeled a part of her search for solutions into collecting.

While she didn't write music, Frankie intuitively understood it. With her voice or her violin bow, she naturally knew the need for the subtle interplay of repeated theme and continual variation, the assonance and dissonance that make music beautiful. And she brought this to collecting. Collectors want their assembled objects to rhyme. They want beauty, and meaning, to arise out of sameness within difference. Frankie's brass rubbings are all the same, but all different. The collection in her curio cabinet was composed of many different things, but if my mother fits in the mold of many obsessive collectors, and I think she does, in her *wunderkammer*-style display of objects Frankie sought a harmony.

I remember watching her one afternoon put some new pieces on display in our home—a few broken, curved, blue-green pieces of nineteenth-century Sandwich glass that had once probably been cup handles. The Sandwich glass factory in Sandwich, Massachusetts, was once famous for its quality work, and today intact glassware is quite valuable. The factory was long gone when

Frankie learned that a side lot on the property, next to a salt marsh, was once used by the glass business as a dump for broken pieces. In the late 1950s she took friends out to the area and they brought garden trowels and dug around retrieving bits of buried glass. I remember, when I was just a kid, Frankie once filled a small, clear bottle with a colorful assortment of shards and stood it on a kitchen windowsill. Sunlight would sparkle through the multicolored glass. I liked that.

The day I remember her adding Sandwich glass to her collections shelf was much later. I was probably in my late teens. She was being very meticulous about placement of the glass, and I was struck by that. It was being placed next to some arrowheads and feathers, if I remember correctly. I was drinking a soda, and between swallows I said, "Who's gonna know what that is?"

"It's Sandwich glass," she said with authority.

"I know what it is," I said. "But who else is gonna know? It's just broken hunks."

Frankie didn't say anything. Then I said, "How come you're just putting it out with other stuff for people to see now? You've had Sandwich glass around for years."

She didn't look up from what she was doing. I remember that. "I don't know," she said.

After a pause, she said, "It just seems to me I need them now."

After another pause, she said, "Before it's too late."

Too late for what? As a wise-guy teenager I thought I ought to know, so I didn't ask.

If I had asked, what would Frankie have said? Perhaps she'd have said something like this: All these things, old and new, valuable and worthless, natural and man-made, have been collected here, arranged, stilled by me in an ever-changing world, made melodious by me in a life of discord, because if I failed to do this it would be an admission that life is nothing but a messy tumult, a pointless, disconnected pandemonium of things and happenings out of my control that leads directly, and too quickly, to death.

And she might have added, And I can't stand the thought.

No, Frankie would never have articulated anything like that. She couldn't have even thought that. Collectors don't think like that, just people thinking about collectors, or a son thinking about his collector mother. Frankie said what she said, and that was it.

For some individuals the search for the philosopher's stone goes on. These people haven't been called alchemists for ages. And they no longer hunt for a way to turn base metals into gold. Now they're called collectors. And what they seek in their efforts is to grasp underlying reality itself. And something else. They yearn to prolong life. A collection—a thing fixing objects, freezing decay, interrupting the flow of time—is a subtle attempt to cheat death.

The English rocks were never a part of Frankie's *wunderkammer.* They were hidden away. They weren't a part of a larger collection shaped and shown in hopes of revealing a lasting meaning to life. They existed to give her meaningful hope for life everlasting. Frankie alone needed that particular rock collection, everyone else be damned.

Rocks from Corfe Castle, from Hadrian's Wall, from Tintern Abbey, and the rest. Fourteen rocks from a timeless geology before history, taken from an ancient history context long, long before the present. Rocks that are calling cards from forever. Frankie's private collection of philosopher's stones.

saturday, march 15

I've called ahead and taken a B&B in Holdenby, a village on a map but not a village I ever actually find. Not that that matters. I'll be staying at a sheep farm operated by a handsome young couple, Catherine and Steven Holt. The building on a creek was a mill in the 1700s. Steven looks like a sheep rancher from New Zealand. When *Returning Frankie's Rocks* is a major motion picture, Meg Ryan will play Catherine, though if the two went head-to-head in a screen test on looks alone I'd wager Catherine would win. She's drop-dead lovely. Naturally, I fall instantly in lust. Steven Holt would be played by Sam Shepard.

Who would play Frankie? Diane Keaton, maybe. Robert Redford could play me. Dream on, Dana.

So I've chosen to stay in a village named Holdenby. One of my childhood homes was Holden, Massachusetts, a small town in the central part of the state just north of Worcester. Honestly, I don't make the connection between the two town names until I pull up to the massive three-story stone farmhouse. Now the decision sets me wondering. And traveling as I am so intimately with the memory of my mother, it sets me remembering.

$\mathbf{W}$hat little I remember.

We lived in Holden, Massachusetts, for just a year. I was five years old, turning six there. It was 1953. Frankie would have been thirty-six years old. My dad, it seems, was gone a lot. He was unhappy at the paper company where he was working. He went off a lot to find another job.

Our house was a new, plain, two-story white wood-frame home in a post-war subdivision. Across the street were woods on soggy wetland soil. We were on the edge of town, and the woods were a deep, dark labyrinth. I remember, just a few yards into these woods there was a huge rock. A glacial erratic, I guess it was, maybe six feet high, ten feet or so wide, a remnant from the retreating ice sheet of the last ice age. But in '53 it had no fancy name like that. It's name was just "The Big Rock."

After a rain, pools of water would collect around the base of the rock. Moss covered one side of it. It was my primary play site. Or at least my favorite. All the kids on the street climbed all over it. It was a fort. An elephant. A mountain. An imposing, silent, alien thing that looked out-of-place in the neighborhood because it was, in fact, out-of-place across from the neat row of Holden homes. And so it was a thing of mystery and enchantment.

When I went outside to play, I remember the repeated order "Don't go beyond The Big Rock." I don't remember who told me this. Presumably my mother. But I don't remember her saying it. I have the vague memory of an inference, that if I did go beyond The Big Rock I would assuredly become lost, because the forest was a place not to be trusted, where children could be kidnapped and never let go. The big boulder thus became a border fortress against all the danger and unknown in the unexplored woods behind it. At the same time, there was a distinct ominous edge to The Big Rock, which only a six-year-old could truly appreciate. While it was seemingly a solid, safe sentinel at the frontier, it was also a mute, cold, massive thing lying at the perimeter between two worlds, and the rock itself couldn't be entirely trusted. Its loyalties might lie with the tangle of undergrowth beyond it, and whatever lurked out there, and not with the manicured lawns and human families on our side of the street. My playmates and I knew this. And so The Big Rock took on an omnipotence, an awesome aspect, of which our parents were absolutely oblivious.

In another time (say, four thousand years ago) in another place (say, Salisbury Plain), The Big Rock might have been incorporated into a stone circle. Or made an altar. Or, maybe, worshiped. The Big Rock is one of the few clear memories I have of Holden.

I remember a few other little things, like being put down to nap on a hard pad in kindergarten, and being lonely and for some reason alarmed. I remember I could never fall asleep. I remember we got our first TV in Holden, and I remember its tiny screen and its miraculous delivery into our living room of Howdy Doody and Buster Brown.

The most major memories I have of Holden, by far the most vivid, are all connected to a single event. The tornado.

In late afternoon June 9, 1953, the black funnel of a F5 tornado—the most powerful category—touched down outside Worcester and for eighty-four minutes it wandered across central Massachusetts. Winds in the tornado's core were estimated at between 317 and 327 mph, which some believe ranks as the highest natural wind velocity ever on the earth's face. Before it dissipated, the tornado leveled a forty-six-mile swath of landscape, killed ninety-four people, injured 1,288, left about fifteen thousand people homeless, caused $53 million in damages, and put to rest forever the notion that New England states don't get tornadoes. Brick and stone structures were demolished and wooden buildings vanished. Telephone poles and trees flew as effortlessly as whooping cranes. Automobiles became airborne (one, reportedly, was found in a tree a mile away from where it had been parked), and a twelve-ton city bus ended up embedded in an apartment building.

The tornado's path brought it through Holden, and it passed about one-half mile from our house.

It's always been surprising to me that I don't remember the tornado itself. My brother Doug had a Little League baseball game that afternoon, and he remembers the game being abruptly canceled and being driven home. Neither one of us remembers what we did at home as the twister churned its way through Holden.

I remember the aftermath. Immediately after, the ground was littered with hailstones the size of Ping-Pong balls. In my little hands they seemed more the size of baseballs. They were everywhere, sparkling on the lawn. I remember running and collecting them and dropping them into a milk bottle.

We had a small picture window at the front of our house, and a smaller window directly in line with it, at the back. During the atmospheric chaos of the storm, a very large bird—maybe an owl—flew full-force into the picture window. Confused and panicky, the bird probably sought refuge in what looked like a narrow tunnel. It smashed into the glass and died. Left behind was a splayed, Rorschach test–like impression of bird head, beak, and out-stretched wings. The image had a grotesque beauty that I remember I found fascinating. Frankie liked it, too. She decided not to wash it off, and the bird's death mask filled our picture window for weeks.

The day after, my mother took me to the edge of the tornado's path. We walked there, is my memory, it was that close. And in memory's eye I can still see what I saw then: a street very like our own, where once there had been a row of modest subdivision houses pretty much like ours, which was now nothing more than a long line of open, concrete foundations. No wood frames, no trees, no cars in driveways or bikes on lawns, just one cellar hole in the ground after another.

My father was away in New York City job hunting when the tornado of '53 took its deadly, twisting journey through Holden. So my mother was alone with my brother and me. She would have sheltered us, protected us, seen us through the danger. But neither one of us has the slightest recollection of what she did. Or what we did together as a family, where we took refuge, or if we even did.

Dramatic or dangerous events are something a kid would be likely to re-member, you'd think. So when one of the most deadly tornadoes in American history cruised a half-mile from our home, I'd expect to remember its pass-ing. There would have been high wind, that hail, preternaturally darkened sky, and ominous noise. There would have been intense adult anxiety for a kid to pick up on. I must have been huddling with my mother, held tightly to her, terrified, down in the basement, somewhere. But I can't see Frankie and can't remember anything at all unusual about the tornado time.

Is it possible we just didn't know, until it was all over? There had been no early warning; the weather bureau forecast that day had been simply "Clearing, with little change in temperature." According to history books, the first tornado warning from forecasters was issued after the tornado had lifted away from the ground and died out. There were no all-news-all-the-time TV channels back then. My brother doesn't remember why his ball game was canceled; maybe it was because it looked like rain. So maybe it was just another late afternoon in Holden with my mother, as ordinary as any other, until an owl plowed into our window, and June hail began to fall. Maybe it came and went and we were all oblivious of the lethal funnel churning through town.

I think, now, this must be the case—that it was just another unmemorable afternoon, with memories of being with my mother as absent as other afternoons, and the only foreboding, portentous presence in my life The Big Rock across the street.

sunday, march 16

I awake to fog in thick clouds hanging over the Holts' sheep pastures. I have a day to myself.

In the afternoon I take a long walk down an abandoned railroad right-of-way outside the village, now a bike-and-hiking trail. Sheep graze on the gently rolling pastureland. As I suspected they would be, scores of families are out, with bikes, dogs, children, packed lunches.

I've brought bread and cheese, and plant myself on a wooden bench along the trail. A couple, aged eighty-two and seventy-five, sit next to me for a spell. They laugh at why I'm in England. Then the wife admits that when they go to the beach in Suffolk, they always take stones. Blue ones, which now line their garden at home. She confesses she also has a collection of stones picked up around England, France, and the United States that she's labeled and glued to a large vase.

"Where did you take the U.S. rock?" I ask.

"Well, it was from a valley along the Columbia River, up in Washington State, wasn't it," she says. Her husband nods.

"That's not like from Stonehenge or Hadrian's Wall, I guess, so I guess that's okay," I say.

"They said it was an American Indian area." She has a guilty look, all of a sudden.

"Well, shame on you," I tease. "Do you want me to take the rock back? Or are you going to do it yourself?"

"Well I can't, can I," she says, "it's stuck to my vase."

9.

from noah to
pet rocks to kim

York Minster

"Noah was the first collector," suggest editors John Elsner and Roger Cardinal in the introduction to their book *The Cultures of Collecting*. And Noah sets himself apart, they say, because he, "perhaps alone of all collectors, achieved the complete set."

"In the myth of Noah as ur-collector," they believe, "resonate all the themes of collecting itself: desire and nostalgia, saving and loss, the urge to erect a permanent and complete system against the destructiveness of time."

A female friend of mine has an enormous collection of pigs: stuffed animal pigs, porcelain pigs, pig-face pot holders, play farmyard plastic pigs. Anything with a piggy to its shape seems to qualify. Does it matter that the pigs be unusual, pretty, or funny, or something? No, she once told me, it matters only that they are pigs.

Noah needed only two pigs for his ark, and then was done with them. For my friend, there's no end to her collection. There are always more pigs out there, more variations of the image theme, new piglets being churned out of Chinese trinket and toy factories all the time. There's no hope of acquiring the complete set because there is no such thing. But that's the point, too. Obsessive collectors don't begin a collection with the goal of reaching an end point. The object quest and the serial nourishment of the collection are what's crucial to the need—the emotional stability—of the collector. They don't want it to end. The end would mean their end.

In this regard, then, Noah was not a typical collector. He didn't want 101 dalmatians. Two was not only enough but the perfect number and the limit. There wasn't room aboard ship for any more, even if he'd taken a special fancy to spotted dogs. But it's interesting that animals were the collection of proto-collector Noah. A variety of scholars have suggested that collectibles, for some collectors, are substitutes for pets. In fact, in some ways they are superior to pets.

Jean Baudrillard calls the object the "perfect pet. It represents the one 'being' whose qualities extend my person rather than confine it. . . . Pets are a category midway between persons and objects."

Maurice Rheims believes, "For the collector, the object is a sort of docile dog which receives caresses and returns them in its own way; or rather, reflects them like a mirror constructed in such a way as to throw back images not of the real but of the desirable."

Philipp Blom writes, "Dogs, much like hat-pins or toy cars, do not run off because their affection is exhausted. It is quite safe to invest one's love in them. Loved in the way their owners want to be, and indulged with as they themselves want to indulge, they are both object and fulfillment of desire."

Influencing all these thinkers undoubtedly was Sigmund Freud. He believed a collector "directs his surplus libido on to an inanimate object: a love of things." This search for love, Freud felt, often takes people to pets, especially cats. And it also takes them to objects in collections. For people who dread loneliness, a collection of "loved" objects lying around, staring reassuringly out from a showcase or shelf, can keep that dread at bay.

In the search for love, let's not forget, a problem for people is that people have been known to spurn people. Love between human beings is notoriously fickle and painfully unreliable. The track record is significantly better for pets, warm, cuddly creatures that rarely fail to wag their tails in greeting or look on at their owners with what seem to be adoring eyes. Never mind the real reason is it's owners who refill food bowls.

The track record for inanimate collected objects is better still. These "pets" never, ever have an off day, are always around (unlike, say, some cats), and are rock-steady companions. A big bonus is they don't need to be fed, given baths, exercised, or taken to the vet, and they never shred the draperies, bark all night, bring in fleas, or pee on carpets.

Is it any wonder, then, that in 1975 a California ad man having a couple of beers in a bar came up with the idea for Pet Rocks. Gary Dahl surmised that people might enjoy an alternative to the hassles of a living, breathing pet, and would pay money for it. He decided the perfect substitute would be a rock. Consequently he brought north three tons of smooth, gray pebbles from Rosarita Beach, Baja, Mexico, packaged individual stones in boxes made to look like a pet carrying case, complete with holes in the side to let the rock breathe, and prepared a "Pet Rock Training Manual," complete with instructions on how to house-train the stone, and make it roll over and play dead. He sold each Pet Rock for $3.95. The Mexican supplier in Baja got one cent per rock.

National TV talk shows and magazines, and reportedly seventy-five percent of the nation's newspapers, jumped all over the story. Within a few months Dahl had sold over a million Pet Rocks. Immediately the envious came out of the woodwork, selling all sorts of copycat crap, including Pet Rock Burial-at-Sea Services. Within a few more months, those burial services became necessary. Pet Rocks were a dead deal and you couldn't give them away.

About three times in the 1950s when I was a kid, our family drove to Florida for winter vacations. My mother's brother, Maurice Jr., was in Jacksonville, and my father's aunt Doris lived outside Miami. The trips always included short visits with them. On one of those trips I did something that became entrenched Hornig family lore.

The story of what I did was told over and over, over many years, to friends and relatives, and on some occasions to complete strangers in supermarket lines or salesmen in the boys' department of clothing stores during back-to-school shopping. My older brother realized the story was told at my expense. He gleefully saw it was the source of considerable embarrassment to me, which naturally led him to perpetuate its telling. My parents, meanwhile, were oblivious to my shame and discomfort, and apparently thought what I did was cute. I was maybe ten.

What I did is, I kissed a snake.

We were somewhere far out along the two-lane Tamiami Trail west of Miami doing touristy things. I distinctly remember three of those things, which is a remarkably high percentage of childhood memories for one day, I'd say, and definitely ranks the day among life leaders in my child memory department.

First we visited a seedy Seminole village and watched a bare-chested man in Indian costume wrestle an uninterested alligator in a concrete pit that smelled of stale fish and sweat. I remember feeling sad. For the alligator.

Then we stopped at another place and took an aluminum-bottomed airboat for a swamp-skimming ride over the Everglades. At some point, far out of sight of anything resembling civilization, a small dry hummock stood out of the wetlands. The airboat driver stopped there. I was put ashore, and then the boat drove off. This was intended to frighten me and amuse the adults, and I suppose tickle the depraved funny bone of my big brother, too, and I suppose it did entertain them all. I remember feeling very scared.

And finally, later that day we visited a rundown wooden building with a peeling painted sign advertising it as a "Reptile Ranch." Inside, an attendant showed us around. At one of the larger enclosures, he lifted out a Burmese python. Its body was twice the length of mine and as thick as one of my legs. It lazily wrapped around the man's torso, and he cradled the python's head in his two hands. I was standing closest, in front of the others. I was quite transfixed. Slowly the guide bent the big snake's head down to me, and said something I don't remember. What I do remember—what everyone in my family long remembered—is that I suddenly bent forward and kissed the python on the top of its scaly head. Then I remember the burst of laughter from everyone. And, then, feeling embarrassed.

In a therapy group thirty-five years later, I was among participants talking about their mothers. Each of us in the group was asked if we remember being held and being kissed. When it came my turn, I shrugged my shoulders. "I don't know," I said. "I can't believe you all really remember being held or being kissed," I said. "I sure don't remember. Why would I remember something that ordinary and uneventful when it happened so long ago? I was just a little kid."

"If you don't remember," said the group leader, "it probably didn't happen."

I've thought of this declarative statement over and over ever since. Because while I don't remember being kissed by Frankie, what I do remember, vividly, is my mother kissing Kim.

We had three main pets in my earliest years. There was a spaniel dog named Teddy. But he didn't last long. He was hit by a car and killed when I was just an infant. And there was a cat named Lucky, who had better luck and lived until I was about five. Lucky's claim to family fame was that he observed my use of the trainer potty and subsequently began using it himself. I remember once seeing a picture of this, in fact. But I don't have it now. Lucky didn't, as far as I know, learn how to flush.

But far and away the family pet most imprinted on my childhood and family life was a cantankerous seal point Siamese cat named Kim. We got him when I was about eight, and he lived for sixteen years. So thinking back, there hardly seems a time when Kim wasn't roaming the homes of my youth, nosing around, and most memorably, crying for attention. Siamese cats are notorious for their loud, babylike cries. Kim's scream was piercing.

Frankie worshiped Kim. She pampered him, held him lovingly, talked to him endearingly, and stroked him, hourly, daily, frequently. She routinely tied twine to catnip mice or crumpled aluminum foil balls and played with him. She bought him scratching posts and cat beds and kitty treats. Kim had Frankie's attention whenever the cat sought affection, and often when he did not. Most notably, Frankie could not hold Kim without kissing him. She didn't shower the cat with kisses, she drenched him over and over again.

Frankie over her lifetime occasionally arranged special photo albums of subjects that moved her—honoring a friend's son who was killed in Vietnam, for example, or snapshots of shows of her exhibited collections, or of special trips. There were three special albums devoted entirely to images of Kim. I rated one album, of baby pictures, put together before Kim came along.

When Kim died, Frankie saw to his burial under the apple tree in our backyard on Cape Cod. Kim had often climbed there. Frankie put a flat stone on the spot. And she cried.

For those passionate about them, relics are alive. They carry some sort of life force inside them. In the best cases, they stir imaginations and serve to bring history alive. In the worst, they are sad substitutes for genuine living things, especially for the warmth and love of other people.

The past recedes like the sound of slower traffic passed on a freeway. But things like Frankie's rocks held something eternal for her, and their sound was forever in her ears.

Cultural writer Susan Pearce sees collected objects as "both signifier, that is the medium that carries the message, and the signified, the message itself. This dual nature of the collection is at the heart of its significance." She sees objects as bridges between this world and the other world, and calls them "external souls . . . physically distinct and separate, but souls because the meaning projected on to them brings them into the interior of the collector's personal life."

The meaning of Frankie's surreptitious rock collection has gone to the grave with her. It had inner life only when she did, and only for her. For me, now, I see only a collection that struck little killing blows at the very things valued for their life force, the ancient edifices across England's landscape. I see stones that look little different from mounted butterflies, wings spread and pinned onto paper, insect souls snuffed out to round out a set and provide the collector with safe, uncomplaining, uncomplicated companions.

The words "material" and "matter" derive from the same root as "mother." In my life, too often, any distinction was hopelessly blurred.

monday, march 17

St. Paddy's Day. I make the three-hour haul up the M1 to the Roman-walled city of York, a droning, dreary push through the Industrial Midlands, passing countless caravans of sixteen-wheel lorries, and being passed continuously by tiny cars going eighty mph, cars that I'd be afraid to take over fifty in America.

My rock today is a two-inch-long, half-inch-thick piece of gray, fine-grade sandstone. It's slightly wedge-shaped and rough-edged on all four of the narrow sides. The two broad faces are very smooth, and Frankie's notation on one side in black letters is *York Minster,* and under that A.D. *670.*

There it is again. A date too early. Construction of the great church was A.D. 1220 to 1480. I remember my reaction at Dover Castle, that Frankie was probably just delusional or ignorant of history, and this time I decide I'll trust her. From my first contacts with folks at the Minster, my trust seems to pay off.

Astrea Hooson, a visitors' services rep, vouches for what the guidebooks say. The Minster was built on a site extremely close to a Roman basilica and a Roman military assembly hall, which was central to the conqueror's military HQ. By the A.D. 600s the Romans were pretty much gone from the area. But they left a lot of stone. A Norman church went up here from about 1060 to 1080 reusing some of this stone, and the present cathedral was constructed on its foundations.

But if Frankie's stone is from the much earlier Roman buildings that predated the Minster at this site, how did she get at material which is buried under the huge cathedral?

The possible answer is revealed after just a few minutes talking with Astrea. She asks the important question. "When was your mother here?" When I say sometime between 1966 and 1968, she gives a knowing nod. Smart lady. She provides me with a working theory.

In 1967, engineers issued a warning that York Minster's sixteen-thousand-ton central tower, built in the mid-1400s and rising almost six hundred feet into the air, was so unstable it could collapse any day. They were that blunt. The tower could fall into a heap at any moment. So an emergency reinforcement, stabilization project was immediately undertaken. Excavations were made deep into the undercroft of the church. In turn, as burrowing work proceeded, an Anglo-Saxon burial ground, the Norman foundations, and eventually the Roman rock remains were coughed up.

Astrea guides me over to the York Minster Stoneyard, the place where all the repairs to the "fabric" of the Minster are done. The yard is filled with huge blocks of new stone, some freshly cut, which are used for any necessary re-carvings or repairs. There I meet John David, assistant to the superintendent of works.

A short man, fifty-two years old, with a close-cropped black beard, John bears an uncanny resemblance to Eric Clapton. He's originally from Wales. It's his job to do the drawings and renderings for every piece of recut or refashioned stone used in a repair or replacement.

John takes a close look at Frankie's rock, and quickly confirms what was evident to me when, earlier, I held the stone up to an exterior section of Minster wall and compared it. It's not the same. "This is a fine sandstone," he says of my rock, "and magnesia limestone is the fabric of the present building. The church stone came from a Permian limestone outcrop which runs north-south about twelve miles to our west." The Romans, however, did use a lot of sandstone, especially a coarse, reddish sandstone they brought from the edge of the Pennines mountain range about thirty miles west of York. In turn, he says, the Saxons reused a lot of Roman building material.

During the late 1960s period when the excavations were done under the church, "a lot of material was being taken out. It was a huge excavation. There were piles of it around, I suspect," John says. "Perhaps this was a piece of worked Roman stone, flagstone, a floor stone. There were archaeologists there at the work site, sifting through, looking for valuable relics. But there was so much material. Certainly not all fragments were considered important."

Of one thing John seems certain. "This certainly came from underneath and not from the present Minster."

He wonders if my rock might have been part of a monument. It looks to him like a piece of a larger slab or tile. "It would have been brought here for some reason," he says, "because it's not from here."

I agree to meet him at his local pub, the Royal Oak, after work tomorrow to talk some more.

I'm finding it hard, nearly impossible, to focus on the mission at hand. On my feelings. I can go through the interviews and data gathering easily. Been there, done that, way too often in my journalism career. But where is Frankie on this trip? She's supposed to loom, or at least emerge, larger than life now in death. I'm following her footsteps but not seeing them revealed.

I feel the way I imagine Frankie would feel if she had to do this trip and return rocks I'd taken. Unfocused. Unable to focus. On the feelings. I go through the motions without the emotions.

It sometimes feels absurd, doing this. More often than not. Then I get reactions when I show up, like today's. People show a delight, a smile, and laugh. They show a sympathy and sensibility to the trip, which, oddly, I worry I'm not carrying out competently within myself. I feel, what is it, fraudulent? Not deceptive. Not phony. Not deceitful. These really are Frankie's rocks found in a dusty box by me, and this really is a journey of restoration and rediscovery. But what, then? Incompetent? Incapable, ultimately, of delivering on the promise, the premise that so seems to delight, so that it's all just talk and nothing more will happen because I won't be able to make it happen?

I find I'm scared.

And lonely. There it is again. A deep loneliness.

My jaw is always tense these days. My upper spine burns. I'm pouring down pints of ale. Staring into space. I'm never anxious to get to the laptop keyboard, and I'm drifting slowly backward on keeping up with entering in notes from my days. I'm increasingly afraid I'll forget context, impressions, the flavor of the trip, or possibly even confuse things. When I do sit down at my PowerBook, I pound out the chronological, experiential narrative, while avoiding any tries to write up the emotional journey. The journal I'm keeping records the progress of the trip. But what about the progress of my heart?

My heart aches.

tuesday, march 18

The sign at the base of the stairs says "No dogs allowed on the city walls." At Micklegate Bar, I climb the stairs up to the Roman wall encircling York and walk to the river, then up to York Minster.

The late-sixties emergency excavations by necessity created a giant hole under York Minster. After the reinforcement anchors were cast and set, there was no need to fill in the hole. Instead, the levels of history and stray artifacts revealed became a subterranean tourist exhibit of their own. A stairway takes visitors down past the medieval Norman level, which is the ground level of present York Minster, then to the Saxon level below that, and finally to the Roman level deepest down. I'm the only person taking in the underground exhibit this morning.

York was the Romans' northern capital. They called it Eburacum, and it was a fortress for the 9th Legion, established on the left bank of the River Ouse in A.D. 71. At the lowest level under York Minster you can actually see an excavated portion of the basilica, or great hall, of the Roman headquarters building. It lies at a forty-five-degree angle to the east-west alignment of the Christian churches built over it. At one spot a plaque proclaims, "Here young Constantine was acclaimed Caesar in AD 306 by the men of his father's legion."

The remains of a painted, interior Roman wall have been restored; it was found deep down here, toppled over, lying face down. A culvert (still carrying water to the River Ouse) and parts of columns can be seen. This buried Roman building, it's believed, was in ruins above ground by about the eighth century A.D. Frankie's rock was labeled A.D. *670*. Who would have told her that?

The folks at visitors' services say I ought to speak with Wilf Mellor. Wilf's worked thirteen years at the Minster as a volunteer guide. But back in the late 1960s he worked for the engineering firm that did the excavation and foundation reinforcement project. He didn't actually do any digging at the site but frequently visited and took keen interest in what was happening.

I reach Wilf by telephone. He's in his eighties now. I ask him, Is it possible Frankie had access to the debris being brought out from under York Minster, and might she have been told what it was, and was she able to take a piece?

"I suspect it would have been possible," Mr. Mellor says. "All sorts of muck and rubble was taken out. They went fourteen feet down. Bits of coffins came out. They used power equipment, and all sorts of foundation rubbish came out. They got rid of a lot of it, because they put that new concrete in there, so a lot had to be disposed of. They looked it over, of course. But a lot was just carted off. I would think there was a great deal of stuff lying about, which your mother could have grabbed. It could be a piece of Egbert's coffin. I can't say it isn't valuable. I'd look silly. What size is it?"

Just a small piece, I tell him.

"Oh, good," he says. "I imagined you staggering through with this big sheet of stone. Jolly good," he says. "I'm glad you've brought it back. Though it's hardly been missed, I suspect."

Later, on the street I meet Tino Little, a slender man in his thirties with a close-cropped blond beard and a head of hair shorn so close it's just stubble. He has an engaging, open, friendly face and a cheerful disposition. Tino is in charge of York Minster's Centre for School Visits, and is immediately intrigued with Frankie's rock and my journey.

He wasn't even born when the huge reinforcement opening was created under the Minster. "But I understand," he says, "there were huge spoil piles outside the cathedral. A railway was moving stuff out. Much of it was just going to the tip." "Tip" is English-speak for landfill, or dump. Looking at Frankie's rock closely, he says, "It's conceivably a piece of roof tile, or floor tile, I'd think."

Tino then makes a confession. He too has a piece of York Minster.

"You don't," I say.

"I do," he says. A workman gave it to him. The stone piece was removed during some renovations of a long-gone royal apartment at the top west end of the Minster.

Tino turns and points high up at an inside corner of the cathedral. The stone came, he was assured, from the garderobe built up there for King Edward I.

"From the what?" I ask.

"From the garderobe."

Following in the footsteps of ancient Israelites (who used the term "House of Honor") and ancient Egyptians (who used "House of Morning"), the English and Americans have always used euphemisms and slang to refer to the place one deposits bodily wastes. There is, in fact, no correct term in the English language. The two most common words these days are "bathroom," the room where you bathe, and "toilet," which actually means the process of dressing. In England, "loo" and "W.C." (for water closet) are ubiquitous terms, though in especially polite company you might hear "closet of ease." "Crapper," a slang expression, bridges the Atlantic, but the Brits hold bragging rights on its derivation. Thomas Crapper, 1837–1910, was an English sanitary engineer who invented a forerunner to the flush toilet. Back when York Minster was built, the thirteenth century, prior to plumbing, the proper term was "garde-robe," a rather elegant euphemism for a small, stone overhang that allowed the royal user a clear, unobstructed drop to the ground outside.

"I like to think the king may have come into personal contact with my piece of garderobe," Tino says, proudly. "I've made it into the base of a table lamp."

The Royal Oak pub is just around the corner from York Minster and seems to be the local watering hole for many of the tight-knit community of folks who work at the magnificent cathedral. When I show up to meet John David, the stone czar, I'm surprised yet delighted to find Tino Little there tipping a pint, too.

Together, we all agree that it certainly looks as though Frankie visited York Minster in late 1967 or early 1968 while the excavation of the giant building's undercroft was under way. The date she put on the rock, A.D. 670, was prob-ably suggested to her. "Somebody was probably digging and was at one of the piles of material, and your mother spoke to him, and he said the spoils were coming from a layer under the church of that date," says John. "Whether it was from that early, who knows?"

"And who cares?" I say, paying for a second round of pints for us all.

What matters is what Frankie thought. And she thought she'd acquired a stone from the last days of the Roman Empire in Britain. She loved the no-tion of Roman occupation and ancient emperors; she had hunks of Dover's Roman pharos, Colchester's Balkerne Gate, and Hadrian's Wall in her collec-tion; she began collecting Roman coins in England, and later became a devoted fan of the PBS *Masterpiece Theatre* series "I, Claudius." She had a thing for Romans. And yet, around 1967 she did visit Rome—a city where ancient mar-ble fragments are lying out in the open—but there were no pieces of the Colosseum in her rock collection box, nothing picked up on Palatine Hill, no shards found around the Baths of Caracalla or mementos from Circus Maximus. Odd, I think. Why nothing from the Romans' very own Rome?

The fact that this York rock had for almost two thousand years been entombed underneath the great medieval cathedral, and was only being brought back to light as Frankie stood there, must have thrilled her. But that context—what she could have told about the rock, imbuing an otherwise ordinary-appearing piece of sandstone with a story to stir imaginations—was never to happen. The stone was buried again, this time in a cardboard box in a dusty Osterville loft, left alone, and forgotten. The remembrance of York Minster was buried along with its story until I showed up that day, digging around through family stuff.

And now, here we are in the Royal Oak, passing Frankie's rock back and forth. It has new context, as well as our spirited speculations about its old context. How long will this new life last? Not forever. Its overland and overseas odyssey distinguishes it from some run-of-the-mill shard of a locally consolidated aggregation of mineral matter, but the days of interest in this plain old rock are numbered. We decide in the pub that the time is not quite yet.

We all agree I can't put the rock back under the cathedral. It took the excavation to reveal a rock for Frankie to take, but now the excavation is an exhibit itself. It's clear there's no place to reinsert it.

"I'd like you to leave it with me," Tino says. He's the top guy dealing with school visits to the Minster, so his role is education, and Tino is inspired, he says, to figure out some innovative way to incorporate the little rock into his talks to kids.

"Children are natural collectors," he says. "They can relate to what your mum did." He's unsure whether the message, though, will be that taking rocks from historic ruins is wrong, or something focusing upon the stone's passage from place to place, person to person. He senses there might be some parable he could dream up using the rock as a prop—perhaps something like "The Roman Rock's Great Adventure."

Tino seems serious, although it might be the tasty Abbot ale. At any rate, I can't think of any better passage for Frankie's York rock than entrusting it to this charming young educator. If Frankie's taking rocks leads now to teaching, inspiring, or entertaining kids, it will have unexpectedly led to something important. Frankie, I think, would approve of that.

With emotion, I give the stone to him. Tino can see I'm full of feeling to be giving it up. He grips it in a fist. "I promise to take good care of it," he says. I believe he will.

wednesday, march 19

After a foggy early morning, the sun breaks out bright, and it's unseasonably warm yet again. The stretch of clear, pleasant days is becoming uncanny. It's entirely out of character for Britain.

Without my York rock today, I feel strangely as though I don't belong here anymore. John David has invited me to the Minster's stoneyard to see the master masons fashioning replacement pieces for deteriorated Minster stone. Upkeep and restoration is an ongoing job. Scaffolding is a common sight along the sides of the Minster as rock pieces crumbling from centuries of wind and weathering are carefully measured, catalogued, and removed. In the stoneyard, stonecutters follow templates and drawings produced by John to reproduce replacements following, as precisely as possible, the original designs.

"I'm the practical man on the stone side," says John. "We can't allow deterioration to go too far. Safety is one reason. We can't have pieces of York Minster falling on the heads of tourists. But it's also important for history. We need to keep the detail of the stonework there for future restorers."

When new carved stone is installed in place of the old, a decision is made. Pieces deemed historically important, principally those with ornamental shapes, go to the museum. Other stone may just be thrown away.

Throughout the workrooms of the stoneyard are blocks of glistening white limestone in different stages of shaping. When the new pieces are inserted in place of the old, they will look bright and new. That's of no consequence to John David. "The Minster wasn't designed to look decayed. It was designed to look clean, attractive. It was built, remember, to draw people to it. Pilgrims. It performs the same function today, though now the draw is more tourists."

"So if I come here in a thousand years," I say, "it's possible you and your successors will have removed every single original stone from York Minster's facade and replaced it with a modern copy? It's being slowly transformed into a replica of itself, isn't it?" I ask. "When does it stop being the original?"

John David smiles, and shrugs. "When does it stop being? That's an easier question to answer. When it falls down. Or in the case of the Minster, when it's no longer performing the same function as the original. Take an old castle. It's not performing the same function as the original. It's not supposed to, anymore. People like that it looks old and lost and gone. So how do you preserve it? You keep sticking it back together to keep it looking like a ruin. I'm glad I'm not in that business.

"York Minster isn't a ruin," says John. "We're preserving a function. A cathedral. If we wanted a ruin, we wouldn't have shored up the undercroft in 1967."

"And Frankie wouldn't have had a Roman stone to steal," I say.

"And you wouldn't have anything to bring back," he says.

"And I wouldn't be here talking to you," I say. "And I've genuinely enjoyed meeting you, John. It's been a pleasure. So I'm glad you're doing what you do."

And I mean it.

At an Internet café I retrieve an e-mail from Melissa Viney. She's received a commission from BBC Radio 4 to do a radio piece on me and the rocks, and is now anxious to make sure we link up.

I have dinner at the Rise of the Raj. Alone.

I'm sad I'm so alone.

10.

crying, and becoming
a horse

Hadrian's Wall

I need to tell you, it's embarrassing, as a grown man, a man over the age of fifty, for crying out loud, so to speak, to be sitting in the Cape Cod Mall Cinema complex watching *The Lion King* and find myself crying. And to not be able to keep from sobbing silently over an orphaned cartoon lion cub and the touching moments of his arduous Disney journey. Crying, like a six-year-old. Crying the way I did when I saw *The Bad News Bears,* the story of the Little League team of losers that overcomes all odds, and wins; as I did seeing *Billy Elliot,* about the motherless coal miner's kid who abandons boxing lessons for ballet, and soars majestically; as I did seeing *Mr. Holland's Opus,* about the music teacher who has a positive effect on a bunch of discordant teenagers. Crying the way I do at most movies, in fact. Hardly tearjerkers, the majority of them.

It's damn disconcerting, believe me, trying desperately to suppress deadgiveaway, baritone-deep guttural sniffles at G-rated family films. It's hard not to get self-conscious trying, nonchalantly, to make it appear as if my fingers are scratching an itch when they're actually wiping aside the flows under my nose and eyes, hoping the remaining wet will evaporate before the theater lights come up. No one else is crying, that's part of the problem. The bigger problem is I'm an outwardly callous, often cynical, grown-up man weeping because a make-believe boozy coach has handed the bat to the team's clumsy kid and told him to pinch-hit in the bottom of the ninth with the game on the line.

It isn't just movies. I cry reading the daily newspaper or watching TV news. Stories about off-duty policemen who teach autistic kids to ride bikes. Or Red Sox players being good role models and lecturing youth groups about fair play. Or listening to the middle school principal praise honor roll kids at an assembly ceremony. I cry at the exchange of vows at weddings of children of friends whom, in truth, I'm not that close to.

It wasn't always like this, the crying at the drop of a hat. I didn't cry seeing *The Parent Trap* on a first date when I was seventeen. I didn't cry at assorted sappy cinema stories and scenes through college, or through my twenties and thirties. But as I slipped into my forties, suddenly I began this crying.

I didn't notice the onset. It wasn't until I started some counseling, and my therapist, a woman named Nancy, observed, "You've got a lot of sadness in you, don't you?"

Her comment took me by surprise. I've always been considered upbeat, good-natured, happy-go-lucky. "I do?" I said. "What sadness?" I asked Nancy, as I wiped away the moisture under my eyes at that moment. We'd been talking about my mother.

Nancy told me to do some homework. She asked me to keep track of the details of the times I get choked up and teary. So for the next several weeks I did that, making careful note of the content of what it was I was reading or watching at the very moment I felt that flush behind my eyes and reached for a Kleenex.

It turned out to be lots of things, the various crying themes. Yet tragedy wasn't one of them. Neither were evil, dishonesty, cruelty, or injustice. Oddly, it wasn't what was wrong with the world that was making me sad. It was what was right. Assembling the themes under a general mental tent, I noted among them: sacrifice, fairness, modesty, nurturing, camaraderie, heroism, true friendship, loyalty, mentoring, and unconditional love. And I was able to see that most of the stories, not every one, but by far the most, involved adults in interaction with children.

I didn't need Nancy to point out the obvious. I wasn't crying about what was happening to these cartoon animals or screen kids. I was crying about myself.

The family lore on the early childhood Dana is that he was an insufferable crybaby. When I got old enough to comprehend and to care, my parents would tell me stories of my hair-trigger crying reflex. They were remembering nostalgically, I guess, and retold the stories with good humor. Yet they made it clear that, at the time, my crying was a pain in the ass.

I could not bear to be left alone with anyone other than my parents, my brother, or my uncle Oscar, apparently. There were no other exceptions. When they tried leaving me with some other relative or a friendly neighbor, I began to bawl my head off the moment they were out the door and I did not stop until they reappeared. Nonstop crying. Family friends whom I've known all my life corroborate this about me. People asked to babysit suffered my shrill outbursts firsthand, had to endure them while my parents were away, and remembered them well. So I guess it's clear. My parents weren't making this up. When they went away, I went berserk.

Frankie was fond of telling the story about how wonderful it was for her in the weeks following my nearly fatal encounter with the jaws of a horse because I could be left alone and didn't cry. I was four years old at the time. We'd gone to visit Aunt Hazel and Uncle Willard in Attleboro, Massachusetts. They had a field behind their house where a neighbor's horses were pastured. As we drove up—and this is among my earliest memories—I was excited about feeding the horses. I had a lump of sugar. I can almost see the sequence of events run through my head like a grainy, faded newsreel clip. I remember running up Hazel and Willard's front walk, greeting them at the door, being fidgety and anxious to see the horses, then moving through the house to the back door, trotting down their backyard's slight incline to a gate, slipping through the gate, sugar lump in hand, and running toward the closest horse. I remember all this quite clearly. Then I remember nothing.

My brother was behind me. When he saw what happened next, he ran for help. The horse had opened its mouth, grabbed my waist, picked me up, and thrown me down. Then the horse picked me up by the head and began to shake me. I probably owed my life, the doctor said, to the double-layered snowsuit I was wearing. I had the hood up. I guess it was cold.

I was still in the horse's mouth when the adults came running. My father was not there, so it was Oscar and Willard who decided that a tug-of-war over my flapping body was a bad idea. Instead, they quickly decided, something had to be done to get the horse to drop me. Williard ran and got a long two-by-four. Each man then took an end, and they proceeded to ram its narrow edge into the horse's throat. Quick thinking. It worked. The horse gagged and spat me out.

Other than nasty bruises to my side and lacerations to my scalp, I wasn't seriously hurt. Physically. Thank you, snowsuit. Psychically, that's another story. For the next several weeks I thought I was a horse. I refused to eat at the table, walked around the house on my hands and knees, and whinnied and neighed in place of talking. No one went to child psychologists in those days; they probably didn't exist. So my parents consulted a pediatrician. His advice was to humor me. He said traumatized individuals have been known to take on the attributes of the traumatizer—the best example being children beaten by a father who then imitate, or "become," the father. He didn't know of cases of kids becoming horses, but it was worth waiting to see if I snapped out of it.

Of course I did (although to this day I hate horses and have an inordinate fear of them). While it lasted, though, I was a docile, quiet foal. For Frankie, at least, it was a fine time. She used to relish telling people how convenient a time it was because she could simply build a corral for me out of chairs and pillows, put a bowl of food on the floor, and leave me alone. And best of all, she could ask other people to watch me. I wouldn't cry.

When I asked her later in life, Frankie thought that after I stopped being a horse and began walking upright again, the hair-trigger crying thing eased off and went away. I became much less likely to cry when my closest family wasn't around. The horse bite, maybe, fixed this in me. She wasn't sure. But she thought so. Either that, or it was time to outgrow crying anyway, she felt.

Frankie believed that children outgrow things. She also believed you don't coddle kids. And she believed showing affection to your children was bad for their development. She came to believe these things because in her own child-hood emotional neglect had been a fact of life, and in part because in the 1940s she bought the gospel of a then popular child-rearing guru who taught that a mother's love was a dangerous instrument.

We tend to forget these days the profound impact Benjamin Spock had on new parents and their children when he gained popularity in the mid-1950s. His best-selling child-rearing books were downright revolutionary. Spock be-lieved kids need love, and need to be shown love. This was brand-new think-ing. Prior to this, books had taught mothers to treat their children more like, well, workhorses in training than little people in infancy.

I was born in 1947, my brother three years before that. As we came into the world, Frankie brought no positive lessons from her own childhood to moth-ering. Her instincts were clouded. Her mother had been an unloving tyrant, and she'd grown up with that. Plus Frankie had seen firsthand that those rep-resentatives of God, the nuns of her schooling, believed beating and berating to be healthy tools in dealing with kids. She didn't buy this, I know. Frankie was way too gentle. She never hit me, my brother, or anyone. And she was never verbally abusive to any children. Yet she must have been confused.

Friends who knew her as a young mother have since told me they wonder if Frankie liked the role, or even if she especially wanted it. But she had the role of mother and tried to meet it. Unprepared by her own experiences, and anxious to be modern and listen to experts, Frankie read and relied on a pop-ular child-rearing book. I'm not sure which pillar of beastly parenting it was whose suggestions she followed. I do know Spock wasn't around yet. And I can personally testify these were dark days for American newborns. There was a behaviorist named John B. Watson, who emerged in the 1930s as a leader of a strict-discipline, lax love school, and he wrote a parenting guide. I suspect he was the guilty guy, because before Frankie died she lamented, on videotape, that she had followed a certain child-rearing philosophy, and then she described it. It sounds very much like the ghoulish teachings of Mr. Watson.

The videotape was made in 1979 at the public-access studio of the cable tel-evision provider on Cape Cod. I had taken a course there, and was qualified and free to use their floor cameras and studios to produce whatever video show I wanted, wacky or serious, short of indictable political sedition, commercial advertisements, or porn. It was the idea of my brother's wife, Nancy, that we shoot a show entitled *The American Family*. (This Nancy is not to be confused with my later therapist, although I think Doug's wife secretly saw the video as a kind of therapy for Frankie, Big Doug, Little Doug, and me.) Nancy offered to be an interviewer, and it was decided we'd shoot three parts. In one, she'd talk with my mother and father. In a second, she'd speak with my brother and me. And in a third, she'd interview all four in the family together.

To be clear, we never imagined the video as a serious piece of work. At least brother Doug and I didn't. For us, it was a lark. Frankie and dad Doug took it more seriously. Nancy, I'm not sure. Anyway, after the first two pieces were taped, we all became so mortified at saying sensitive things about each other on-camera that the segment with the whole family was never done. This was alien territory, speaking of our feelings, and Nancy was posing probing questions about our family relationships and our histories together.

The videotape, as far as I know, is the only existing record of my mother on film or video with sound. She died before VCRs and home video cameras became commonplace. A few reels of silent 8mm film surfaced after her death. Some show Frankie in England (no shots of her taking rocks); others show her on Cape Cod doing mundane things. None of it is very interesting. So *The American Family* is it—the sole chronicle of Frankie in voice and moving pictures. I wish, now, we'd filmed the third piece, all four of us. Times have changed. But for this mid-twentieth century American family, no film whatsoever exists of us all together.

In the film, Frankie is sixty-five years old. She's dressed in a turquoise blouse, blue plaid pants, and brown loafers. Her hair is wispy, gray-brown, and lofted in a short perm. Her face is lined. When she speaks, Frankie is tentative, soft-spoken, shy. Her lips frequently purse, like a little girl's might when she's trying to be cute.

Nancy asks Frankie if she's pleased at the job of parenting she did. Frankie furrows her brow, and purses those lips, thinks a second, and replies in a high voice, which is almost squeaky at first:

"Well, no, not really. I mean, today they have Dr. Spock compared, in our time, to a person who was very strict about putting them to bed at a certain time, feeding at a certain time. I mean, to suck your thumb was bad, they called it 'bad habits,' and you had to wrap their hands. And if they cried, or anything, you weren't supposed to pick them up, that was very bad, and there were bottle holders, where you turned them on their side. It was a very bad thing to give them too much attention, which I think was probably not good. There were all these strict rules; all this giving them love and everything, you didn't do it. The child was supposed to adjust to your routine. If there was a playtime, it was between such hours, and that was it, you didn't break that."

Frankie is asked if her boys were problems. "Never," she says. "They were very easy to raise." But then she adds, "I think if I had to do it over again, I think I'd talk to them more if they had problems. I guess maybe we waited for them to talk, and if they didn't talk, then nobody talked. Whereas I know some parents would sense their child was having problems and would automatically be the ones to approach. Whereas probably our reaction was, well, if they want to talk they'll talk, and maybe that's not the right thing."

She's quiet a couple of seconds. Then she says, with sadness in her voice, "But, see, you don't know."

Everyone is quiet for a couple more seconds. Everyone on-camera is hanging on those words. Viewing the video, I hang on them, too.

She's right. You don't know. What do we ever know?

Finally, Frankie purses her lips again, and finishes, "There's a gap on both sides, created unwillingly. But then there's nothing you can do about it."

Nothing but cry.

thursday, march 20

After two hours of motorways I'm into Hexham, a few miles south of Hadrian's Wall and about 20 miles west of Newcastle-upon-Tyne. The Tyne is a river. Hexham is also on the Tyne. Why they don't call it Hexham-upon-Tyne I'm not sure. Maybe you've got to be a big city to deserve to boast you're upon. Otherwise you're just beside. I begin hunting for lodging in Hexham-beside-Tyne.

I'm carrying two rocks that once had rested somewhere in Hadrian's Wall. Where along its length, I'm not absolutely sure. The other sites on my trip are all in one place. But this one is stretched out some eighty Roman miles, which is seventy-three modern miles, and I'm not certain where Frankie visited the wall along its long run across Northumberland and Cumbria. I do have a solid clue. In sorting through Frankie's collection of photo slides years earlier, prior to throwing most of them out, I made note of some. Frankie, true to form, had carefully catalogued her pictures on paper lists on the inside covers of her slide trays. Here I found snapshot IDs for "Hadrian's Wall, near Housesteads, looking west," and "Roman Fort at Chesters."

So, it was not too hard to decide where to come back with Frankie's rocks. The closer you get to Newcastle-upon-Tyne to the east, the less wall is left, and the more dense the modern population centers around it. Far in the other direction, to the west, remnants of the wall gradually disappear altogether as you pass over the Pennines highlands range. The west side of the mountains is stone-starved, so over the centuries wall stone was stolen wholesale as free and easy building material. And closest to Carlisle and the Solway Firth, at the extreme west end, the wall wasn't built out of stone to begin with. It was built of sod. So it's not surprising it's the midsection of Hadrian's Wall, the best-preserved, that Frankie visited. Visually it's the most dramatic. It's where Housesteads Fort and Chesters Fort are. It's where I've come.

When I leave, my suitcase will be considerably lighter. The two Hadrian rocks are by far the two largest Frankie took in England. The biggest weighs three pounds. It's irregularly shaped, dark-brown, quartz sandstone, about six inches along its longest axis, but jagged and ragged and not highly weathered anywhere. The smaller rock, about a one-pound piece, is of slightly lighter sandstone with a couple of white veins. It's rough and irregular on five of its six faces. One side, however, is relatively smooth, and appears to be weathered. It may have come from an exposed spot.

After checking into a B&B, I immediately head for the wall. I'm a sucker for these cool Roman engineering feats. Hadrian's Wall is where Emperor Hadrian, around A.D. 120, decided the northernmost limit of the Roman Empire had been reached, and that this frontier needed proper posting. Stone here was hauled up on muleback from a quarry on Fallowfield Fell, a half mile away. I understand the magic in these stones. The wall is a masterpiece. Of all the rocks in my mother's collection, these two will be the hardest to part with, despite the welcomed lightening to my luggage.

friday, march 21

Mike Collins is staff archaeologist for Hadrian's Wall. He works for English Heritage, the government-funded preservation group that oversees the site. The bespectacled, wispy-haired, thirty-two-year-old is alone, rummaging around his Hexham office, making coffee and trying to retrieve messages off a telephone answering machine that keeps repeating them over and over, when I show up unannounced early this morning. He has the habit of clicking his tongue when he's looking up information.

Mike is delighted at my story, and invites me to sit down and talk. Examining Frankie's rocks, he decides they're unlikely to be facing stones. In places where the wall is widest, parallel facing blocks were filled in between with rubble. "It looks more like rubble," he says.

The rubble core of the wall is exposed in many places these days. The core is open, mainly, because between about A.D. 600 and 1950, local people helped themselves to as much stone as they needed.

Stone walls, wherever they are these days, seem to suffer variations of this same scavenging problem. The granddaddy of them all, the two-thousand-mile-long, two-thousand-year-old Great Wall of China, is losing rock at an alarming rate. Some blocks are taken by local villagers to repair homes, others are trucked away as raw material for building roads. Between 2001 and 2002, for example, an entire thousand-yard section disappeared in Zhangjiakou, reportedly dismantled by peasants paid $2 per tractorload by a construction company. Unlike great churches or castles, walls wander over great distances and are difficult to police.

Closer to my home, New England's picturesque stone walls are similarly disappearing. Several centuries ago, landowners would have hugged, praised, and given astonished thanks to anyone willing to haul away the stone littering their landscapes. The rocks were in the way. Today is a different story. Fieldstone, especially stone antiqued by lichens and years of weathering, is so valuable in construction now that companies will pay farmers for their walls. And many are selling. Other old stretches of walls are vanishing at night—while small new walls suddenly appear around shopping centers and upscale trophy homes. Robert Thorson, who's written a book about New England's stone walls, estimates over one-half of the region's original 240,000 miles of stone walls remain, and that unless tough preservation laws are passed and enforced, "the fabric of the landscape in which we live—the patchwork quilt of abandoned farmsteads—will unravel, one stone wall at a time."

Stone walls just won't stay put the way they used to, is the point. And so it has been with Hadrian's Wall. "Much of the dry stone walls, field boundaries, and even farm buildings in the area are built out of stone the Romans quarried and hauled to the line to make the wall," Mike Collins says.

Mike encourages me to put Frankie's rocks back into the wall. It should be easy. Along most of its length preservationists have made no effort to hard-mortar the wall to keep it together. It's left loose, so the wall can "breathe." English Heritage isn't much worried about tourists picking it over. Today, Mike says, "the vast majority of visitors wouldn't dream of taking home a piece." It's unlike the 1960s, when Frankie came here, when environmental consciousness was different, he says. That was another era. He wasn't even born yet. But that's what he understands.

As if to emphasize the point, he mentions, "You know, in my dad's garden there are bits of Battle Abbey."

Probably the most spectacular surviving section of Hadrian's Wall is the three-mile run from Housesteads Fort west to Steel Rigg. The wall is often elevated there, snaking over Peel Crags, Hotbank Crags, and Cuddy's Crags—a crag is a steep, rugged ridge of rock. Gently rolling farmland landscape to each side is broken by these rough ridges, and the crags have inadvertently served to preserve long, uninterrupted portions of Hadrian's handiwork. Farmers over the centuries were less inclined to climb the precipitous crags to scavenge for building blocks. Plus the prevalence of exposed veins of rock lower down meant they didn't need to. Where the wall follows the rugged crags, there are expansive, scenic views.

Deciding to return Frankie's rocks to this stretch of wall means I'll be replacing stone where it is needed least. But hey, I'm an ambassador here, not a builder. My little additions will never make up for the serious subtractions near Heddon-on-the-Wall, Cawfields, Birdoswald, Hare Hill, or any of the other regions in either direction. Yet even here at its midsection the wall is hardly pristine. Even high on a crag, there are unlimited spots to add to the depleted mass of this magnificent stone frontier.

Housesteads is the most popular place to begin hiking this stretch. If Frankie did take these stones from this region, it was probably from Housesteads. I doubt she hiked away from the parking lot very far. Frankie wasn't a hiker. But I'm going to begin my hike at the other end of this scenic stretch. Steel Rigg is in the middle of nowhere. There's a small parking lot there to serve wall walkers, a trash can for litter, and little else. At eleven this March morning, the day after the vernal equinox, I'm alone, and begin hiking east.

Over the course of the day I'll see ten other people, despite a pale blue, cloudless sky, and temperatures that will rise into the high fifties. At Housesteads, I imagine, the tour buses will have arrived and I'd be jostling right now with jokers from Georgia as I try to find a solemn spot and a quiet moment to put Frankie's rocks back to rest. From here at Steel Rigg, I'm able to do it in near solitude. Which is a good thing. Because I'll cry.

I hike east for about an hour. At a point about four hundred feet high on the ridgeline on Peel Crag, I pick a spot. There's a fresh breeze, keeping things cool, but there's bright sunshine. While the wall has been quite tall in places along my hike—over my head in some cases—here it's crumbled and low. A line of fence posts and three drooping lines of barbed wire follow the wall along the south side. I'm on the north, where soft, winter-whitened grass lies in whorls on a slight slope rising to the stones. It's not a section much photographed by hikers following the path, I suspect. With more dramatic wall scenes in either direction, here most people probably turn their attention to the vast yellow-brown patchwork pastureland views both north and south. Or they enjoy the view of Crag Lough, a lake curling around Peel Crags far below like a cobalt-blue kidney bean. Or maybe they gaze at a heavily forested portion of fir-green Northumberland National Park off in the direction of Scotland, or watch hawks hunting in spiral flight in airy space at eye level. Hadrian's Wall here gives way to its setting.

Which is fine by me. I've no interest in tourists admiring my stone repair. Or having them wondering why this piece of rock seems a little less mossed or messy. Or, God forbid, having someone pick Frankie's rocks out of the wall a second time, only to find her handwriting on the wall, so to speak. This low-lying, less noble-looking section was no less important than anywhere else along the line when Hadrian's legionaries piled blocks to bisect Britannia. So I figure it's no less deserving of my attention now.

I take off my black windbreaker and spread it on the ground. I lie back and stare at the sky. I'm in no hurry today. I'm not being battered by rain squalls. I'm not in the company of a custodian. I've made no promises to leave my rock with the front office. I've got all afternoon up here. The sun feels good on my face.

I've brought lunch: two Grandma Wild's shortbread biscuits, a banana, two tangerines, and a Coke. I eat slowly. When I'm done, I consider throwing the banana and tangerine peels off the nearly sheer north cliff face. They're biodegradable and will disappear quickly. But I balk. It doesn't feel right. All of this is disappearing, I think, gazing around at all I can see. The open landscapes, giving way to farms and developments. The landscape's contours, being lost to erosion, settling and plowing. The flesh of the fruit, my skin, me, and Hadrian's long stone wall, too, all disappearing. It's all just a measure of scale. A measure of time. At this instant, though, it's all here as it is, and the moment should not receive my litter, organic or not. In these moments, the litter will exist. So the peels go back into my backpack. I'm not the one to judge which disrespectful, harmful, or unsightly things done will wear away in a reasonable length of time and are therefore okay. Neither was Frankie.

I spend a long time on the ridge thinking about my mother.

The thoughts are strays. Nothing binds them together. I do nothing to bring them in, or organize them, or interpret them. I just randomly remember Frankie . . .

Frankie . . .

Arriving at the houses of her friends, unexpected, her habit of just walking in and announcing herself by pursing her lips and letting out a loud "Psssst!" I can hear her.

Expressing to a friend one afternoon, with pride, that she had never, over several years, ever changed the oil in her brick-red Henry J.

Cuddling and kissing a blind poodle named Pierre, an elderly friend's canine companion.

Scolding me for using a fresh towel after each shower, and teaching me that towels could be reused a number of times.

Picking her up from Suburban Hospital, after I got my driver's license, at the end of her three-to-eleven P.M. nursing shift, looking tired and older, and speaking little, driving her home.

Watching her playing bridge, lining up salted peanuts next to her on the card table in order to keep track of trump.

Standing holding a placard on the sidewalk outside the front of a five-and-dime department store in Osterville called Eaton's, which had just opened—picketing the place because, she said, "it just doesn't belong in our village."

Her nicknames for everyone, I can hear them still—for adults, Good Paul, Poor Betty, Mrs. M, Goonada, Good Dave; and for kids, The Thing, The Creature, The Germ, The Horrible Geek.

Her nickname for me, The Nane. I can hear it.

I'm sad. And very, very lonely.

The breeze is blowing more strongly now. It's getting cold. Grass stalks are waving; the old, silent gray-brown Roman wall is a still, flowing presence. I'm all alone, teary. The wind will dry that, and the tears will go wherever it is they go. It's time to give back the rocks.

I wedge the larger of the two rocks Frankie took into a cranny on the wall's low north side, the rock's narrow end in, its wider butt end facing out. The rock fits solidly into the slot. It looks a little out-of-place because light patches of lichen show on many of the exposed stone surfaces around it. But it's just a matter of time before Frankie's piece gets dressed like that, too.

I wedge the smaller rock into an appropriate gap on the other, south side. It too looks a little naked next to its old lichen-dressed brothers and sisters. But then it's a recent returnee with a clean, fresh-scrubbed uniform, looking like a ballplayer inserted into the lineup late in the game. It looks just fine there. It fits. It's taken a long time, along a very long route, but it's back in Hadrian's Wall.

For a long time I look at the returned rocks with affection and melancholy. When I stop looking, I know, I'll be giving up responsibility for them. When wildlife rehabilitators finally release a river otter or a coyote after taking it in after an injury and nursing it back to health, I imagine they feel the way I'm feeling now. It feels a little like abandonment.

Though the stones are returned, I don't want to leave. I pace around. I lie back down on the grass, then get up again, and pace again. I'll never see these stones again. They're not old friends, not at all. But just as they contained for my mother the magic of their Roman handlers, they held for me the handling of my mother. As they contained a little bit of Hadrian for Frankie, they held a little of Frankie for me. She chose to take them, singling them out. I've chosen to put them back, singling out this spot. To her they were special. By my actions, I reject that, and so I reject Frankie's imaginary, symbolic world.

I should have been in that special world of hers. I should have been the magic in her world. I should have been the true mystery, the subject of her attention, and hope, and construction. I do reject the rocks. I love them. But I hate them. I hate all of her collections. They had my mother's attention and appreciation and I didn't. They were fawned over, handled, studied, admired, organized, coveted, protected, and shown off. I got little of this. They had my mother's heart, and it left little of her heart for her little boy. There wasn't enough heart to go around. And when some was freed up, another collection popped up.

I'm crying now.

For the past eighteen days I've been running around England, site to site, rock return to rock return. Today I'm sitting still. It's what Frankie should have done more often—sit, look, listen, feel, experience. The present has no end.

I feel lost up here. I feel as if I've just buried something precious to me and will soon turn my back on its resting place. It's easy to say I hate the rocks. It's hard to ignore their symbolic connection to my mother. Upwind a few cows low. It sounds close, but the animals are just dots on the distant hillside. The herd seems to be marching to a stone-wall corner, probably to a gate. But from this height and distance, it looks like a fan-shaped wedge of particles being drawn slowly, inexorably toward a drain.

The sun has become low. It's getting chillier. It's still an hour back to the car park. Frankie's rocks are back in the wall. My pack is much lighter. I'm sad. Reluctant to leave. But I begin walking away. I don't look back.

11.

everyone touches the rock
from the moon

Tintern Abbey

"There are plenty of ruined buildings in the world," wrote Scottish poet Hugh MacDiarmid, "but no ruined stones."

That depends on how you look at it. For example, say, when it's the very looking at it that gives the stone its reputation and then it suddenly stops looking like what you thought it looked like. When that happens, people think it's ruined.

A case in point is what happened to the Old Man of the Mountain, the 40-foot, head-to-chin profile of a craggly-looking face formed out of five layers of granite on a ledge of Cannon Mountain near Franconia Notch in the Granite State, New Hampshire. Receding ice-age glaciers twenty thousand years ago carved the face, which Native Americans recognized, colonialists revered, and modern tourists flocked to see. But nothing lasts forever. Countless repetitions of winter freezings and thaws, plus ordinary gravity, caused the Old Man's nose, upper lip, and chin to crumble and fall away in May 2003. "The Great Stone Face," so called by Nathaniel Hawthorne, was suddenly gone, leaving citizens mourning a lost countenance of strength and defiance that provided the region with inspiration, and no small inflow of tourist dollars. For weeks after the collapse, people brought flowers to what was formerly the best viewing site, and said tearful good-byes to the visage in their memories. A remembrance day was held, and people cried.

The cliff face had never been considered an ordinary crag. "It seemed as if an enormous giant, or a Titan, had sculptured his own likeness on the precipice," Hawthorne had written of the Old Man. Patriot Daniel Webster had said, "Men hang out signs indicative of their respective trades. Shoemakers hang out a gigantic shoe . . . but up in Franconia Mountains God Almighty has hung out a Sign to show that in New England, He makes men!" In truth, the Maker was just making mountains, and then going about the business of wearing them away. But this fact of fate didn't stop the governor from setting up a task force to explore the possibility of gluing the profile back together, or perhaps chiseling out a new one. Reason eventually prevailed. Nature was just being nature, the governor decided, and government couldn't compete with that.

Some rocks, however, quickly found their way into the Old Man's ongoing souvenir-collectibles universe. The mountain man's profile had long been printed on ashtrays, shot glasses, thimbles, key chains, and scads of other tacky stuff. The face is cast on the flip side of the state's quarter coin, that insidious scheme by the U.S. Mint to transform ordinary pocket change into a collectible by issuing fifty different quarters, carefully parceling them out over years. Old Man items have long been collected and traded. So with the face suddenly on the ground in the gorge below, rock pieces naturally began to show up on eBay's auction site. Two-dollar bids were winning a tiny piece along with, reportedly, a "certificate of rockthenticity," until the state's attorney general stepped in and declared the artifacts were government property and their sale illegal.

What a spoilsport! Everyone agreed the Old Man was gone. Gone as an image, vanished, flown away, finished. What fell wasn't the work of a famous sculptor. There were no crafted pieces of stone that could be retrieved and reassembled or shown in a museum like Greek or Roman torsos missing heads and arms. What fell was rough, natural granite. It lost every semblance of specialness the moment it became dislodged from the Cannon Mountain ledge. Context was everything. So why not allow some folks to make a few bucks selling off bits of rock? It isn't like New Hampshire residents couldn't use the income. Or that the state couldn't stand the outflow of a little granite.

On the ground, the stone is worthless. On somebody's shelf in Alabama or Ohio or Arizona, it takes the Old Man's memory and message out into the lives of people again. Not quite like viewing his jutting jaw and furrowed brow in place, balanced on the mountain, but in another important way, and probably the only way the stone can have any special meaning now that it's off the cliff. By becoming a part of a family.

Modern technology and the faceless, emotionless institutional interactions that dominate modern day-to-day life—a cultural crisis in human connection—have left many people hungering for ways to touch, literally touch, what they feel to be truly meaningful. History is one of those meaningful things. So is legend and rarity and aura. Putting the Old Man's rock remains in people's actual hands would fulfill a need many people have.

At the National Air and Space Museum in Washington, D.C., there's a hunk of moon rock on display. The moon rock was brought to Earth by astronauts on the Apollo 17 mission. The first moon rocks, of course, were kept in biological isolation for fear they might harbor some nasty, alien organism, which, if released on our planet, might consume civilization. But they found the moon rocks were just inert, lifeless, four-million-year-old examples of volcanic basalt, fundamentally the same as basalt here on earth. So the only thing unique about the rock put on display was where it came from. Which amounts to everything.

The museum put up a sign in front of the moon rock that read, "You may touch it with care." According to museum guards, everyone touches it. Everyone. Absolutely everyone.

The need to touch special rocks may satisfy an unsettled, primal need. This, again, is psychiatrist Werner Muensterberger's area of expertise. "The wish or longing to own or possess an object points to a person's deep-rooted though usually unconscious need to be and remain—and I mean this literally—in touch," he has written. "This need may go back to earlier contact with a doll, or teddy bear, or any object, as long as it gives his owner pleasure."

Frankie had deep-seated touching needs.

Frankie took at least two rocks from historic sites in America over the years before she went to England. By the time I got to high school, she had a piece of petrified wood taken from the Petrified Forest National Park in northeastern Arizona. And she had a stone labeled *Mesa Cacoma Pueblo adobe wall,* also, of course, taken on a visit to the American Southwest. They may have both been taken on the same trip. I don't know. I don't remember when they showed up in our house.

People visiting the federally protected Petrified Forest Park have been putting pieces of its stony wood in their pockets since tourism began there. The Park Service estimates that even today about one ton of fossilized wood is stolen each month. Back in the late fifties or early sixties when Frankie would have gone, it was probably almost expected. Maybe that was okay. I remember the glistening piece of rock-hard wood. I remember being amazed by it. I remember it led to my learning how wood turns to stone. There was benefit to its taking. Its role on planet earth was artificially expanded beyond mute mineralogy to include show-and-tell.

I don't remember who told me about petrified rock, though. I don't think it was Frankie. More likely it was my father. Frankie didn't teach me things. She spoke fluent French, yet Frankie never spoke French to me or my brother growing up. It would have been the most natural thing to teach us. When I was a little kid I'd have been a captive student and quick learner. I could have ended up bilingual. Instead I suffered through C's and D's in high school French class, and switched to Spanish in college. Today I resent that Frankie didn't pass on to me the most useful, innate educational gift she had, her native tongue. It seems like such a wasted opportunity.

She was knowledgeable about so many of her collections, her hobbies, her projects, her causes. But Frankie reserved explanations for guests, or for groups outside our home. Sometimes I watched Frankie putting together poster boards or displays for exhibits, or watched her catalogue assorted collectibles. She never drew me into her interests. Did I want to go there? I'm not sure. Probably I didn't give her the impression I did. I was shy. I was supposedly the slower learner of her two sons, so I had an image to uphold—a slightly dullard image, which, I'd come to realize, was enormously useful in avoiding the pressures, expectations, and criticisms in the matters of doing better in school, working harder, and achieving more. I left that role to my ostensibly brighter brother. And, too, around my mother, I probably postured myself with the detached diffidence of any normal mid-twentieth-century American kid. I wouldn't be surprised if Frankie felt I was indifferent to what she was doing. But the truth is, I was intrigued by Frankie's eclectic, scatter-shot interests, and if she had stopped, stepped outside her manic cone of self-conscious activity, and tried to interest me, I like to think it would have worked.

I'll never know, because she never tried. Of course, neither did I.

The petrified rock was a useful show-and-tell. The Pueblo masonry was more like the English rocks—a formless relic from a historic-building site that she took and then set aside. I remember seeing it when we lived in Maryland. It wasn't hidden. But it never was given any life. It was never examined, explained, debated, or even admired. It just sat there. On a shelf. The Pueblo people were descendants of the Anasazi culture, among the oldest on the North American continent, and the little piece of adobe wall could have told a story, if there had been a storyteller. It had a story to tell. But Frankie, apparently, was satisfied with its silence. Possession alone, it seems, was all that mattered.

He was writing about museums, but John Hale could have been writing about collectors like Frankie when he said that "thoughts, feelings, actions . . . are the stuff of history, not sticks, stones and bombasine. . . . When the raw material does not contain traces of thought, the doors to the past remain closed." There was a veil over that Pueblo piece. It had something to say, but I heard nothing.

David Lowenthal wouldn't be surprised. "Unlike history and memory, whose sheer existence betoken the past," he wrote, "the tangible past can not stand on its own. Relics are mute; they require interpretation to voice their reliquary role."

Frankie was not an interpreter for me. She was a collector. She was a doer. She was perpetually busy, and I was just this little guy hanging around. I wasn't in the way. I never felt that. But neither was I a participant in any of her interests. So with me, growing up, there was only silence on the sense of what the Pueblo stone meant to my mother, what power it held, why it sat on a shelf in our home.

I guess it should be no surprise to me that years later she'd leave everyone in the dark about a collection of formless stones taken surreptitiously from across the English countryside.

The petrified wood and Pueblo rocks, along with her collecting susceptibility, presage the English rock collection. Yet what they don't do is explain why a robust collection of this sort was stimulated overseas, and not back home. Frankie visited numerous historic sites in America over my childhood years, without finding the need to carry away physical mementos. There was the Pueblo piece, but it's an exception. She didn't add pebbles from Mount Vernon or Colonial Williamsburg, a stone flake (or vial of water) from St. Augustine's Fountain of Youth, or a stalactite sliver from Luray Caverns. We lived a long time outside Washington, D.C., yet Frankie apparently felt no urge to possess pieces of its famous monuments or buildings. She was a President Kennedy fan, but took no dirt from his tomb at Arlington or paint chip from the white fence around his summer home in Hyannis Port, just miles from where she summered on Cape Cod and later retired.

It seems that Frankie just didn't care about America's rocks and relics. Well, why should she?

I've come to consider something about my mother that I never had before. I think she was as much a European as an American.

This never occurred to me, growing up, because all the outward signs—the frozen dinners, suburban hairdos, TV shows she liked—suggested that Frankie was a typical American housewife. But that childhood of hers, for which I had only the vaguest feel, was immigrant-influenced, and was filled with customs and rituals rooted in the Europe of her ancestors. Its effects wouldn't have been easy to cast aside. Frankie was brought up, I think, in a way that left her straddling the Old and New Worlds. And while her socialization and assimilation were locked onto the models of magazine advertising spreads and network American family TV shows, invisibly her heart and soul might have carried along a deep spiritual connection with Europe.

America was all around her, probably too much around her. Its rocks maybe weren't old enough. The English rocks suggest she needed physical and emotional connection to specimens of an ancient European past.

It's telling, I think, to look at her friendships when I was growing up. She had plenty of WASP American friends, for sure. She made friends easily. But compared with all the other moms I knew, she had an enormous number of ethnic friends, people who were very different from the majority of families in the communities where we lived.

Many of her closest friends were Jewish. While they weren't exactly foreigners, their homes and lifestyles preserved Old World culture. More directly, Frankie befriended an unusual number of genuine foreigners. Some of the closest were an elderly Belgian couple and a French couple who lived around the corner. Frankie's fluency in their language made this understandable. But her closest friends included an Irishwoman, a woman from India, a Chinese couple, a young Iranian doctor, a young Greek doctor, a Turkish woman, and an English couple. These weren't just acquaintances. They became her intimate friends, keeping up with Frankie even after returning, in some cases, to their native countries.

If Frankie did have a long-held need for a physical and emotional connection to specimens of an ancient foreign past, she might have collected all these people to her as the only available substitutes in suburban America. It's odd to imagine collecting human beings, though serial lovers are commonplace practitioners. In fact, maybe Frankie's need here wasn't much different from a promiscuous lover's. She had a longing for intimacy with something beyond her grasp, something she didn't understand and couldn't define. It wasn't flesh, but it had something to do with people. She was lonely, I'm certain, a condition that gnawed at her insides since childhood. She needed love but didn't know how to accept it. There was a hole in her life, and collecting fills holes . . . temporarily. To be fulfilling, the collector must keep at it, acquiring again, and again, and again.

saturday, march 22

I'm headed to Wales, six hours away. I'll be traveling something like two hundred miles, the longest single driving stretch of my trip, making my way to the vicinity of Tintern Abbey.

I listen to the radio for half the trip. Mindless talk. I need the company. Gotta get out of my head, gritting my teeth, thinking of Frankie, this trip.

I drone past the industrial midlands tri-gauntlet of Liverpool, Birmingham, and Manchester, this time on their western side. Gray, ugly landscape and sky. At the turnoff toward Southwest Wales, the green and beauty return. Once I am over the border that funny Welsh language shares road signs with English, like Spanish is on display in Miami. I check into a B&B just up from Llandogo on the River Wye (the Afon Gwy, if you're more comfortable with Welsh).

That night in the Rose and Crown pub in Tintern, I see a poster on a pillar at the right-hand corner of the bar. It's headlined, in very large type, "Echoes in the Stones," and under that, "Tintern Abbey."

Well, yes, there are echoes in the stones I'm carrying. Echoes of my mother. But how is it that they've been expecting me?

Reading the small print I find it isn't Frankie Hornig's echoes the good folks of the Wye Valley intend to hear in the romantic, roofless abbey in late July and early August. It's the echoes of the ancient past, the voices of Cistercian Order monks, Henry VIII, Thomas Cromwell, the Black Death, the Industrial Revolution, Victorians, Turner and Wordsworth, and the World Wars, all brought to life in theatrical vignettes, with costumes, chanting, incense, and song, in an elaborate nighttime celebration capped by the pyrotechnics of some serious fireworks.

Holding Frankie's stolen Tintern Abbey stone in my hand, I bring it close to my mouth and whisper, "Don't take offense, Ma, it's only your echoes I'm here to hear."

A party of three men and three women are sitting nearby. They can't hear what I say. But I'm a stranger in a small village, and they're locals, and they've been watching me. Now they demand to know why I'm talking to a rock.

I point to the poster. "You've got your echoes in the abbey's stones, and I've got my echoes in the abbey's stones. And, to be honest, I was telling my mother yours have got nothing, as far as I'm concerned, over hers."

Six sets of eyes stare silently at me for what seems quite a long time. This is not standard talk for country pubs, where the most provocative exchanges amount to praise for extremely tidy maiden overs thrown by cricket bowlers, or the relative merits of American over Japanese diesel tractors. Tourists telling their mothers things through rocks is odd behavior. I can see it isn't going down well. So I join their table and tell them about Frankie's rocks.

Grins return to one and all. "Bloody good," says one of the men, wearing the worn overalls and exhibiting the weathered face of someone who has come upon his fair share of rocks outdoors, and surely knows his fair share about tractors. I have been in Great Britain almost three weeks at this point and finally someone has said "bloody good" to me. About time. Even if this is Wales.

Frankie's rock is passed around. It's jackstone, two of the local guys decide. That's a limestone-sandstone aggregate that looks like concrete, they tell me. Jackstones are also little pebbles or stones used in old-time versions of the kid's game of jacks. Back at home, my geologist friend assessed the Tintern Abbey piece as low-grade brick, a clay-based sand within mud. Could the men in the Rose and Crown and the geologist in upstate New York both be right?

It sure looks bricklike. It's about three inches by two inches, by just under an inch thick, brown with orange highlights. It is jagged and irregular on three sides. But one edge is flat with a hint of being very slightly concave. One long side is slightly rough, but still relatively flat, as if it was an embedded side. The other large side, though, is definitely the interesting side. It has hints of ornamentation.

Hints of a design. I hadn't noticed this back in the States. It's suggested to me here, now, in this pub. I find myself excited. This side of the stone is quite flat and shows a band of white across one corner. The band appears to be arching slightly, as if it's part of a large circle. Another line of white is on the inside of this. Below this is a smudged area of white upon which Frankie had written *Tintern Abbey*. It's impossible to tell if the white smudge has shape. Beside it, though, is an intriguing white shape that looks sort of like a white rabbit, with a little nose sticking out from under two larger ears. Or it could be a foot, and the rest of the animal is obscured. The white areas are clearly superficial, set into depressions in the brick—just as red Wessex clay tiles used in the abbeys were imprinted in the thirteenth century, using a wooden stamp mold while the tiles were still malleable, the resulting pattern filled with contrasting white clay, and then glazed and fired.

"Looks like part of a floor tile," says one of the men.

"It does, aye, it does," says another of the men.

And, for sure, it does.

sunday, march 23

Floor-tile fragment. That becomes my working theory, which I take the next morning to Kate Arnatt, head custodian for Tintern Abbey. A wholesomely pretty woman of no more than forty, with blue eyes and blond hair piled atop her head, Kate works for CADW: Welsh Historic Monuments based in Cardiff. Custodians are not janitors in Britain. They are people entrusted with the custody of something special, in this case an abbey founded in 1131 and laid to ruin by an Act of Supremacy order of Henry VIII in the late 1530s. Kate is site manager and curator, and she lights up with excitement when I show her my rock/tile and tell her my story.

"It's almost definitely a floor tile from the abbey church," she says, turning Frankie's find in her hands. "Or possibly from the chapter house." She draws her finger along the white outline. "It looks like the indentation where a design used to be. A border design, maybe."

Tiles of all designs, combined in decorative groups, were used to decorate the floors of Tintern, she says. They often were donations. Anxious about the afterlife, abbey benefactors would adorn tiles with their personal heraldries, a shield with three clarions or three chevrons, perhaps, and see to it the tiles were laid somewhere in the church. Other designs might show a mounted knight, Saladin with a horse, or hunting scenes like dogs biting at the feet of fleeing deer. Fleurs-de-lis were popular. The monks themselves, shunning garish display, favored simple geometric patterns.

"A lion's foot!" exclaims Kate, suddenly. "One of his paws. It looks like a lion's paw. I remember seeing one in that pose. He was a lovely lion."

Kate is looking at the intriguing area where I'd seen a rabbit's nose and ears. Now I can almost see what she sees. The famous lion passant pose, the beast walking with one forepaw raised, its tongue sticking out, a heraldic staple. This white spot could be one of the paws. It could be. Or maybe not.

There are almost no floor tiles left in Tintern Abbey. Most of the ruin's floor is now grass or gravel, open to the sky and the weather. A few tiles remain in the chapter house. They are different from Frankie's, but similar. A photo of a sample tile known to have come from Tintern is shown in the guidebook. It shows two doves, on each side of a bough, within a circle. The designs are white on pale-orange brick background, identical to the broken piece I've brought back to Tintern.

How on earth could Frankie have gotten access to a piece of floor tile here? I ask Kate. "Stick your head around the corner of that wall and you'll be able to see why your mother had a chance to take something," she says. Around the corner is an assortment of stone rubble piled under a galvanized steel overhang. All of it has come from areas of the abbey disturbed during maintenance or preservation work.

I tell Kate my mother would have been here in the late 1960s. "A lot of work was being done then," she says. "A lot of material was dug up, and there was no place to store it. A lot was lying around. A lot was reburied. It's easier to preserve stonework if it's in the ground. So that was done. During the time it was dug up it was exposed, waiting to be interpreted, catalogued, evaluated.

"When I was a young girl"—which, guessing at her age, would have been shortly after Frankie was here—"I remember seeing a pile two and a half feet high, to the left of the gate, containing fragments of floor tiles. It was in the process of being sorted. Which is why I know what they look like. I saw them there. The quality of this," she says, still holding Frankie's specimen, "is rougher, much more rugged, thicker, more basic than more modern tiles. They were more higgly-piggly back then" in the early days of the abbey.

"I'm guessing a lion's paw," she says. "Wow!"

Later, I'm sitting at the far eastern abbey wall, looking back at the sunlit ruins. It is quiet. Just a handful of tourists roam around. The outbuildings—like the abbott's house and hall, monks' dayroom, kitchen, and latrine—have been reduced to little more than stone-wall outlines. But the tall, defiant walls of the abbey nave, presbytery, transepts, and crossing, the heart of the church with its rows of solemn, pointed-arch window holes, stand majestically against a background of steep, evergreen-covered hills. The low remains of the infirmary are closest to me. Frankie, I'm sure, would have walked there, her interest kindled by her nursing career and the room's hospital role.

Frankie was not alone in dismantling Tintern. By the late 1530s it was declared perfectly legal to pillage the place. King Henry VIII takes responsibility for that. He decided that, after God, he was top dog at the Church, and for all practical purposes he put the pope and Rome out to pasture. With ties to the Catholic Church, abbeys around Britain were seen as papist strongholds. Henry decided the simplest solution was to confiscate them, and gradually gut them. Henry's henchmen took Tintern in 1536, and rather swiftly all its valuables were carted away to the king's treasury. Royal plumbers melted down the lead on the roofs. More mundane materials like timber, ironwork, and glass were auctioned off to local folks. Then the abbey shell was left to vine creepers and rock collectors. Like so many ancient stoneworks in Britain, Tintern, too, served for years as a convenient recycling source whenever a stone wall or cattle pen or new cottage called for raw material. The smaller, lower outbuildings were easier to smash up and cart off, and so were the first to go. The larger, most lovely part of the abbey was relatively spared.

By the Victorian era, Tintern Abbey became celebrated as a decaying shell of great, wild, romantic beauty. J.M.W. Turner and Edward Dayes did famous watercolors of the picturesque, ivy-clad, roofless ruin. Poet William Wordsworth wrote his famous "Lines Composed a Few Miles Above Tintern Abbey," and it became fashionable for travelers to take boat trips down the River Wye and picnic on the abbey grounds.

At least one of these visitors thought a little more laying to waste would be beneficial. The Reverend William Gilpin, who published a best-selling Tintern guidebook in 1782, felt there was room to improve the storybook scene. "Though the parts are beautiful, the whole is ill-shaped. . . ." he wrote. "A number of gable-ends hurt the eye with their regularity; and disgust it by the vulgarity of their shape. A mallet judiciously used (but who durst use it?) might be of service in fracturing some of them."

Frankie, I imagine, had she been around at the time, durst do it.

Sitting here, the audio tour asks me to imagine the abbey with all its walls and roof in place, the ornate pulpitum still in its liturgical setting, the monks' dormitory still with its second story, the cloister arcades still standing. The visitor's tape asks me to imagine Tintern in enclosed darkness and monastic silence, spaces built for contemplation but now open to sunlight and tourist chatter. It isn't easy.

I've been trying to imagine my dead mother here, alive and animated, agitated, active, her camera around her neck, eyes flitting between this archway, that stone window, the next thing to snag her restless attention. It's not easy to do. It's like I'm in a skeleton, a big gray whale's skeleton on a beach. It has grandeur. But it has so much decay, too. It's the past, history, death. As Frankie is dead and in the past. I can't recapture her here. I've got to go into my heart to do that. And my heart has been so hurt. It makes imagining Frankie here, back then, or right now, as difficult as imaging a white-cloaked, Cistercian monk on a processional walk down the eastern aisle, its floor tiled with the images of lions. The two are strangers to me.

I've come here to express my love. I can do that. And I've come to find, even in the ghostly way I must imagine Frankie's presence, that inside her, in her own inwardly sad way, she too loved me. I'm sure she did.

It's time to leave Tintern Abbey. But before I move on, Kate Arnatt introduces me to Tintern's stonemason, Alan Cornish. He's in his thirties, clean-shaven, and wiry, and has a handsome, friendly, open face. He's wearing a watch cap and overalls, and has been doing maintenance work high on a scaffold along the outside, south wall of the nave.

Stones with stories are not strange in these parts. Like much of Britain, the Wye Valley has its share. Up river, for example, the Buck Stone once stood. It was a massive, top-heavy boulder that used to wobble on its axis. It was a sacred Druid site, people said. Walk around it three times at sunrise, they said, and a wish would be granted. No longer. In 1855, six brawny good old boys toppled it from its natural plinth and it shattered. Also close to the river above Tintern is the Staunton Longstone, a standing stone or "menhir." Folklore held that if pricked with a pin at midnight, this stone would bleed. Just up the valley to the northwest in Trelleck are Harold's Stones. There are three of them—the tallest twelve feet high—erected ages ago for unknown reasons. What is known is that Harold's Stones possess supernatural powers. Just touching the stones once caused a couple of dowsers to be flung through the air.

Frankie's Wye Valley rock isn't quite in this league. But it has its own story, which I tell to Alan Cornish. Then he examines the stone. He knows stone, I can tell.

Alan concurs with the Rose and Crown guys, and with Kate and me. "It's a tile," he says. "A fired tile, not natural out of the ground, is it?" All the stone used to build Tintern, he says, is sandstone. Drawing his finger along the white part, he says, "It's part of a circle, in'it? Definitely man-made. A fired tile, in'it? A little overburnt. That's the gray inside, in'it? A little overdone."

Alan takes me into a dingy, dusty storage shed across the parking lot from the abbey's tourist entrance. Inside are many chunks of abbey stone, some showing the carved hint of a column or archway. Along one wall are about twenty plastic, 100-pound grain sacks, all filled to the brim with pieces of floor tile taken out of Tintern. Alan and I pull out pieces of similar thickness, and similar red and gray brick coloration with white-clay embedded high-lights. Some show clear designs: a bird, circles, decorative ornamentation.

Turning a piece over in his hands, Alan says, "Floor tile. Looks like your mum's piece, dun'nit?"

Back in Kate Arnatt's office, I hand her Frankie's tile. Kate had asked me to leave it with her. She wants to show it to CADW's archaeologist. But mostly she wants to be able to pull it out to show other people—school or tour groups, perhaps—a prop whenever it seems appropriate to teach about preser-vation or provide proof that in one case, at least, something taken from Tintern Abbey found its way back.

Kate holds it firmly in both hands, recognizing that I'm giving up some-thing very emotional and meaningful to me.

"I'll take good care of it," she says. "I'm glad to have it. We don't get many visits like yours. None, actually. Thank you."

As I leave, I walk with Alan Cornish back to where he is working on the abbey fabric. He agrees, they haven't had any other sons bringing back rock.

"But you do get these eccentrics coming around, don't you?" he says. "This bloke comes to one of the churches where we was working, and the scaffolding was up, and he asked permission to do a rubbing of the bell. He goes around rubbing bells. That's odd, in'it? Another fellow came round, didn't he, and was measuring the width of trees. I don't understand this sort of thing. Far as I'm concerned, I'll take a good motorcycle, eh?"

12.

rocks as fetish objects and totems

Tintagel Castle

A mode is the manner in which you do something, and to English museumologist Susan Pearce there are three basic modes to collecting: systematics, souvenirs, and fetish objects. There's crossover and overlapping of all three, and it can be difficult, sometimes, examining someone's collections, to declare with certainty what fits into one mode and what's another. Yet generally a collector focuses upon one or another of the modes.

Frankie staked solid claims in all three.

The most classic collecting is what Pearce calls the systematics. Fine art collections are mostly in this category. Or carefully compiled collections of books or specimens. With systematics, an intellectual relationship between the collected items and the collector is strong—or at least the collector gives the appearance of possessing deep understanding of his/her stuff. Ms. Pearce believes that systematics "presuppose a two-way relationship between the collection, which has something public (not private) to say, and the audience, who may have something to learn." With systematics, arrangement of items is important, and a collector's understanding of what he/she has is often more important than feelings toward the items. With systematics, other people are likely to care about and value what the collector has assembled.

Several of Frankie's collections seem to be systematics: her music boxes, say, or the Hummels and monumental brass rubbings. Her most classic systematic, probably, was her plate block stamp collection. She had thousands of American plate blocks—those four-stamp corners from a sheet of postage stamps that bear the sheet's printing number. Her plate block albums go back to 1940. That year she saved, and carefully protected in cellophane, five pages of one-cent to three-cent blocks commemorating James Whistler, Samuel Morse, Industry-Agriculture for Defense, the Pan-American Union, the anniversaries of the Pony Express and Wyoming Statehood, and more. For the next thirty-eight years, until 1978, this collection was rather diligently kept, although in no case completely. Frankie never made certain in any year that she acquired all the blocks released by the U.S. Postal Service. That wasn't her imperative, which nudges her outside the company of hard-core systematic stamp collectors. But she assembled most new releases, invested a great deal of money and time in it, and developed considerable expertise in this hobby.

Frankie's plate block collecting stopped short in 1978. She never bought a block or added another album page from then until her death in 1983. I don't know why she stopped. I never heard any explanation for it. She and my dad retired to Cape Cod in 1977, and once settled on the Cape, Frankie turned to something she'd long neglected, her musical talent. She took regular voice and violin lessons, sang and played with church and conservatory groups, and practiced quite a lot. Perhaps in retirement she didn't have time for stamps, with all her renewed musical commitments.

Souvenirs, the second general collecting category, is the most common type of collecting. People travel, people buy trinkets and kitsch to remind them of where they've been and what they've seen, and maybe even to bring back sensations of being somewhere. Souvenirs take the collector back in time. Or, put another way, the souvenir object carries the past into the present and future. That's its main power. Buy a little metal Big Ben at a Victoria Street souvenir shop and it helps transport into later moments the tones of the towering clock's toll, that time when twenty years earlier the visitor stood on the banks of the Thames. Beyond this, it has little value. One mini–Big Ben might evolve into a collection of any sort of Big Ben replicas, shifting the souvenir mode somewhat. But it's more likely the collection will grow with the addition of a miniature plastic Eiffel Tower, a dried calabash shell with a maiden doing the hula carved on it, a three-inch lobster trap replica with "Bar Harbor" written on its side, or a snow globe with Mount Rushmore's four solemn faces inside.

In a souvenir collection, the opposite of systematics, one person's souvenir is another person's junk. Souvenirs make lousy exhibits, in either museums or people's homes, because they hold simply no interest for other people. They don't carry an observer back anywhere. Only the owner is transported. Photos of cities or travel sites visited are often just souvenirs, despite what the traveler thinks. Which is why people's slide shows put their friends to sleep. Clyde and Martha standing in front of the Baseball Hall of Fame. Who cares.

Frankie took thousands of photo slides and prints of places she visited, and virtually the entire collection was souvenirs. It was, I think, her major method for amassing an essential storehouse of souvenirs, so that she would know she had at hand tangible tickets back to where she'd been. Her cup plates, postcards, coasters, guidebooks, storehouse of hotel stationery, and assorted trinkets picked up in souvenir shops—and Frankie had picked up her share of these—were other time machines for her use.

Susan Pearce's final category of collecting is fetish objects. These are objects that are lifted out of their historical or cultural surroundings or context and given new importance within the worldview of the collector. They are building blocks in the collector's efforts to constuct some sort of meaningful, and necessarily soothing, private universe. But unlike souvenirs, which superficially sort of do the same thing, with fetish objects the collector "is subordinated to the objects," in Pearce's words, "and it is to the objects that the burden of creating a romantic wholeness is transferred."

With souvenirs it's just the opposite. The objects are maidservants and have a secondary role as the collector constructs "a romantically integrated personal self." The collector simply arranges souvenirs delightedly at her feet. But she bows at the foot of fetish objects.

"Fetish" is one of those words that isn't much used except when describing someone as weird. As in: He's got a foot fetish. Here are the three definitions given the word by my dictionary:

Fetish: (1) An object regarded with awe as being the embodiment or habitation of a potent spirit, or as having magical potency. (2) Any object, idea, etc. eliciting unquestioning reverence, respect, or devotion. (3) Psychol. Any object, part of the body, etc., that, although not of a sexual nature, causes an erotic response or fixation.

Many of Frankie's collections were clearly not souvenirs. The Makonde African wood carvings, for example. She didn't pick them up in Africa. She never went to Africa. She never visited Asia either, yet she had an eclectic assemblage of Asian artifacts. And the smattering of Mesoamerican items Frankie acquired, including A.D. 600 red clay Incan figures—which, Frankie noted in one memo book, were "believed to be imbued with spiritual force, in the dwelling place of a spirit." None of these things were picked up at gift shops during trips. But were they systematics or fetish objects? It's hard to say. In no case did Frankie studiously explore the history or cultures from which these things came. There was no quest to expand them as collections, or ideology applied to them. Such a focus would be expected of systematics. So it's my guess these were fetish objects—her fascination with their possible inner power, with the ancient hands that once held them, moved her to acquire and keep them.

Her Greek and Roman coins were fetish objects, I feel certain. She didn't collect these coins the way she collected her plate blocks. She had no scholarly or numismatic interest in them. She simply saw them in London shops, held their antiquity in awe, found a powerful need to possess them, and found it was possible to acquire them, hold them in her own hands, and take them home, if she simply came up with the asking price.

I found among her things a book about Roman coinage. In it Frankie had carefully stapled two handwritten lists. The headline atop one list was "Have." Twenty-six coins were on it, each carefully noting its face (usually an emperor), the reign, the coin's reverse image, and what she had paid for it. "Claudius II (268–270) Neptune holding dolphin £2," for example. The headline on the other list was "Want." It held twenty-one face-reverse designated desires. Nowhere was there any attempt to prioritize or interpret her collection, to balance it or focus it. She never arranged it to be shown or for comparative purposes. She didn't "Need" certain coins to complete something, and she ignored coins that a true numismatist would have considered important additions. Her word was "Want." She desired a rogue's gallery of ancient Roman heads—Brutus, Commodus, Pius, Titus, Agrippa. She had a list.

Some of the earliest peoples of civilization collected the skulls of ancestors in the hope of obtaining their life-force powers. Native American warriors took and displayed the scalps of slain enemy fighters, co-opting for themselves the spirits of the defeated. Subterranean church vaults across the world today contain countless skulls of martyrs and saints, kept as hedges against disrespecting their mana. Short of the real deal, a powerful spiritual presence is frequently found in representational images, and the power is amplified when the relic image has survived for centuries and a collector can hold in her hand what passed through the hands of ancients. Frankie, I think, wasn't carefully assembling a coin collection. She was head-hunting.

Finally, of course, there's the English rock collection. If that isn't a collection of pure fetish objects, I don't know what is. The rocks aren't minerals lined up for examination and comparison. They were secretly, silently kept, the opposite of what either a systematic or souvenir collector would do. The English rocks, as collected objects, are not subordinated to Frankie. They are on a higher plane for her.

I can think of no other explanation for gathering around herself raw, unworked rocks from castles, cathedrals, and prehistoric circles except this: possession of them allowed Frankie to go on powerful inner journeys. So do souvenirs, so do systematics. But when the object is full of imagined magic and held in reverence, it's a very different ride. For Frankie, I think, the rocks were tickets to take her somewhere else. And my guess is that place was kinship. My sadness is that she didn't need to take rocks to gain kinship.

A passage in Philipp Blom's book *To Have and to Hold* struck me when I came upon it. He wrote,

> *Relics form a bridge with heaven and immortality; other objects bridge space . . . bridge time . . . our distance from nature . . . or from genius. . . . A church may be interested in a stone because it belonged to its original foundations, or because it was thrown at St. Stephen, the first Christian martyr. It may also be thought valuable, as by one anonymous collector, because the Empress Elizabeth, Sissi, of Austria had stumbled over it. The col-*

lector in question was not interested in the stone as stone and would have bought a rake if that had been the imperial obstacle. In much the same way, the other collectors seek a special significance in the object, and it is only this meaning it carries that transfers value to it. It is this moment of transcendence, of the possession of transcendence, that makes every collected object, be it a matchbox or a martyr's fingernail, valuable. Every collected item is, to some extent, a totem.

I had a small, carved totem pole in my bedroom as a child. It was painted red, black, and yellow with the obvious brushstrokes of mass production. It came from the souvenir shop at that Seminole village we visited in Florida on one of our visits in the fifties. I didn't know at the time what a totem pole was, except that in real life it was something considerably larger that Indians made out of tree trunks. My little totem pole had two eagle's wings at the top and several glum faces carved into its miniature girth. It stood for years on a shelf in my room, next to a couple of raked, customized cars with moon hubcaps I'd made from kits and painted candy apple colors. The souvenir was meaningless to me. It didn't remind me of Florida or the Seminole reservation or alligator wrestling or anything. I certainly didn't know that a totem is an emblem for a clan, a symbol for kinship, and that totem poles were monuments Indians erected to honor their heritage. If I'd known that, I might also have known that totem poles are relics from Northwest American and Canadian tribes, not the Indians of southern Florida, and that therefore the tourism trinket in my room was a fraud.

It's a short stretch from fetish to totem. If fetish objects are regarded with awe, carry a strong sense of spirit, and are worthy of respect and devotion, aren't totem objects, too? Doubly so, I'd say, because totems carry the direct connection to ancestors, and respecting one's elders is an early life lesson taught around the globe.

Respecting her mother was, for Frankie, a lifelong struggle.

A totem pole is a totem object because it has meaningful images carved into the wood. Roman coins have meaningful images pressed into their silver sides. Frankie's rocks have no images on them at all. But I don't think that matters. As bridges over space and time, they could carry Frankie on trips of transcendence, out and away from her own loneliness and pain, far away from her own past, into a different past. And Frankie needed to get far back. She needed to get to clans and spirits way before her own creation.

Plymouth Rock and its pious Pilgrims just would never do. Frankie needed the philosopher's stone, some base material worked by the ancients, to help put her in touch with the kernel of creation and the meaning of life.

It seems possible to me, and I'm aware it's in a weird way, that Frankie took these rocks to find the mother she never had.

And now I'm on a similar mission, taking them back.

monday, march 24

Tintagel and its castle sit just above the Bodmin Moor in Cornwall, on ever-windy coastal bluff-land above the Celtic Sea. No major roads lead to Tintagel, a remote place along a sparsely populated section of rugged coastline. The way is not even well marked. I need to navigate my rented Renault along a bunch of narrow B-roads through pasturelands. High hedgerows along the roadsides obscure visibility and throw off my orientation. I have to repeatedly consult my road atlas.

I'm trying to follow signs to Trewarmett, which is just before Tintagel. This requires carefully ignoring a succession of intersection arrows pointing toward Tresparrett, Trevalga, Trethevey, Trefrew, Tremail, Treknow, Trewalder, and Trebarwith. Along a six-mile stretch of A395 just before this, I'd passed cutoffs for Tregadillett, Treween, Trewint, Trewen, Tresmeer, Tregeare, Treneglos, and Tremaine. It isn't easy to keep things straight on such a tremulous trek. Finally the B3263 brings me into tiny Tintagel village. Fortunately for my trembling brain cells, early in the twentieth century Tintagel changed its name in order to capitalize on growing tourist interest in the famous castle, which was known as Din Tagell, meaning the "fortress of the narrow entrance." The village used to be called Trevena.

After settling into the Pendrin Guest House B&B, I walk to the castle. It's late afternoon and by the time I get to the castle its administrative offices have just closed. English Heritage has jurisdiction here. I meet Patrick Riordan on his way out. He's deputy custodian for the site. His boss is on vacation. A man in his fifties, with a dark, short beard and thick, dark hair, Patrick listens to my story, looks at Frankie's rocks, and in an even, gentle voice says, "Well, all right, then." And then he smiles. So do I.

"It's slate, I figure," I say, as I rotate my head and slate fills my field of vision every direction I look.

"It would be, yes," replies Patrick.

He's going home, but he agrees to meet me at the castle in the morning.

Frankie took two Tintagel rocks and both are slate. The castle is slate. The homes and walls in the area are slate. Roofs are slate. Animal pens are slate. A fourteenth-century house in the village, which was the post office building in the nineteenth century and is now a historic monument, is made totally of slate. Quarries in the area have been excavating slate for a thousand years. This northwestern Cornwall corner of landscape bleeds slate the way Purbeck bleeds limestone and Dover bleeds chalk. The low-grade metamorphic rock has been thrust to the earth's surface here for all to see, quite dramatically along the rugged coastline, and for all to use.

Both of Frankie's pieces are clearly labeled *Tintagel Castle.* One is almost round, three inches in diameter, but thin in that way slate's flat planes flake. The other piece is more interesting. It's four inches long, an inch wide, and a half-inch thick in the middle. But the stone is bowed almost like a little barge, its bow and stern ends coming up to sharp, straight edges. The rock has what's called a slickenside surface, clearly exhibiting the geologic folding that this part of England has undergone. The present landscape was the bottom of a shallow sea 350 million years ago. Then, like a mud pie bakemaster hand-fashioning a giant geologic layer cake, long-gone mountain rivers deposited mud and silt to the sea bottom, then shoreside volcanoes added ash and lava, and still later, intense heat and pressure from earth upheavals compressed it and folded it and flipped it all over. The slate, which once was the bottom layer, is now extruding from the tops of the cliffs. Fissures and faults run all through it.

While Tintagel Castle is in a serious state of decay, this is one site on my trip where the loss of rock isn't due to pilfering by rock-needy neighbors. Slate doesn't form easily into blocks. It breaks; it can be broken by hand along its layered planes. It's best used piled up in thick sheaves, as Tintagel was. And the abundance of slate lying all around meant there was no reason to go down to the castle to steal stone.

No, Tintagel wasn't reduced to ruins by needy humans. Just as human hands can break and flake the slate, so too can the pounding sea and fierce storms that relentlessly batter the Cornwall coast. The narrow land bridge to Tintagel headland, where the castle was built in the 1200s, was originally much wider and more level than today. But the ocean's forces have dramatically eroded the isthmus, and the headland is close to becoming an island. In the Middle Ages a large portion of cliff collapsed, and other major rockfalls occurred in 1840, 1918, and 1989. Each of these falls took significant portions of the castle's courtyards and fortifications along with it.

Everyone acknowledges that Tintagel's days are numbered. As the English Heritage guidebook puts it, "In the long term, Tintagel is a wasting asset."

In the big picture, then, the loss of Frankie's lifted pieces of slate does not loom large.

Before dinner I stop in at the Tintagel Toy Museum and Shop in the center of the village, where thousands of vintage Dinky and Corgi and Matchbox toys are on display. The place is obviously the marriage of someone's obsessive collecting of British metal toys with his/her hope that drawing curious people in will lead to the sale of new Dinky, Corgi, Matchbox, and other toys. Many of the older trucks, airplanes, or soldiers are not for sale, but some are. Collectors would find the place a must-see.

For me it is a must-see, too. I'm a sucker for these die-cast metal cars. After Mini Coopers were reintroduced a few years ago, I bought a metal model. It reminds me of my days in Swinging Sixties London when Mini Coops were a mod's motorcar of choice (only to be salaciously satirized in the wildly popular Austin Powers movies at the end of the century). I also recently found a Made in China metal VW Karmann Ghia, something I've been searching for for a long, long while. I had a white Ghia convertible in the late sixties. It was my first car, and I adored it. The miniature model was yellow. I repainted it white.

To this day I have a few of the old, vintage English-made Dinky metal cars displayed on a shelf in my dining room. A yellow Austin-Healey 3000, a Hudson sedan, a Peugeot 203, and a 1950s-era, blue and gold Ferrari and a red Maserati, my two old racing friends. Behind the playground at Rosemary Elementary School in Chevy Chase, Maryland, there used to be a hard-packed dirt hill. In fifth grade, a bunch of us boys fashioned a series of weaving gutter tracks down the bank. During recess we'd gravity-race our Dinky race cars. My Maserati was a regular winner.

I still have those few Dinky cars, and a modest collection of Dinky army trucks, tanks, artillery pieces, personnel carriers, jeeps, and armored cars. I saved them from one of Frankie's yard sales. But my extensive collection of Matchbox vehicles is gone. After I went away to college, Frankie put the Matchbox metal toys in another yard sale and sold them. Never mind that she almost certainly sold them for a fraction of what they were worth. Never mind that today they'd be worth much more. What I mind is that this collection of solid, timeless pieces of my childhood, filled with memories, were taken away from me without a passing thought to whether I ought to be consulted on the matter. I mind that my army Dinkys nearly suffered the same sell-off fate. And I mind that my mother, a passionate collector, a person who fully understood a person's attachment to things, did this. I'm at a loss to understand it. Except in a way that seems inescapable, yet painful. That once again, in this way as in so many other ways, Frankie didn't have me in her thoughts, in her mind, or my feelings in her considerations.

I mention to the clerk at the Tintagel Toy Museum and Shop that I'm enjoying seeing all these wonderful old metal toys because I once had so many of them myself but that my mum put most of them in a yard sale, and now they're gone.

"Well, I hope you've forgiven your mum," she said.

I nod. But I wonder if I have.

tuesday, march 25

In the morning, in my room, I'm holding the thicker of Frankie's Tintagel rocks, the barge-shaped one, and as I idly torque it between my hands it snaps in half. Slate will do that. Now I've accidentally done it to one of my special-delivery items. Now, unexpectedly, I have three rocks from the coastal castle.

There's an odd feeling in this. Frankie stole two rocks. I came to return two, not three. I find myself surprisingly unsettled by this. It makes me feel a little like an accomplice, adding to the destruction of the site's stone. I feel a little guilty. Yet as I walk to the visitors' center to meet Patrick, I decide that if it has any meaning at all, the rock split is a reminder of the impermanence of everything—things here, things back home, things carried away by Frankie or carried back to Cornwall. The cracking, flaking, breaking-up of the cliff rock upon which Tintagel was built is not somehow separate and distinct from a single specimen of the same rock, placed in a museum case, or in a cardboard box over a cottage garage, or in a son's hands. The time lines of decay may vary, setting by setting. But the time of decay always comes.

In lifting this rock away from wherever it lay thirty-six years ago, my mother was not a sole force of destruction. She was just one among the many, past and present, working upon this exposed headland. Forces infinitely more powerful than Frankie made the slate, and then lifted it from the underground, and then eroded everything around it to expose it to the castle builders. They, in turn, separated it from where it was embedded and put it in a wall, subjecting the mineral material to the abrasive friction of handling and working. Wind and weather, frost and fire over the next thousand years did their part in transforming the rock whole into an infinitely expanding subdivision of smaller and smaller parts. Then one day Frankie took her two rocks, probably breaking them away from larger constituent pieces. A little more size and shape was shed, no doubt, during the years the rocks were with her, jostling and rubbing in transit against companions from Hadrian's Wall, Corfe Castle, and all the others.

And now this morning, one piece has become two in my hands and I'm now carrying three. But I know the three will become four, and then eight, and finally, a million or more years from today, these rocks will be a million grains of sand on a beach here that has not yet been born. And here where Earl Richard of Cornwall built his Fortress of the Narrow Entrance, and out of the same geologic material, some futuristic child will build a wicked-cool sand castle.

It's inevitable. Still, today I'm taking my three rocks back.

It's off-season, midweek, and despite yet another blue-sky, warm day, there will be few visitors to Tintagel. So Deputy Custodian Patrick Riordan is doing double duty. I find him taking entrance tickets at the wooden bridge that spans the chasm between the castle's mainland and island courtyards.

"You've used the word 'stolen' a couple of times when you talk about what your mother took," Patrick says, as we get talking. "I don't see it that way. It's the ecological protection movement which makes it frowned upon now. It's made it wrong to pick wildflowers, pebbles from the beach, all sorts of things. But I don't see this as stealing, because I don't think your mother saw it as stealing. It was souvenir gathering, something to remind her of her journeys. The rocks were a form of diary, a concrete diary. And this was an innocent pursuit before the late 1960s.

"Stealing has a negative connotation. You can't be retrospective in your views," he says. He thinks for a few seconds. "Especially if it's based upon a need. Taking the rocks may have represented a fear of the future, never being able to return. As well as reverence for the past.

"You're being too hard on your mum," he says. "She needed to take the rocks."

"I hope everybody doesn't need to take rocks," I say. "Unless everybody brings them back."

Souvenir stones have been taken, Patrick admits, calling Tintagel "a contemplative site which lends itself to wandering around. So it lends itself to be picked over, it does."

It also attracts some people with more than casual tourist interest, and more interest in possessing its stones. "The Merlin association, the legend aspect of the site," Patrick says, "brings a very strange collection of people here. We see a vast array of ideas of what the site represents. It seems to represent different things to different people."

For some, a visit to Tintagel is a pilgrimage, Patrick says. It's a spiritual thing. It's a place, some people believe, imbued with mystery and magic. King Arthur's story starts at Tintagel.

King Arthur. Frankie. The two click in my head.

The better-known aspects of the Arthurian legend all come later: King

Arthur's mystical court at Camelot, his Knights of the Round Table, the Sword in the Stone test revealing Arthur as rightful king, his beautiful Queen Guinevere, his magic sword Excalibur, and the Quest for the Holy Grail. The man had to come from somewhere, though, and that's where this coastal castle comes in. If the legends are to be believed, either Arthur was conceived in Tintagel or born here, or perhaps both. Or maybe as a newborn he was handed over to Merlin the magician at the castle's gates. Whatever version, Tintagel over the ages has consistently been identified with the beginnings of Britain's most romantic, courageous, chivalrous, and spiritually pure figure.

It's quite possible, of course, King Arthur never existed. He's never been historically proven. And Tintagel wasn't even built until long after Arthur was purported to have lived. But from Geoffrey of Monmouth's twelfth-century *History of the Kings of Britain,* to Sir Thomas Malory's medieval narrative *Morte Darthur,* to Alfred, Lord Tennyson's famous poem *Idylls of the King,* to the drawings of Aubrey Beardsley, to the Broadway production *Camelot,* no one particularly cares about what's true. Tintagel's keepers, from its first days to today's custodians, as well as the village chamber of commerce, have never had the slightest interest in dispelling the myth. Just as it was good for Earl Richard's eleventh-century karma, it's good for Cornwall's twenty-first century economy.

With such an association, is it any wonder rocks have left the premises?

With such an association, it strikes me, is it any wonder Frankie took two rocks? This is what clicked earlier. Frankie was into Camelot, big-time. The thought comes again, then goes as my attention is drawn back to Patrick, who is still talking.

Patrick Riordan recalls rocks being returned on two occasions. Both by post. In both cases, he says, the people who took stones from Tintagel felt they'd been followed by bad luck ever since, and were nagged by worries. "They indicated they hoped the act of returning the rock would correct the feeling," he says.

"Did it?" I ask.

"I don't know," he says. "They never followed up."

As I'm leaving, Patrick begins reflecting on my visit. He's a thoughtful person. He's unsure what he's feeling, but it involves his father. He's uncertain what he wants to say, but he still says something. It seems he says it more for himself than for me. There's an unmistakable tone of sadness in his voice.

"You know, with my father, he was from Ireland. He began his life on a farm in Ireland, and came here, and so I was living just outside Tintagel on a farm too. I think you tend to see where you are as your final place. The completion of a circle. He was completing his. But I was beginning a new circle. Here was a starting point. What you're doing completes your mother's circle. But I suppose it begins a new one for you."

He's not looking at me. He's gazing out at Barras Nose, the barren headland just west up the coast.

"Life is more than two dimensions," he says. "Life is more. And completely frustrating when you're trying to work these things out."

I'm alone when I replace Frankie's two, which have become three, pieces of slate. I'm alone again with her memory.

I decide against trying to place the rocks into a crumbly castle courtyard wall, or within one of the foot-high outlines of the Dark Age dwellings scattered around the grassy dome of Tintagel Island. I go to the extreme western end of the island bluff by the edge of the sea. This is as close to America as I'll get on this trip, I think, and the clearest unobstructed line over the water. At least until my airliner ascends out of Heathrow in about a week and lifts me homebound beyond this point.

It's unseasonably warm for a Cornwall March. There's a moderate breeze. I stare out to sea for a long time, my mother in my thoughts, the rocks in my pocket. Over two hundred thousand visitors a year come to Tintagel. Only a handful are here today, and all of them are roaming around the ruins. I'm alone out here at the extreme edge of the site.

I walk around a black sign, its white letters proclaiming "Cliff edge" and its triangular yellow warning graphic showing a human silhouette falling off a cliff. I climb down a little. It's a safe enough place, if you're not afraid of heights, and keep your balance.

The sea crashes noisily into the rocky, sawtooth shore about two hundred feet below. Here, and to the right and left, and behind me on the mainland, sheets of slate flow down the headland in arrested waves, looking like wavy onion-peel lines of altitude rising on a detailed topographical map. The exposed rocky foreshore resembles the random rippling of the sea itself, except the one is gray-brown, the other blue-black, and one is frozen motion, the other motion that never stills.

I have a strong urge to fling the rocks off the sheer cliff into the sea. I resist the urge. It feels too defiant. You throw things away when you don't want them anymore. I want these stones. I don't want them the way Frankie wanted them, prizes or mementos or talismans or totems or whatever possessed her to want to possess them. I want for them. I want for her.

I'll leave them together. I considered splitting them up. But no. Frankie took them together, they've spent decades together in a dark box, they've taken on that part of Frankie that all the rocks have after such a stay with her, and now they've come back together. It's no time to separate them. Two, made three by me, metamorphic peas in Mother Earth's pod; what unique, horizontal travel stories they could tell all the kadzillions of tons of flaky slate slabs around them whose only dramatic journey in three hundred million years has been vertical, and whose definitive common trip is back to dust.

Slate overhangs grassy tufts where I finally sit down. No surprise, that. I lift the tufts a little and wedge the three stone pieces in hard. They settle snugly against solid slate all around. I camouflage the stones, as if they need it, covering them partially with sod. When I stand up, I see they've disappeared back into the Tintagel landscape.

I'm sad again, and close to crying.

A small fishing trawler passes a half-mile off the headland, beating against the southwesterly chop. I stare at the boat for several minutes, the wind taking off the moisture in my eyes and keeping my vision clear. For some reason, the very last sentence of F. Scott Fitzgerald's novel *The Great Gatsby* has stayed with me ever since my mother made me read it when I was a boy. It's a novel filled with loneliness and loss, and with dreams of what might have been. The last line comes to me now:

"So we beat on, boats against the current, borne back ceaselessly into the past."

13.

the fossil police are history

Lyme Regis Interlude

What's a few rocks?

On and off during my journey to return Frankie's rocks I'd hear this question posed in various ways by all sorts of different people. Is anything really lost if a few stones are taken? Does it really matter? Are sites actually harmed? Is a little stone stolen actually noticed in the big picture of weathering and decay?

In *The Past is a Foreign Country,* David Lowenthal suggests that perhaps there is actually value in taking pieces of antiquity. "To own a piece of the past," he says, "can promote a fruitful connection with it." Lowenthal reports that an adherent of such thinking was English writer John Fowles (who, let's remember, wrote a best-selling novel in the 1960s entitled *The Collector,* the story of a psychotic butterfly collector who decides one day to add a beautiful young woman to his collection). Speaking specifically about fossils found near his Dorset home, Fowles felt that what tourists "pick up and take home and think about from time to time is a little bit of the poetry of evolution," and so, if it is part of a natural process, it can't be considered a crime.

This wasn't what I believed. It wasn't how I was raised. "Take only pictures, leave only footprints" was the mantra I memorized in the 1960s. And by the time I became a Cape Cod newspaper editor I was a bedrock preservationist. My typewriter frequently railed against the bulldozing of historic buildings or landscapes during the Cape's convulsive growth spurt in the 1970s and 1980s. Even little losses—a stone wall, a traditional view, a section of ancient way, a dilapidated cranberry bog house—added up, I felt. Alone something lost might barely be noticed. But over time . . .

I worked for twenty years at the Cape weekly newspaper called *The Register*. During my time there an anonymous reader once sent me a copy of a letter he had sent to *Yankee* magazine, a folksy New England periodical. The letter referred to an advertisement the letter writer had seen in *Yankee*. A reproduction of the ad where it appeared on a page of ads in the magazine was enclosed.

Tucked between ads for the Earfriend cordless miniature AM radio, hand-painted geese in a peach basket, and personalized kilt pins was an ad this person found offensive.

"Heritage Rocks" was the advertisement headline. "Authentic rocks from the beaches of Plymouth, America's Home Town. A piece of history for Thanksgiving, a perfect paperweight or knick-knack. No two alike. Each bearing the famous 1620 date and accompanied by letter of authenticity. $7.95."

The ad, this anonymous reader thought, attests "to the fact that the beaches of Plymouth are being sold at the rate of about $15,900 per ton" if each rock weighed one pound.

"Down here on the Cape, we cherish every pebble, stone, rock, and boulder as a deterrent to erosion, a problem, I believe, shared with Plymouth," this person wrote. "After all, if the Indians had removed all the rocks from the Plymouth shores before the arrival of the Pilgrims, Plymouth might not now be America's Home Town."

Actually, logic would suggest that if the Indians had in fact removed all Plymouth's rocks, then a skiff full of tired Pilgrims rowing ashore from their anchored mothership would have been more likely, not less, to come ashore there. Beaches are always better for shore landings than rocks. For that matter, there were certainly beaches in Plymouth in 1620 and no one has ever explained why the tired seafarers chose a slippery rock for their famous first footfall in New England. The Pilgrims' own journals never mentioned landing upon a rock. That story didn't begin circulating until the early 1800s. A century before that, the story goes, an old man who objected to town plans to build a new wharf pointed out the rock, which was in the way. The old guy claimed the rock had this Pilgrim landing history, and insisted it couldn't be disturbed. It was saved. But the rock was also moved, with oxen and pulleys, and in the process it split in half. Later it was moved again, and broke again. And over the years, vandals have chipped off pieces. So today Plymouth Rock is maybe one-third its original size, and rests in a location twice removed from where any forefather or foremother might, or might not, have stepped upon it.

Now, on the matter of commercial sale and transport away of natural resources, the Heritage Rocks concept was nothing new to Cape Cod. Gift shops used to sell canned Cape Cod air, for example. Seashell ashtrays and ornaments made of local scallop or quahog shells can still be acquired. And untold quantities of beach sand every summer day depart the Cape's shores for faraway places, affixed to deflated beach balls in the trunks of cars, wedged in between the sawtooth treads of jogging shoes, or captured at picnics by the sticky tops of mustard jars.

And before getting too high-and-mighty about people taking natural stuff away, it's worth remembering that without transport of environmental resources, many places would not exist. In the matter of Cape Cod, for example, it was a very big jogging shoe indeed—the great glacial ice sheet—that pushed up the place, not entirely unlike a sunbather settling on his towel pushes up a mound of sand with his heel. It makes you stop and think. Very big forces lurk around out there. And this always leads me to wondering about the tyranny of the small event versus the inevitability of the colossal event.

Glaciers or hurricanes removing Cape Cod sand, or littoral drift replacing it, are not small events. They're big. Bigger than we are. There's nothing we can do about them. And theirs is no tyranny anyway, only natural forces at work. But when people pocket rocks from historic sites, there's a direct, chronic dismantling of something. I always assumed the danger to Corfe or Dover or Tintern would lie in the tyranny of small events. Not in Frankie. In thousands, hundreds of thousands, millions of Frankies. I've become a lot less sure.

Plymouth Rock still sits in its sunken shoreline portico. School buses on field trips still arrive and children stare at the rock, bored. "How do they know this is the rock?" they ask. The question can't be answered. Plus the kids aren't told this is only a portion of the legendary boulder, and it's not lying where it was said to be lying when the Pilgrims arrived, so it's not the same rock, nor is it really where they arrived. But I suppose the teachers try to suggest it isn't the rock that matters, anyway. The rock is a symbol for something far removed from geology. The rock is about a story and an ideal.

Shouldn't stories and ideals be lifted up and spread around? Wouldn't the true tyranny be to keep the rocks out of people's hands when their hands are the first and most direct route into their hearts? Won't the sharing of symbolic bits of geology lead to more understanding, across generations and communities and societies, and more harmonious lives for all?

wednesday, march 26

I'm a couple of days ahead of schedule and decide to take a couple of days off and vacation at the shore. Cadbury Castle, Glastonbury Abbey, and Avebury Stone Circle are still ahead. Studying a map I see that Lyme Regis, down on the English Channel indentation of Lyme Bay, is more or less on the way. I've been interested in going there ever since reading John Fowles's terrific novel *The French Lieutenant's Woman*. The interest was rekindled when Fowles's name came up in my much more recent reading about collecting.

Fowles lives in the Lyme Regis area, and the cliffs all along this stretch of Dorset coastline are full of fossils. Tourists visiting the area have long enjoyed taking the fossils. At one point, though, local authorities felt this was destructive and ought to be stopped. They sought to form fossil police to apprehend fossil takers.

Fowles, who sat on a local preservation board, surprised everyone and spoke out against separating tourists from the cliffs, prohibiting fossil picking, and forming a force of fossil cops. He said, Let the tourists take the fossils. This went against a preservationist's knee-jerk logic. In fact, his opinion prevailed, and today the taking of fossils along Lyme Bay's beaches is perfectly legal, fossil hammers are sold in shops, and posted signs inform visitors that they are welcome to gather fossils, but to beware they don't get caught by the huge tidal changes.

The most prevalent fossil is the ammonite, a once extremely abundant, spiral-shaped mollusk that floated in the warm Jurassic seas covering portions of Britain 175 million years ago. Ammonite fossils abound in the Lower Jurassic seacliffs around Lyme Regis. When visitors leave there with fossils in their suitcases, more often than not they carry home ammonites.

I decided I ought to take a look. I wasn't sure I would actually collect any fossils. I wasn't sure I should, given the nature of my trip to England. But maybe I would.

Lyme Regis is very crowded when I get there. Once again it's sunny, hazy, and hot. Hot, at least, for March. It's been now weeks of clear, blue sky and sunshine, I realize. England's notoriously overcast, wet weather has been absent. After the first nine days or so of my trip, past about Dover, I've been enjoying an unbroken string of mild, clear, sunny days. I was prepared for much worse. I've experienced the best. In fact, I'll learn later, this March will end as the sunniest March in Britain since records began forty years ago.

It's the fine weather that has drawn people out today. Lyme is popular with English people as well as overseas visitors. The congestion when I arrive is mostly due to English day-trippers—pensioners and people playing hooky from work. By late afternoon, the mob will thin out. But at first, I need to jostle my way around to find a room.

Low tide is at 6 P.M. Britain is so far up into the northern latitudes the tides here are bears. They go way, way out, and come way in. Sailboats here are built with double keels so they can settle into the mud when the tide recedes, resting, balanced, upright. Around low tide is best for fossil hunting on the beach along the West Dorset Heritage Coast, more commonly called the Jurassic Coast, fronting Lyme Bay. Blame John Fowles. About 4 P.M., I head off. For once this trip I'm not returning rocks. Instead, I head off to collect rocks. I feel a little guilty.

I walk east, navigating around tidal pools, slippery exposed rocks, and prim, elderly local ladies carrying prospector's hammers. After an hour poking around, I find almost no fossils. Just a couple of broken fragments. But I'm not disappointed. I'm fascinated by the inexorable erosion of the cliffs. Signs warn visitors not to climb the cliffs, or even to get too close, because at any second huge hunks of the cliff face could come crashing down. And it does. While I'm there, I'm startled several times by a fierce rumbling sound, and instinctively I jump seaward, even though I'm not too close to the cliffs. With a roar, enormous chunks of the cliff collapse. The cliffs are eroding at an observable rate. Literally observable. I watch it happening. And as the sheer landscape slides away, it carries untold numbers of fossils with it, returning them whence they came 175 million years ago, back into the sea.

John Fowles was right. Take the fossils, if you can find them. Why not? At the rate Black Venn, the Spittles, and the rest of the colorfully named cliffs are coming unglued, it sure seems like no souvenirs will be here to comb for in a lifetime or two.

I'm unexpectedly witnessing, I realize, Mother Nature returning rocks. It's something she does deliberately well, even if much more slowly than a human mother's son by jet plane and rented Renault, over a month. The ammonites, annelids, cephalopods, brachiopods, plesiosaurs, trilobites, and all the other various creatures entombed in stone here were once free-floating or free-swimming. But they died, and Mother Nature collected them up, buried them, pressed them into rock, and then ever so slowly she lifted them in a giant geologic arc and is now dumping them back into the sea. It's been happening at a relatively glacial pace, for sure. But this last stage is happening at a quantifiable rate, right before my eyes.

It makes the journey of Frankie's rocks look like just so many stones idly skipped across a tranquil duck pond.

Fossil collectors here don't so much add to the destruction of this natural national monument as they provide it with infinitesimal interruptions. These aren't harmful. They're simply random little side trips the fossils in rocks take on to Milan, say, or Michigan. John Fowles's point was that some youngsters or in-laws or neighbors at these new resting places might become inspired by seeing the fossils. They might develop a heretofore unrecognized interest in paleontology or geology or history. Or word might spread of what a wonderful place the Jurassic Coast of England is. Some greater worldly good, and even some additional tourist dollars, might flow from interrupting a single rock's return to the sea. Better that than simply exiting with the next outgoing tide.

If, somehow, the cliff face at Lyme Regis could be frozen in place, like a waterfall in winter, and kept that way forever, would taking the fossils then qualify as a no-no? Is it okay to take them, in other words, only because more are continually being shed from the cliff and there's no stopping the shedding?

It would stand to reason they shouldn't be taken in that case. If all the Jurassic fossils at Lyme were confined to a sole, static, exposed headland, then it would cease being a dynamic system and would become a sort of museum display case. People would have to come to see it, and if those who came stole the fossils there would eventually be none left for others to see. Isn't this what Frankie did—steal rocks from nonrenewable, historic showcases frozen in time, diminishing each of them by a small degree? She did. But if Lyme's coast conjures any insight for me, it's that all these old, fragile things, crumbly castles or crumbly cliffs, are helpless in the face of nature's forces. Museums can put things under glass in humidity-controlled cases. But not much can be done at Hadrian's Wall or Dover's pharos or Tintagel Head to stop what time and nature insist upon eating away. Frankie was just a blip on the screen. Few of the structures to which I'm returning rocks will be around in a couple of hundred thousand years.

Staring up at the collapsing cliffs beside Lyme Regis, I wonder if politically correct preservation really matters. Everything is transitioning into something else, though the time lines differ. But instead of fretting about practical obstacles to preservation, wouldn't my energy—all our energies—be better spent learning about the past, and passing along its inspirations and lessons to the next generation? What survives isn't stonework. That won't survive. What can survive, one hopes, is ideas.

It wasn't right to remove two sizable rocks from Hadrian's Wall. I know Frankie shouldn't have done that. But I think Frankie's bigger crime is that she hid the rocks away. While her assembling this larger rock collection was a bad idea, it was made much worse by becoming surreptitious. I've only learned about Hadrian's Wall on this journey to return the rocks. And it's led to a whole new appreciation for the aspirations and organization of the Roman

Empire. Frankie could have been the teacher. Other people's lives in Maryland or Cape Cod could have been enriched, and perhaps nudged in different directions, if Frankie had pulled out her rocks from Hadrian's Wall or Corfe Castle or Salisbury Cathedral and shared with folks the excitement she felt possessing stones with such magical pasts. She could have shown them in the Osterville Library display case, or taken them into schools.

Or for starters, she could have shown them to me. Sharing her passion for the rocks would have been sharing something with me, and considering a childhood where she shared so little with me, I think I would have welcomed handling the stones. I know I would have cherished the chance to connect with my mother.

Like all the stony ammonites people take home from Lyme Regis, Frankie's rocks could have been valuable side trips along their journey into dust. Instead, she brought them, temporarily, to a dead end.

West is not the direction that is supposed to be best for finding fossils. But my fossil-finding failures to the east turn me in the other direction. After scrapping around near the base of the cliffs, I finally pay closer attention to the surf line. I'd heard it said the waterline is the best place to look. It is. I begin to find ammonite after ammonite, small to large, one-sided impressions of the creature's whorl against hard stone backgrounds. Then I find complete, spiraling pieces of whole shells distinct from the muds that once held them.

Over the next two hours I collect twenty examples of ammonite fossils. My pockets begin to sag. My luggage, I realize, will regain some of the dead stone weight I'd been shedding replacing Frankie's rocks. I smile at the irony: My trip to replace historic stone is about to include taking away some geologic history. Frankie focused on rocks turned into structures by ancient peoples. I'll be carrying back ancient creatures turned to stone by Nature herself. My mother took pieces of man's history on the landscape; I'm taking pieces of the history of life on the landscape.

I shrug my shoulders and turn to leave the beach. I am not feeling the slightest twinge of guilt now. These fossils will go on display on a shelf I've got in my house. It's my own modest *wunderkammer*, containing a few bird skulls (including an albatross skull I picked up in the Bay Islands off Honduras), as-sorted seashells (including a chambered nautilus I found in Western Samoa), a whale tooth, an arrowhead, some weird coral tubes I found on Bonaire, and other naturalia. A few ammonites will join the display, and I'll show them to people and tell them my story. Others I'll pass on to kids I know, or to friends. Visiting Lyme Regis has helped with what gift to bring back for people. In every case, the rock fossils will be shared. Unlike Frankie's rocks.

I'm depressed tonight. Lonely, again, as usual. Sick of bad, expensive food, eaten alone. At least there's blues on the stereo at the pub.

I need something. Some fix. What kind? I'm tired of this trip. I gave up my annual visit to Tobago for this trip. Bad trade-off. Wandering, wordlessly, by design, with a purpose but without a plan. Alone. Like I felt growing up. Lonely. In my different bedrooms, with my cowboy blanket, customized plastic model cars, and triangular pennants from St. Augustine, the Statue of Liberty, and the Washington Senators thumbtacked to my wall. My pennant collection, which I started because my cousin Nancy had one. I wanted one. To keep me company. To remind me of her.

I was alone. My father, serious, absorbed in his work, his reading. Frankie, scattered, distracted, absorbed by her hobbies and collections, regularly down in the dark with a migraine, barging back and forth with her projects when she wasn't in pain. I was invisible. The movement of my household, of my family, passed me by each day as if I were a gecko in a terrarium. My father might scold me for something, my mother would dole out food, my brother would denigrate me or tease me or take something away from me, but it would all happen as if in passing—attention that was almost incidental as all three of the older people in my family went about their routines.

And I watched. Lonely.

14.

rocks borrowed for one brief, shining moment

Cadbury Castle

In his book about British collectors, Clive Wainwright said that in the seventeenth and eighteenth centuries questions were commonly raised about people obsessed with the simple stuff of antiquity. An antiquary was viewed as "an eccentric lover and collector of objects rather for their age and historical associations than for any aesthetic merit," and what, after all, is the point of that?

Unlike Europe, colonial America had no shared cultural past, so the country had no aged ruins to distract people. It became a country of entrepreneurs, not antiquarians. The American ethos for modernity, for looking ahead, to the future, to progress, became admired by many overseas, while the value of Europe's own preserved past was sometimes called into question. Johann Wolfgang von Goethe weighed in on the matter in 1812 with a poem about the United States titled "America, You've Got It Better."

In this poem, Goethe notes that America has "no decaying castles" and is not bogged down by "useless old remembrance."

Goethe's point is that the past, with its prejudices and polarizations, can get in the way of fresh new beginnings. History, and an abundance of its ruined rock remains, can be a drag. They can be nagging reminders of things often best left behind. Inherent in a medieval castle, for example, may be the fact of serfdom, or a time of tyranny and cruelty. Many objects in museums are there because of past regimes of pillage and conquest. Bloodshed and death are frequently a subtext of relics.

There's something to be said, Goethe seems to be saying, for the clean slate of America's fresh New World, unsullied by the bloody hands of ancients.

Frankie couldn't have cared less about any of this. She wasn't an antiquarian. Not in the student or expert sense of the word. She didn't admire old rocks. She didn't think deeply about what past they served or what they meant. She simply wanted them, needed to have them.

French philosopher Jean-Paul Sartre has suggested that we "want things in order to enlarge our sense of self, and that the only way in which we can know what we are is by observing what we have." When Frankie took a look at her English rock collection, I don't think she saw examples of history. She certainly didn't see beauty or artistry, craftsmanship or cultural artifacts. The rocks were just plain rocks. Yet she wouldn't have seen geology or paleontology or archaeology either. What Frankie would have seen—what it was about possession of the rocks that would have enlarged her sense of self—was the rocks' silent, invisible associations.

Prehistoric, Roman, and great church associations were some that seemed to matter to Frankie. Yet another association that I think mattered to her as much as any others was celebrity. From her childhood adoration of movie stars, to her adult fixation on important people, especially the Kennedys, renown mattered to Frankie. Especially romantic renown. In the absence of access to the actually famous, which few people have, objects of association must suffice.

The author of a 1928 essay on collecting, Bohun Lynch, wrote that in childhood he had "a piece of chalky stone with 'From Nazareth' written upon it, given me by an evangelical aunt, and some 'ever-lasting' flowers picked upon Majuba Hill during the first Boer War by an uncle who led the retreat across the Ingago." Lynch scoffs at valuing otherwise worthless items solely because of their purported associations—like, say, "the pin that touched the ruff that touched Queen Bess's chin."

Yet valuing things by association, especially the association to celebrities, both famous people and events, is a theme running consistently through people's passion for collecting.

In the Smithsonian Institution are trimmings from President Lincoln's hearse, and the tobacco plug Admiral Peary carried to the North Pole.

At one time it was possible—perhaps it still is—to buy glass vials said to contain Elvis Presley's sweat. Supposedly the King, at a concert, perspired heavily on a stage floor that was covered with wood shavings, and the precious liquid was distilled from this. Meanwhile, a small Ball jar of Elvis's hair, clipped and saved by the singer's former hairstylist, sold for $115,000 at auction in 2002.

Wood fragments of the holy cross upon which Jesus was crucified began to appear in collections, and to be traded, in the Middle Ages, and the phenomenon continues to this day. When skeptics computed that tons of trees would be needed to account for all the purported hunks of cross, true believers in the church came up with a simple explanation: whenever an ax cut out a piece of wood from the cross, the cross miraculously would renew itself.

More than three hundred pieces of memorabilia from Jack and Jacqueline Kennedy, offered by a pair of the First Lady's former attendants and peddled at auction in July 2003, included a container of Jackie's face powder, and a pair of Jack's Navy-issue boxer shorts from his PT-109 war days (high bid, $5,000).

Following a federal fraud and racketeering trial in 1999, the IRS seized the first and most famous brothel in Nevada, the Mustang Ranch, and eventually auctioned off its contents. Nude paintings of absolutely no artistic value sold for $1,000, and Mustang jackets went for $400 (compared with the $30 price a customer would pay when the place was running). When Hugh Hicks of Baltimore died in 2002, his collection of lightbulbs totaled more than sixty thousand. Included were bulbs with celebrity associations: headlamps from Hitler's Mercedes-Benz, for example, and a dashboard light from *Enola Gay*, the aircraft that dropped the atomic bomb on Japan.

Examples are endless. Celebrity sells. The stuff of celebrity has always made for collectibles.

The bulk of Frankie's collections don't fit in this category. And Frankie rarely sought autographs, or even snapshots, of famous people, the two easiest ways to assemble a collection of direct associations. She was not a classic celebrity hound. But celebrity matters to every collector.

Most specifically, what matters is her own celebrity.

For collectors, there is always a tug between two motivating but opposing influences: imitation, the desire to fit in, which leads to collecting things other people collect, to join their club, to match their expertise; and individuation, the desire to stand out, which leads to acquiring strange, valuable, or rare things that no one else has. The more obsessive a collector, the more powerful the pull from those poles. Frankie's shelf openly displayed examples of both—cup plates, which are hardly extraordinary items, next to a Tang Dynasty bronze mirror, for example. Actually, the opposing sides are built into most ordinary collections—Frankie's dolls, fans, or lace, say—where by its nature a common, shared collecting theme is differentiated only by the specific items in an individual's hoard. Most collectors try to have it both ways.

Frankie yearned to be accepted. A childhood of ostracism by her mother and siblings left a troubling hole in her life. In knowing she had collected things that other people also had, her sense of self, of belonging, was soothed. Yet Frankie also yearned to be unique. Until her retirement, she suppressed the two things that set her far apart from most people, her voice and her violin. After retirement, when she took up music again, nothing pleased her more than the praise and celebrity she quickly gained within the local church and conservatory circles where she performed. When I was growing up, though, it was never music. Instead, she sought unique acclaim for her charitable work, her nursing commitment and skills, and her collecting.

It's never been easy to fit Frankie in a box. Psychologists would suggest that obsessive, insecure people trying to navigate and achieve equilibrium in the tug-of-war between those opposing poles—the needs to fit in and to stand out—use the objects they collect as substitutes for personal contacts or personal achievements. They're an easy way out. Frankie, though, had numerous, devoted friends. She was widely loved. While lots of her friends found her "a little nutty, a little kooky," as one told me, they all considered her "a wonderful friend." Frankie wasn't afraid of friendships. Likewise, she achieved many things with the good works she did, her volunteerism, her caregiving, her fundraising, and she was widely praised and admired for her help.

Frankie didn't depend on her collections to imitate the contact with people and personal achievements she sought. They weren't substitutes. But I think she was so needy for acceptance and renown that she turned to every possible means of fulfillment. Her collections didn't stand in place of anything, they were additional assistants on a multifront mission.

She was hedging her bets. The collections were hedges. Hedges against nothingness.

Celebrity comes out of uniqueness, not conformity. The English rocks conformed to slate or limestone or sandstone standards and would fit in any mineral collection. But this is obviously not why Frankie took them and cherished them. In place at their heritage sites, the rocks also conformed to the historic entity, the solid shape preserved at the sites. But Frankie lifted them out of the sites and took them away. They weren't valued for their place in a historic whole.

To Frankie, these were rocks with famous reputations. They had celebrity associations. In her active mind, Frankie could imagine ancient peoples—this Roman officer, or Druid priest, or medieval knight—constructing, handling, leaning against, whispering conspiracies next to, or chanting incantations beside this wall, this stone circle, or this castle.

In holding the rocks, Frankie could feel their celebrity. In possessing the rocks, she could feel celebrity bestowed on herself.

friday, march 28

At breakfast this morning, I meet Betty and Harold, an older couple from Birmingham. Betty lets out a high-pitched giggle when I tell her about Frankie's rocks. I detect a blush as she confesses that she, too, has taken rocks from places she visited.

"But mine are all mixed up," she says. "I didn't even mark them, and I've forgotten where I picked them up."

"Where did they come from?" I ask.

"From all about, really, aren't they? The odd place. Castles, beaches, places I liked and wanted a keepsake." Betty lets out a heartier laugh. "Though now, of course, they're not much of a memory, because I've no idea where each came from. Harold hates the beach, don't you?" she says, turning to her husband.

"She's always picking up things, bringing them home," he says.

"I am not!"

"She is. She'd bring home the Rock of Gibraltar, I think, if you could fit it in the boot."

My suitcase weighted now with new stone—okay, fossils—I set off from Lyme Regis to find Cadbury Castle, off to the northeast in Somerset. Rain has returned, but it's gentle, the air warm.

When I first went through the rocks in Frankie's collection, this one mystified me. Her hand lettering on the stone simply said *Cadbury*. A rock from a chocolate company? Rock candy? Looking up Cadbury in my *Lonely Planet Guide to England*, all I found was Cadbury World, which is up near Birmingham. There you can see eight hundred chocolate bars a minute being "wrapped and dispatched," the guidebook informed me, and the story behind the crème egg is there revealed.

Frankie's Cadbury stone is shaped like an oversized axhead shim, a slender wedge about 3 inches long and a half-inch thick, tapering from a one-inch end to a half-inch end. The color of the cuneal piece is mostly light gray and walnut tan. It doesn't look the least related to crème eggs.

My other useful reference resource, the English Automobile Association's superb *Treasures of Britain*, contained a small entry for Cadbury Castle. So I knew such a place existed, somewhere in Somerset, as I began my March journey. Yet I wasn't sure exactly where, or what, it was. And when I thought to ask, several of the Heritage and Trust people I met along the way knew nothing about the place either. So by this point in the trip, it truly intrigues me.

What was such a relatively obscure stone doing alongside Frankie's chunks of famous Salisbury Cathedral, Tintern Abbey, Dover Castle, and the others? All of Frankie's other rocks came from relatively well-known tourist destinations. When I pull into the little parking lot for the castle site in South Cadbury, I am totally alone.

There's no gatehouse, no entrance fee, no gift shop or guards or guides. I won't see another person for the next hour and a half, as I hike up to the flat-topped hill site, wander across its 18 acres, and envision the long views over farmland that I suspect are out there behind the ground-covering mist.

Stonehenge pulls in close to a million visitors a year. Cadbury World is packed with screaming, sweet-toothed children on holiday weekends. Cadbury Castle, it looks to me, would be lucky if it ends a year with an attendance number in four figures. But Frankie had come here. More to the point, she'd taken a stone from here. Why?

I begin nodding to myself, as I silently hum my best guess: *In short, there's simply not / A more congenial spot.*

The last stone I returned was at Tintagel, reputedly King Arthur's birth-place. I came to Cadbury oblivious to its history or tales. Now as I begin to learn about the tall hill, I learn something intriguing: Cadbury, too, has staked out for itself a significant place in the Arthurian legend. It's believed by some that Cadbury was the location of Camelot, the seat of King Arthur's Court.

Again, as at Tintagel, memories of Cape Cod Melody Tent come to me. The summer Music Circus, as everyone called it, was an entertainment mainstay of warm months in Hyannis. It originally featured all the classic musicals of Broadway, like *Oklahoma, My Fair Lady,* and *The King and I,* performed in the round under an orange-and-white canvas tent. One of Frankie's all-time fa-vorite shows was *Camelot.* She saw it every time it came to the Music Circus. She bought the record album of the Broadway musical score and played it over and over. She sang its songs around the house.

She was taken, too, with modern Camelot. The world of President John Kennedy, his glamorous wife, Jackie, their adorable children, and the uplift-ing spirit surrounding their White House days and public life came to be called Camelot, and Frankie fully felt its mystique. She collected piles of mag-azines with Kennedy stories. She took every visitor to our Cape Cod home to see the Kennedy Compound in Hyannis Port. She went to local horse shows when Jackie or Caroline was riding.

The moment John Kennedy was shot, I was in eleventh-grade geometry class. After they made the announcement over the PA, they sent us home. I walked home. I found Frankie in front of the TV, crying.

Millions of Americans cried, of course. But this was one of the few times I saw my mother cry. It made me so uncomfortable, I went outside to throw a football with friends.

Frankie went to Washington for Kennedy's funeral and she stood on the side of Constitution Avenue to watch the caisson carrying President Kennedy's casket pass, the riderless horse walking alongside, the long, somber line of dignitaries in black marching behind. I didn't go, so I don't know whether she cried then, too. Later, she frequently visited Kennedy's grave site in Arlington Cemetery.

Frankie was enchanted with something she identified in Camelot, both the Broadway and Kennedy versions. Something in the Camelot story was pure and good, nurturing and protecting, chivalrous and heroic. Her early childhood hadn't provided such a place. In those days, sad and lonely days, such a pure and shining place as Camelot must have been a dream. As she watched the assassinated president's funeral procession, her sadness must have been compounded by the melody and words from Lerner and Loewe's musical playing in her head, as it had so often been played in our living room.

Henry VIII had a nosy antiquarian named John Leland, and he's the fellow who was supposedly the first to connect Cadbury with Camelot and King Arthur. In 1542, Leland wrote, "At the very south ende of the church of South-Cadbyri standith Camallate, sumtyme a famose toun or castelle, upon a very torre or hille, wunderfully enstrengthenied of nature. The people can telle nothing ther but that they have hard say that Arture much resortid to Camalat."

Observing the site, Leland remarked, "Truly me seemeth it is a mirackle in bothe Arte and Nature." Well, I don't know if it's exactly a natural and artistic miracle, but the big, green, flat-topped hill looms impressively up from the treeless floor of the plain around it. It's definitely a dominant landscape feature in the area.

The only interpretative amenity at present-day Cadbury Castle is a plastic-covered placard at the edge of the car park. From it I learn the hill has long been valued and used for its strategic height and location in Southwest Britain. Ancient trackways that converge there indicate it's long been at a crossroads of human movement, and archaeological digs show settlement since 3000 B.C. A Bronze Age village on the summit had grown into an extensive hill fort and town by the Iron Age, a center of trades and trade, and probably focus of a religious cult. By around 500 B.C., the fort featured four huge stepped earthen banks as its main defense. Today these embankments are the only visible historical remains.

The town was cleared around A.D. 70 during Roman occupation, but a massive refortification was done by Britons after the Romans departed. Around this time, A.D. 500 or so, Arthur enters the scene. Not for sure. Nothing is for sure where Arthur is concerned. The scant historical record for Britain for this time shows its landscape divided into "kingdoms," and Celtic lore, later on, tells tales of a bunch of battles of local Britons, led by someone called Arthur, against invading pagan Saxons. Arthur won the day, and it's reasoning, not historical record, that suggests he would have used Cadbury as his base. Everyone before him had, after all.

At the bottom of the car park placard is notice that "Cadbury is a scheduled Ancient Monument on privately owned land." And that the site is "protected under the 1979 Ancient Monuments Act, and under no accounts should any excavation be undertaken." Frankie was here before 1979, so she couldn't have violated the '79 Act. Finally, the placard says, "Archeological excavations were undertaken here, 1966–70." Frankie was certainly here then. Precisely then. And the dig would have gotten considerable press coverage.

I stare up at the big, solemn hill. Excavations were under way at York Minster when Frankie was there, at Housesteads on Hadrian's Wall when she visited, and at Tintern Abbey, and now here at Cadbury. Was it piles of excavation debris lying around open on the ground that were for her too much of a temptation? If she encountered the piles in sequential stops at the historic sites, was it these coincidental excavations that actually caused Frankie to begin collecting her rocks? I have no idea in what order she visited the sites to which I'm returning rocks. But it seems likely York and Hadrian's Wall were visited in a weekend trip north from London. And Tintern and Cadbury aren't far from each other. I wonder.

A narrow, steep dirt path leads up to Cadbury Castle. After passing through a kissing gate, the path cuts through the undulating, earthen bulwarks, built about when ancient Athens was entering its classical age of law, philosophy, democracy, architecture, and art. We know so much about classical Greece because so much was recorded in stone. As I emerge onto Cadbury's broad hilltop, the Acropolis crosses my mind. The setting is similar. Except there's no marble Parthenon standing on this mounded citadel, and no congested, modern city at its feet. The hilltop is broad, richly grassed, and empty. Sheep graze here and there. Below is tiny South Cadbury, a village of scattered farms and a solitary stone church. Stone, however, wasn't used at the hill fort to give the place permanence. And lack of stone contributes to the fact that we know little about the Durotriges, the people who, it's thought, used this spot as capital of their territory. Stone artifacts are not a part of their legacy. But Frankie found a rock. Gazing around, I can't imagine the spot from where it was taken, or where now to put it back.

Not one building or wall, or even a tree, breaks the open site. Only the earthen ramparts suggest the place had anything to do with human habitation. Here and there I see little holes sunk into the turf. Probably the work of animals. Or perhaps a sign relic hunters with illegal metal detectors have been up here.

There's no clear or appropriate place to return my mother's stone here. No one to give it to, or to comment on it. I'm alone. It's my ceremony, my choice. I would have liked someone official to take a look at this piece of Cadbury. Jon Nickerson, my geologist friend who had examined it on Cape Cod, pointed out a pinkish tinge around two exposed edges, and a trace of white that he thought could be mortar. Under a magnifying eyepiece he found a tiny piece of scallop shell embedded in one side. "Looks like a local mud," he thought, "made into an impure, crude brick."

They certainly had bricks by King Arthur's day. Maybe this was a brick fragment found during the late 1960s excavations, which was when they revealed both the defenses added to the hill fort around A.D. 500 and the possible foundations of a cruciform church. Arthur was the area's first Christian leader, if he was a person at all. So a cruciform church would be something he'd want erected at Cadbury. Did a debris pile in '67 or '68 contain some of this? Did Frankie think it did? I'll never know.

I'm sad again, in this breezy, barren place, letting go of yet another of my mother's special collection. I decide to replace the stone in a rampart, the only man-made feature on the hill. All the ramparts are grass-capped now. The east mound is the most shaped. I select a spot where it's about 8 feet tall.

I find a small gash in the grass where rich, brown topsoil is exposed. I press the stone in, then cover it with loose dirt collected from some of the other exposed holes. Then I rip a fresh divot of turf, a hunk like the ones my five-iron rips from fairways when I'm hitting bad golf shots, and I press the clod down to cover the hole. To cover the rock.

Frankie's piece of Camelot is back at Camelot. She only borrowed it, for one brief shining moment.

Before leaving South Cadbury, I stop in at the little thirteenth-century church close to the base of the castle hill. Frankie's passion for brass rubbing took her to small parish churches across England. I wonder if this church has any monumental brasses on its floor. If it does, maybe that's what brought Frankie to such a remote location. Maybe it wasn't Camelot lore at all.

But the church has no brass.

While I'm at the church, about thirty minutes at the most, several people come and go. They are the only people I've seen since stopping at Cadbury. They aren't tourists. They've come to visit grave sites in the small churchyard. Headstones stand between budding trees, a tulip, a yew, and a ginkgo. Two young women come and water the heavily flowered grave of their mother, who died in 2001. An elderly couple come to water the grave of their daughter, Dawn, who also died in 2001. She died at age twenty-six, leaving a little boy and a little girl, whose pictures lean against the headstone. A short, husky man in his thirties comes and leaves a potted plant at Daphne's grave. Daphne was his mother, and she died in 1998. Fresh flowers are stacked up against several other stones in the cemetery. All this strikes me as a great deal of remembrance activity for such a small, remote churchyard. I'm curious.

I stop Daphne's son as he's getting into his car to leave. Delicately, because it is, after all, a question concerning departed loved ones, I ask him what's going on here.

"Mother's Day," he tells me. "I can't get here Sunday, so I came today. I guess the others needed to come early, too."

I give him a quizzical look. "Mother's Day is Sunday? I thought Mother's Day is in May," I say.

Now it's his turn to look puzzled. But he's quick to judge my accent. "You're an American?" he says. I nod. "Maybe it's different in America. In England, Mother's Day is in March. It's this Sunday."

"Cool!" As soon as the expression is out of my mouth, I can't believe I've said that to a stranger who has just left his dead mother's grave. But that's what comes out. It's what I suddenly feel. Seeing the man's blank look, I quickly try to explain. "That's cool, because I didn't know that, and the reason I've come here to South Cadbury from America is to remember and honor my mother. And here you are," I say, gesturing toward the flowered headstones, "remembering and honoring your mothers. And, well, it strikes me as quite a coincidence. But, you know, appropriate." Then I tell him about the rocks.

I'm not sure he understands. He is probably thinking I've mixed up the date for Comic Relief. Daphne's son drives away.

I think it is very cool. Mother's Day has come early for me. And it comes while I'm experiencing a month of mother's days. Now spread before me in this little churchyard are bouquets of flowers left for a variety of remembered mothers. While behind me, high on Cadbury's hill, I've left my own memorial to a lost mother.

As the plaque on the hill told me, Glastonbury is 11 miles to the northwest, and it's there I head next.

I must be honest here. Again, I had no idea, as I set out, that I was heading to yet another haunt of King Arthur—the third in a rock-returning row.

Neither did I have the slightest idea that my Renault was propelling me to a New Age adherent's mecca, where globally significant energy lines run through you like spiritual spears, storefronts look as if they've been transported to town through a time warp from 1967 Haight-Ashbury, and priestesses, enchantresses, and goddesses outnumber Her Majesty's ordinary women-folk wherever you turn your gaze. I had no idea. I truly didn't. I thought I was going to a place famous for its ruined, late twelfth-century abbey. *Glastonbury Abbey*, says the handwriting on Frankie's rock. It doesn't say anything about pagans, cult-religion pilgrims, white witches, or ley lines.

My first clue that Glastonbury is a draw to far more than people interested in the historic abbey is the difficulty finding an available room. Place after place is full up. After several B&B referrals, I wind up at Hillclose, where Penny and David Riddle rent rooms. Hillclose is close to Tor Hill, and is located on Street Road. That's really its name. Street Road. It leads to a town named Street, a ways down the road. A good thing Street, the town, isn't named Road, or I'd be staying on Road Road. And things, I soon discover, are weird enough in Glastonbury without that.

They say Glastonbury has always attracted seekers and bohemian types. There has always been something drawing people here, some silent voice or spiritual energy. It had a mysterious power on neolithic peoples first, then became a Celtic sanctuary, then a Christian holy site. In modern times, servicemen who'd seen quite enough of civilization on the battlefields of World War II came here after the war to find some new meaning to life. Hippies and flower children came in the psychedelic sixties. And now Glastonbury is a New Age melting pot, filled with bojangled, incense-waving, pierced people in purple pants and flowing, flowered vests. Exploring the small downtown, a woman in her forties walks past me barefoot. England, in a city, in March, barefoot? I see one person after another with a long, single braid of hair hanging down from above a temple, draped over a breast. I figure this must have significance.

One shop window after another makes it clear this isn't your ordinary place of blokes wagering on football at Ladbrokes and ladies serving scones at tea. This is a different England. A place of clairvoyant readings. The Schnider Sect. Toe rings. Healing crystals. Sensual oils and attars. World herb and tinctures. Faeries. Priestess enchantress training. Immersion ceremonies.

Posters are up here and there for "Goddess Conference 2003: Celebrating the mystery of the Nine Morgens, the Nine Ladies of Avalon," 30 July to 3 August.

I was in college in the late 1960s and did my share of exploring lifestyle alternatives and the expansion of consciousness. I once had hair down to my shoulders, grooved to Incredible String Band and Donovan songs, read stuff like Jack Kerouac's *The Dharma Bums* and Carlos Castaneda's *The Teachings of Don Juan*, and sat up many a late night listening to various glassy-eyed, flaky friends drone on about astral projection, biofeedback, planes of reality, I Ching, and transcendental meditation. I have my own mantra. My horoscope's been cast and I know my sun and moon are both in Aquarius. And to this day, I spend more time trying to understand mindfulness than trying to make a decent living. So, hey, I think of myself as pretty hip, okay? I'm not exactly Mr. Chips. But on the streets of Glastonbury, I'll tell you, I feel like a positively banal, middle-aged, pencil-necked geek.

So what was Frankie looking for here?

The abbey? That's what she probably came for. But what did she find here? Avalon.

I'm going to guess she didn't realize it when she came. I'm going to guess, too, that it made her heart race and made her hands grab for a talisman to take home.

That evening, in a local pub, Tony tries to convince me I shouldn't put Frankie's rock back. Tony runs a scaffolding business and looks like a character out of *The Hobbit,* with his short stature, big ears, and bald head. He's no Frodo, though; he's a former Royal Marine who served in Aden in the late sixties.

Tony expresses an opinion I've heard more than once on this trip. But he's more adamant about it than most. "You're bleedin' daft," he insists. That's a pretty strong assessment, given the crowds walking around this town. "The rock's importance now isn't that it came from the abbey. It isn't important that it come back to us. We don't need the rock. The rock's importance is that it came to you, from your deceased mother."

I've brought the stone into the pub with me. Tony turns it over slowly, gently in his small, thick hand. Watching him, I recognize the way he's handling it. This stranger is handling the rock with great respect, almost with reverence. It's not, I realize, respect for the stonework of the great abbey, standing tonight floodlit, in ruins, across High Street just yards from where we're downing pints. It's respect for my mother. Tony's turning the stone the way I've turned more than a dozen stones in my hands over the course of this trip. Not like a rough, solid, stolen rock. Instead, like the desiccated confirmation rose I found pressed in the pages of the 1929 Bible engraved "Yvonne R. Franco" in gold on its leather cover.

Carefully. Respectfully.

"It's got your mum's handwriting on it," Tony says. "I'd say it's yours, mate. I wouldn't take it back. I'd take it home. It's yours now, not Glastonbury's."

15.

collecting is about memories, remembered or not

Glastonbury Abbey

 Collecting is about memories. Even, I think, if you don't remember the memories.

Or even if the nature of the memory changes.

I went through so many saved things, accumulated objects, after my mother died, and after my uncle Oscar died, and after my dad sold the Cape Cod house where the three of them had been living and moved into an assisted-living apartment. We had to shed a vast collection of family possessions. Frankie and Oscar could be of no help with memories now. My father, nearing ninety, presented with specific items, remembered little.

Frankie collected handmade wooden boxes, and I put an assortment of things inside one and brought it to my home. There are other things; there were too many things; Frankie's stuff, mostly, a few of Oscar's things, some of my dad's. Some things, sorting through, I couldn't bring myself to sell, give away, or throw away. It became a new collection; my collection now; a collection of family things. Which mean little to me, except in imagining. And except that I know they were somehow important enough to my mother, my dad, or my uncle to make it this far, through moves and lives lived, to me.

Among the things inside the wooden box:

A silver pocket watch and chain, with "OHH" engraved on the back. Oscar Henry Hornig. It was my grandfather's.

A little metal gold ball the size of a marble, with cast stitched seams intended to make it look like a baseball, engraved with "NA Townies '35" and "OHornig." This was my uncle Oscar's. He was a star shortstop for the North Attleboro town team.

A small letter opener with a mother-of-pearl blade and a bronze handle in the shape of a longhaired, knightly banneret with a sword held across his chest. Imprinted in cursive script on the blade is "Paris."

A pin depicting crossed American and French flags with "France forever" written under them.

An aluminum disk the size of a silver dollar with a real Indian Head penny dated 1901 securely in its center. "Lucky Penny Pocket Piece" it says on one side, "Good Luck Souvenir Pan American Exposition Buffalo, N.Y." it says on the reverse.

These things were once connected to memories. The direct memories are now gone. This doesn't mean the things lost their significance. Most have value to collectors of commemorative pins, letter openers, antique timepieces. In someone else's collection, though, Oscar's little honorary baseball would undergo a transubstantiation, losing its ability to conjure up the deft play of OHornig over that thrill-filled 1935 season, and taking on the memories—the personal past and representational stage setting—of its new collector. It would all change.

At least with me the silent gold baseball conjures up strong, affectionate memories of Oscar. He taught me to play baseball, and gave me passion for the game and for the Boston Red Sox. The man is still there. Oscar still is in the baseball. In the hands of a stranger, however, the memory in this memento becomes entirely different. It becomes the new owner's history. Maybe he had a childhood of losing play, ridiculed at-bats, humiliations on the mound? Maybe a childhood spent in the shadow of an overbearing, athletic father or brother? Perhaps the circumstances under which the little gold ball was acquired? Always the reasons it was acquired. These become the object's new story.

The new collector will have no memory of the memories that plucked this piece of memorabilia out of the torrent of otherwise unselected ephemera that swept through O. Hornig's life, and sweeps still through mine, and through everyone's life, that relentless rage of things, possessions, stuff. Most is crap, is lost, let go, cast off, thrown away. Not in this case. It was tangible memories that turned this piece into a survivor. I have it now.

Collecting is about memories, even if the collector doesn't remember the memories. And now I'm talking about the original collector. It sounds like a contradiction in terms. But just ask Sigmund Freud.

Freud knew a thing or two about the unconscious. About buried memories. He developed techniques for excavating down into people's unconscious, in the hunt for repressed memories—sort of like an archaeologist on a dig looking for valuable buried historical fragments. Freud also knew something about collecting because he was himself a collector. He collected people's stories, their dream texts, their memories, yes. But he also sought and saved ancient Egyptian, Greek, and Roman objects. By the time of his death, he had something like three thousand pieces.

Freud directly connected his collecting to his psychoanalytical work. He kept his collected classical objects in the rooms where he saw and treated patients, the workplace where he studied and wrote, not in his living spaces. He saw collectibles as symbolic of inner conflicts in people, touching on the anxiety over fear of death, struggles with narcissism and sexual repression, and a wide range of nasty psychic holdovers from early childhood. Freud saw his relics, scattered about his office, as soothing to patients, evoking connection with the past, as well as triggering nostalgia in people, a helpful doorway, he felt, to past feelings. And inasmuch as collections are an objectified, ordered world created by people as substitutes for the "real" world around them, and the relationship to objects replacements for relationships with genuine people, Freud felt collections were keys to effacing the past, a crucial step in throwing personal demons out of the cluttered mansion of the mind.

As John Forrester put it, Freud's collections "remind us that psychoanalysis is a cure made possible by means of the kind of remembering that makes forgetting possible."

Collecting for Frankie, I feel certain, was about memories. I'll never know what they were. I don't think she knew what they were either. I don't think she remembered her memories. Not consciously. But something within that cranial nerve net where memories are stored raged within her, firing off impulses that sent both her mind and her body here and there, frenetically, one minute to the next. She couldn't sit still. Not in anything she did. From the outside, it looked as though she was racing from one vital interest to the next, one serious priority project to another. On the inside, I'm convinced, she was running away from something she was terribly afraid would stare her in the face if she settled down, quieted her mind, and confronted it.

Collecting expert Walter Benjamin wrote, "Every passion borders on the chaotic, but the collector's passion borders on the chaos of memories." I've thought of that often, as I've considered the jumble of disparate collections Frankie had, the intensity of her service to them, the way in which they replaced a relationship with me. My mother kept so busy with these things, when I was a child, I remember thinking they must be so important. What did I know?

Now I know. They weren't important. I wish Frankie could have known that. They weren't the important items in her life. My brother Doug was. My dad was. I was. Her friends and her good life were.

I think back to childhood and try to remember. It makes me nostalgic . . .

. . . for mornings slurping Cheerios and making believe I'm reading the cereal box, when I'm actually watching my mother out of the corner of my eye talking to herself in the kitchen, complaining about a recipe she's reading that she can't imagine following.

. . . for afternoons standing on the street corner by Rosemary Elementary School with a white safety patrol belt across my chest, which my mother would always launder for me the night before so that I'd look crisp, clean, and official, and stand my post proudly.

. . . for evenings watching *Gunsmoke*, sipping ginger ale out of my father's shot glass, listening to my mother humming downstairs as she listened to Brahms.

Somebody once said nostalgia is memory with the pain removed. I suppose this is why Freud listed the eliciting of nostalgia as the central of three functions served by collected objects (after evoking the past, and before effacing the past). If remembering the past hurts, who wants to go there? So if the nostalgia in objects caused pain, nobody would collect objects, and Freud wouldn't be able to suggest they could help people leave the past behind.

Nostalgia is a longing for things far away and long ago, and it carries the connotation of better times, usually familial times, when ice cream cones with jimmies were an elation on a summer day, children skipped to school swinging book bags, life was simpler, and homes and families were warm and safe. Yet the Greek root of the word is quite different. *Nosos,* "a return to native land," and *algos,* "suffering of grief," are its combined parts. Years ago, nostalgia was seen as homesickness, an affliction for which there was a range of treatments, from leeches to emulsions to opium.

If she became nostalgic in surrounding herself with collectibles, Frankie's memories of childhood would have been grief-filled, unless she removed the pain. She would never have relished memory of what was. She would have become nostalgic only for what might have been. Somehow, her seashells and stamps and English rocks must have helped her remake a painful past into a better place.

Frankie suffered at the hand of a cruel, unloving mother. My experience growing up—her mothering of me—barely compares. Frankie was a model mom and saint compared to Bah. But I'm nostalgic, too, for what might have been.

Collecting is about memories because memories are nothing else but an accumulation of life experiences amounting to a big collection of things seen, heard, touched, smelled, tasted, and learned. Everyone collects memories, like it or not. It goes hand in hand with living. You can't escape it. In turn, it's generally accepted that a life's worth can be calculated by tallying up the depth of experience and richness of accomplishments—the totality of what amounts to collective remembrance.

Collecting is about memories, too, because memories are subject to loss. Experience is subject to forgetting. It's a built-in problem. Alzheimer's disease, dementia, and ordinary aging take a toll on memories. So do drugs and alcohol. So do brainwashing, torture, political propaganda, social pressure, practical expediency, egotism, false flattery, and, ultimately, death. And so does childhood injury. I've forgotten everything immediately following the moment that Attleboro horse latched on to my head. Trauma will do that. So will simple unhappiness.

Objects aren't as vulnerable to loss as memories. That's why so many people collect souvenirs. And why so many children, afraid they're losing their parents those first days they're aware of being put down in the crib and left alone, grasp to them objects that stay close, like stuffed animals or security blankets. And it's why so many people with lost childhoods become collectors. Nobody wants to lose things. Especially important things. And what's more important than a childhood?

Since finding the box of English rocks, I've been struggling to remember my childhood. It only took fifty-plus years to get around to it. That's not so bad. Some people never get around to it.

Sometimes you need objects to stimulate memory, and Frankie's rocks have been that for me. They are guides. They are tools. Traveling around England, I won't just be returning rocks. I'll be re-collecting my mother. Re-collecting: collecting again, rediscovering, ordering, valuing, holding close to me a second time now a woman I once adored, never physically held close, and have now lost.

Collecting is about memories, finally, because collecting is about re-collecting.

Remembering.

What shocks me more than anything, as I've gotten into this, is how amazingly little I remember.

saturday, march 29

The clocks get adjusted for Daylight Savings Time tonight. Spring ahead. Fall behind. It's spring. I'm to go an hour ahead tomorrow.

Like Mother's Day, the date here is different from America, which adjusts clocks April 6. I fly back to the States April 2. So tomorrow I spring ahead one hour here in Somerset, and a week later I spring ahead another hour at home on Cape Cod. How does that work? It's one of those time-space things, which can leave you scratching your head. How come I lose two hours in this clock-turning thing while folks on either side of the Atlantic who simply stayed put lose only one hour? It seems weird.

Which is fitting, I suppose, because in Glastonbury, as I've said, weirdness is the way of life.

At breakfast in Hillclose B&B I tell my host, Penny Riddle, why I've come to Glastonbury. A small, prim, middle-aged woman with a friendly, round face, she just nods. Penny sees all types. Every sort of seeker, Sufi, supernatural believer, channeler, chanter, born again, and mystic. She's put up daydreamers and night crawlers, veggies and druggies, longhairs and skinheads. She's had guests carrying guns and guests carrying considerable loads of emotional luggage. They've come in sandals and high heels, in Mercedeses and on motorcycles, alone and in jingle-jangle bands. To Penny Riddle, a son returning his mum's rocks is close to boring.

"Leave not one stone on the other," Henry VIII is supposed to have said about Glastonbury Abbey. The order came after that infamous 1534 Act of Supremacy, which led to the rather self-centered king's systematic demolishing of abbeys around the country. As at Tintern Abbey, Glastonbury was mostly knocked down by 1539. Much of its stone, it's said, was used to build the road to Wells, about five miles northeast up today's A39.

"It's mostly been taken away. But I've got a piece in my garden," says Penny Riddle. She shows me. It's a piece of old stone gutter that once diverted rain off one of the abbey's roofs. Now it carries a little rivulet of water which bubbles up from her garden fountain.

At least Penny's piece has been put to good use, I think. Not like Frankie's. Which is why I've brought it back, I guess.

Glastonbury is situated on the Isle of Avalon, so called. It's not an island now. It's about 15 miles inland from the Bristol Channel. Yet this wasn't always so. Avalon is on high ground that juts from the eastern shoreline into the Somerset Levels, which was once a marshy, watery place. Neolithic marsh villages have been found all over the Levels. Romans and later peoples drained the area, but not before earlier people had made the unusual Isle of Avalon setting a special, sacred site.

Central to this sacredness is the odd peak that dominates Glastonbury, a

518-foot-tall pinnacle called the Tor. The Tor is tied to a slew of legends. It guards a gateway to the underworld. Fairy folk are said to live on the peak. Adjacent freshwater springs by its base flow white and red, it's said. Excavations do show that a warrior chief during the Dark Ages perched his aerie fortress on its top.

It is a natural formation, composed of horizontal bands of clays and limestone, with a cap of hard sandstone. The most mysterious thing of all about the Tor is signs of spiral-ring terracing around its sides, as if at some ancient time unknown worshipers used it as a ceremonial circular walkway or three-dimensional labyrinth. The neolithic peoples of ancient Britain certainly made their share of mysterious circles, so add the pathway circles on the Tor's slope to the mix.

But Glastonbury/Avalon is better known for its straight lines. Ley lines, to be precise. Glastonbury, I come to learn, is a sort of Grand Central Station for ley lines.

I knew nothing at all about ley lines. To find out what they are, I turned to the Web, and found a site headlined "Attune to Leylines." The subhead was "tuning into our mother." I don't know about their mother. But I was certainly trying to tune in to my mother, so I paid attention.

Ley lines were discovered in 1921, they say—they being the folks tuned in to their mothers, I guess. It was found (discovered?) that a series of straight lines (or, more precisely, curved lines going in one direction over the spherical globe) linked a great number of earthly landmarks into a network of ancient tracks. Landmarks were often hilltops, used by travelers as reference points on the tracks. This goes back to prehistoric peoples, according to those attuned. The best example is probably the Aborigines of Australia, one living culture that to this day believes in invisible energy lines on the landscape. Their ancestors walked the land in lines, they believe, and sang the world into existence. Landscape features, even rocks, supposedly contain this energy, and their existence is defined by song lines.

What ley lines consist of depends on whom you talk to. They are full of powerful energy, there's agreement on that. Maybe it's cosmic energy, or energy laid on the land by aliens from outer space, or electromagnetic energy, but in all cases it's spiritually enlightening energy. And it gets compounded at intersections where two or more ley lines intersect. These junctions become really cool places. They're energy vortices, sacred sites that can cause people to do things like, well, walk barefoot in an English city in March.

Glastonbury has figured prominently in all this since at least mid-twentieth century, when a researcher found what he believed was a remarkable alignment of a group of ancient sites in southern England. A straight line could be drawn through them, starting at St. Michael's Mount off the coast of Cornwall and running northeast through Brentor, Hurlers Stone Circles, Burrowbridge Mump, Glastonbury Tor, and finally Avebury's Stone Circles. Subsequently, Glastonbury was calculated to be a major intersection of other, albeit shorter, ley line site alignments heading in other directions. Alignment, remember, is crucial to the ancient peoples of Britain; Stonehenge, Avebury, and the other stone circles were alignment devices, it's thought. So the revelation of multiple spiritual sites aligned through the Isle of Avalon crossroads has intrigued folks ever since.

Things got even more interesting in recent years. A British scientist, Terry Walsh, used computers to discover that ley lines through Glastonbury and extended over the planet Earth pass through a stunning number of widely recognized sacred sites around the world. The great circle lines passing through these sites in many cases were four-site alignments with Glastonbury. Walsh also noticed that the alignment lines through Glastonbury were at regular angles of either sixty degrees, in one case, or in another case of four sets at twenty degrees, with four thirty-degree angles between them. In turn, the lines could be shown to create hexagonal and octagonal patterns, which have considerable significance in ancient beliefs.

Now, to this purely paranormal paradigm, add organized religion. Glastonbury lays a very large claim—not in the least substantiated, incidentally—to be the earliest Christian building spot outside Palestine. Joseph of Arimathea journeyed here from Palestine, according to the story, carrying two cruets and the Holy Grail. Traveling with him was a nephew, Jesus. Joseph caused all kinds of miracles on the Isle of Avalon, the story goes, and thus was Christianity given its initial public relations boost and, subsequently, its first extended roots into this new land.

Finally, last but not least, the Arthurian legend is firmly rooted here. In the mid-twelfth century a monk named Caradoc wrote an extensive description of a sixth-century power struggle after the Romans departed and Saxons and

Britons were left to slug it out. Glastonbury Tor and nearby Cadbury were on the front line of confrontations. Caradoc wrote that the heretofore unknown Arthur united the Britons and raised an army in Devon and Cornwall to march on Avalon. He besieged Melwas, a local Saxon king, at his stronghold on the top of the Tor. Romance being what it is, he was also trying to rescue the lovely hostage Guinevere. Or so it goes. Dates for this are given as between A.D. 450 and 540. The struggle culminated, according to legend, with a great military victory by Arthur over the Saxons at a place called Mount Badon, which was probably near Bath.

If in the prime of life King Arthur was running his Knights of the Round Table—and their all-important quest for the Holy Grail—out of Camelot (Cadbury), it was in the moments of death he turned to Avalon (Glastonbury). With all those ley lines coursing through the place, is it any wonder? After receiving a mortal wound in battle, he turned himself into a Christ figure—and perpetuated his larger-than-life status and real-life ideals—by ordering that he be taken to Avalon, where he told his followers he would be brought back to life.

After learning all this, I find I'm more than a little anxious as I pass through the Glastonbury Abbey entrance gate with Frankie's stolen stone in my pocket. Glastonbury, I can't help thinking, is no place to mess with stones.

There is no official at the abbey office to talk with me. Everyone is on vacation. It had been helpful at past sites to show my rock to someone, and conjecture together where it might have come from. That won't happen here. I am once again on my own.

Although she never knew it, Frankie's Glastonbury rock was a "figured stone." Prior to the eighteenth century, that was the English term given to stones containing fossils. This was before Darwin. The word "fossil" then meant something else. The notion of once living things, now extinct, preserved over eons didn't fit with the churchly creed of creationism. So anything that looked like a plant or shell on a rock, it was decided, was just an imaginative, playful God exhibiting His ability to make fake rock "figures" of living things.

Frankie's piece of Cadbury had a single scallop shell in its side, so it was a figured stone, too. Under a magnifying glass, the Glastonbury Abbey rock revealed it is full of crinoids. These were tiny, doughnut-shaped creatures that

attached to the seafloor and radiated feathery, lilylike arms into the water column. Frankie would never have noticed the crinoids with the naked eye, and
she wasn't interested anyway in the geology of the rocks she took. It was only
their magic that mattered. She wouldn't have known, or much cared, that the
two-inch-long, charcoal-gray, triangular rock was fine-grained limestone, and
that the white band slanting through its inch-thick side was a fracture, long
since healed with a calcite filling.

As I wander around, I truly do sense my mother's presence here. Must be
those ley lines tuning me in.

At Tintern Abbey, it was the main body of the church that was left in best
shape after Henry VIII's henchmen and hammers were done and gone. The
outbuildings are mostly preserved only in outline. At Glastonbury, only the
abbot's kitchen outbuilding and the Lady Chapel are substantially standing.

Little of the abbey's once majestic, steepled choir is still standing. Its ceiling is sky, its floor grass. There, marked on the ground, I find King
Arthur's grave.

When I planned this trip, and even as I began my swing through Cornwall
and Somerset, returning rocks to Tintagel, Cadbury, and Glastonbury, I was
unaware that in revisiting these three of Frankie's chosen sites I would be re-
tracing Arthur's life journey, from birth to heroic maturity to death. The fact
that Frankie took rocks from all three simply can't be a coincidence, I think.
She had a piece of Tintern Abbey, so a piece of Glastonbury Abbey would fit
nicely alongside it in the abbey category. But I'm betting this was the farthest
thing from her mind. I think she took a piece of this place because she suddenly discovered, as I have, that she had come to King Arthur's final resting
place. I'm guessing it wasn't until she stood precisely here where I'm now
standing, reading the placard I'm now reading, that she got the urge to take a
Glastonbury rock.

The placard on the choir floor says "Site of King Arthur's Tomb. In the year
1191 the bodies of King Arthur and his queen were said to have been found
on the south side of the Lady Chapel. On 19 April 1278 their remains were removed in the presence of King Edward I and Queen Eleanor to a black marble tomb on this site. This tomb survived until the dissolution of the Abbey
in 1539."

What was once, apparently, a splendid shrine in the center of the choir is nothing more now than an outline in concrete markers. The base of the shrine was rediscovered in 1934. It's unknown where the couple's bones went after Henry VIII's demolition squads left town. It is known where one of the abbey's stones went, though. At least I know. It went home to London with my mother, and later home to America. Gazing at this unimposing grass-topped grave, I'm feeling almost certain that Frankie here was giving herself a rock-solid connection to Arthurian legend, a tangible fragment of Avalon to go along with Camelot and Tintagel.

I leave the grave and walk idly through the grounds for a while. At the low stone outline of the refectory on the lawn, I stop and sit on a bench. Frankie's stone is in my hand and it's having a powerful effect on me. The sun warms my face, and I feel tears welling, and evaporating. I'm tempted to take Tony's advice and take this rock back home. Its replacement value to this ruined site is nil. It does have more value to me, as a memento. Memory often needs a trigger, and just as this rock may have held some of that for Frankie, some trigger for some lonely need, it could prove just as useful to me, later on in life, when I'm old and gray, and this trip and this abbey are years in the past and are only fading memories.

But no, I'm taking none of Frankie's rocks home again. I've come a long way to bring them back. I'm going to put them back. All of them. They complete a circle journey here, now, and it would be a mistake to take any home. This one goes back into Glastonbury Abbey's stoneworks a different rock from the one that came out. Then it was nondescript. Now it has Frankie's imprint all over it. In actual print, by her hand. But more significantly, in its chosen singularity, selective spirit, and long journey away and back. It's different, and yet it's not exceptional, and it won't be an exception for me in dispersing her collection.

I've chosen a spot. The inside wall of the Lady Chapel. At first, I think I ought to bury the rock next to Arthur and Guinevere's grave. But it certainly wasn't taken from there. And, I remember, the placard said the couple's original burying place was on the south side of the Lady Chapel. There's a notch in the south wall of the Chapel, about nine feet off the ground. The hole is diagonally up from an attached half-column, broken off at about eight feet. Perhaps an arch or vault was once attached here. The stone in the wall and the stone I'm carrying are very similar. The notch is about the right shape, triangular, and a couple of inches deep. On my toes and with my arm extended, I can reach it. That high up, it will be beyond the scrutinizing eyes or probing hands of any other visitors who might be tempted to take a piece of the abbey. It will rest close to the legendary king and queen's first resting place. Frankie would like that.

The chapel is quiet now, roofless, in ruins, in sunshine. Even now, stone and mortar are shedding from the wall. Pieces could be picked up from the ground, though none as large as Frankie's. I have to wait about ten minutes for a moment when no other tourists are in sight. When the moment comes, I don't hesitate. I stretch up and shove the rock into the notch. It fits snugly. I step back. An Asian couple has come into the chapel. I pretend to admire the column. The Asian man poses the Asian woman in front of the altar and takes her picture. I take a picture of Frankie's rock above the column.

They smile at me as they leave. I smile at them, and then look one final time at Frankie's piece of Avalon nesting now in the Lady Chapel. I smile again. Then I leave.

All this the way it ought to be. Taking only pictures, leaving only footprints, and rocks that rightfully belong here.

As I walk back to Hillclose B&B following a nightly pint at the King Arthur pub, a young man maybe twenty years old comes out of nowhere in the dark, and stops me on the street. I'm ready to run, but he has a beatific smile and a gentle face, and is about six inches shorter than me. He has close, dreadlocked hair and a blond beard.

What a lovely night, he says. Am I enjoying my stay, he asks.

I presume he's gay and is trying to pick me up. Though I'm old enough to be his father. Maybe he likes older men.

Yes, it's a lovely night, I say, and I walk on, but he walks with me.

He's quiet for a while. Then he says, "I have something for you," and without any prompting or preliminaries or any reason I've given him, he hands me a smooth, amber stone. It looks a little like glass, a little like an opaque gemstone. He calls it a runic.

We're on Street Road now, across the street from my B&B. He wants me to have it, the young man says, "because you're the stone man."

I didn't tell him I'm the stone man. I didn't tell him I'm in England returning stones. I didn't tell him anything. He looks more like the stone man, or at least like a stoned man. His eyes aren't exactly those of a commodities trader, and he's acting pretty dreamy. I refuse to look at his feet, afraid I'll see little cloven hooves. Or pink slippers shedding twinkling dust.

I try to think whether I saw him earlier in the pub, where he might have overheard me talking to someone. I'm almost certain he couldn't have been there. He would have stood out like a piece of asteriated rose quartz on a pile of iron ore in the places I've been drinking.

Then he says this, and I'm not making this up: "When your son brings it back, tell him to place it at the exact center of the tower on the Tor. For the next person."

And then he walks away.

His path, I presume, takes him precisely along a ley line.

I'm ready to leave Glastonbury. It's not my kind of town. I once lived with a ghost named Winifred in an 1880s mansion in Cotuit on Cape Cod. But that was back in the early 1970s. My life since has been pretty removed from the occult and supernatural. About the most mystical thing that happens to me is going six for six at the plate in softball when I've entered some sort of transcendent hitter's zone. I am ready by breakfast to leave the town behind.

But Glastonbury isn't quite done with me.

Two other couples had booked into Hillclose B&B while I was out at the King Arthur pub. My first glimpse of them is at our communal breakfast. They've all gotten to the table before me.

I see Penny Riddle's face first, as I round the corner into the dining room. It shows carefully controlled, mischievous glee beaming from her round head, which floats Cheshire Cat–like from above a matronly, flowered apron. I say good morning to a very young, very conventional English couple. They've just become engaged and will be marrying in the fall. On each of their faces I see a frozen half-smile, just barely masking profound mortification.

As I turn to greet the other couple, Penny, her voice oozing depraved delight, says, "We have a couple of your compatriots with us here this morning." And then I see the pair from Houston.

The plain, quite ordinary woman in her forties would have been entirely unmemorable, except that she is sitting next to a person she repeatedly refers to as her father. Yet this individual has fluffy hair hanging below his shoulders, is wearing a yellow dress, nylon stockings, gaudy earrings, and bright lipstick, and looks to be about the same age as his "daughter." The dark shadow on this Texan's cheeks and the husky baritone of his voice suggest male hormones are quite in abundance. Yet his outfit, inflections, and swooshy mannerisms (including, I'm afraid, enormous enthusiasm for my mission on behalf of my mother) make for a cross-gender mind-bender, which is a little unnerving at 7:30 in the morning with porridge, bacon, and beans.

I'm not sure the English couple take more than a few bites of breakfast before fleeing.

The Texans leave before me, to go walking in the Cotswolds.

When, finally, I've loaded the Renault and paid my bill, and am about to leave, I playfully scold Penny Riddle for subjecting the innocent young English couple to such an indigestion-inspiring wake-up call. "Have you no standards?" I demand.

She laughs. "They were your countrymen," she says.

"Countrypersons," I correct her. "And they're not mine. They're from Texas. I'm from Massachusetts. Different countries."

"I told you we get all sorts, here in Glastonbury. Now you see for yourself. You can put it in your book."

I'd been thinking about this. I'd decided Penny Riddle has a book to write herself. As I pick up my bags and get ready to leave, I tell her my idea. "You know, you should write a book."

"I could, you know."

"I know you could," I say. "All you have to do is take notes. The stories come to you. I'm not sure if it's humor you'll be writing, or horror. But they'll be good stories, either way. You should try your hand at it."

"I've even got a title for you," I say. "Bob Dylan has this song called 'Sad-Eyed Lady of the Lowlands.' You could call your book 'B&B Lady on the Ley Line.'"

16.

dreaming, longing for a mother

Avebury

I remember I had a dream when I was a kid. At least I think it was a dream. Maybe it was a daydream.

I was ten or eleven years old. Whether it came while I was sleeping, or while I was awake, it doesn't matter, I guess. Because it entered my head somehow, that I know, back forty-five years ago or so, and I know for certain that it stuck around for several years after it came to me. I thought about the dream long after, into my teen years. I played with the dream in my head, turning it around, trying out variations, evaluating evidence against it to judge its veracity. I don't think I ever really believed it. I'm sure I didn't. But I'm not sure I ever felt it was completely out of the question either.

The dream went like this:

I'm at our home in Chevy Chase, Maryland. It's evening. My father and mother are in the living room, reading, my dad in his chair, my mom on the couch. I'm sitting on the stairs in my pajamas, halfway upstairs, my knees nearly to my chin, looking down through the balusters at my parents. I'm alone, even though they're sitting there. And then I know—in that way in dreams things become suddenly known without reason—that the two people sitting in the living room are not really my parents.

I understand who they are. They are employees. They have been hired by my real parents to raise me. The reason for this is that my real parents are outrageously rich. They live in a huge mansion on an immense estate, I'm not sure where. The reason my real parents have hired these other two people to bring me up is that they believe it will keep me from becoming spoiled and a snob. They think it will instill better values in me to grow up with these middle-class people, a civil service engineer working for the navy and a nurse, in this modest house on this ordinary street.

My real parents haven't farmed out all their children. I have lavishly dressed brothers and sisters living happily in the mansion, surrounded by tons of neat, expensive toys and stuff. I've been singled out, shipped off, and cut off from my true family because it was felt I couldn't handle the wealth.

Finally, in the dream I know that at some point, when I'm older and judged to be well adjusted, there will be this big, lavish party at which it's revealed to me that my surrogate parents are only stand-ins, and my birth parents step forward, I become acquainted with my well-off siblings, and I accept a fat and juicy bank account that's been waiting for this day.

Looking down at Mr. and Mrs. Hornig in the dream, I'm angry. And lonely.

The dream became a floating scenario in my awake state, as I said. I toyed with it in my mind for years afterward. I didn't think it was true, the dream. But it was an intriguing notion I enjoyed contemplating.

I never thought much about it later, as life moved on. I never thought very deeply about where it came from, what it meant. I just shrugged it off when I got older. I decided it was nothing more than wishful thinking. Dream on, Dana, dream on that you're a billionaire's son and, despite all appearances, you're going to inherit a life of ease and luxury. I wanted a Ferrari. I knew by temperament I leaned toward the lazy. And I needed only to look at Frankie's Brain Book to realize that it didn't look as if I was going to become a billionaire based on my own brilliance. The dream, I guess, didn't surprise me. I had a longing for riches. Who didn't?

Finding Frankie's secret box of rocks sent me searching for childhood memories, and I've been frustrated that I seem to have so few. That comment by a psychotherapist, about if I don't remember being kissed then I wasn't kissed, got me thinking that if I don't remember times with my mother, episodes or events, meaningful interactions, maybe it's because there weren't any. I refuse to believe it. We had a home, I was cared for, the family did things. But where are the memories?

Since finding the stones, the memory of this parents-for-hire dream, and of the weird sort of daydream life of its own that it took on, came back to me. I remember dreams of falling, and dreams of losing all my teeth. These were recurring dreams. Yet they're common dreams. Lots of people have them. They're standard in books of dream interpretation. The dream of looking down on hired parents, though, is out of the ordinary. And it's the only childhood dream that was so set in my memory that I can see it and relate it in detail to this day.

The box of rocks brought it back. Thinking about it now, I realize the dream was never about longing for riches. It was about longing for parents.

I don't feel abused. That's not my history, and I would never suggest it was. I don't feel sorry for myself. I don't feel my family was dysfunctional. I mean, relatively speaking. It can get bad out there, I'm fully aware of that. It can be really, really ugly. Acute alcoholism, sexual depravity, physical violence—some youngsters in some families have it truly bad. Nothing like these things crept into my childhood. I was never a child surviving in the line of fire. My home was generally quiet, orderly, provisioned, conventional, safe. My parents were hardworking, responsible, thoughtful, practical, smart. They cared for their two boys, Doug and me, and did well by us.

But everything is relative. My father's father died in the great flu pandemic of 1918, one of an estimated forty million people who died worldwide. My dad was just four years old. His widowed mother, Ethel, was left alone to raise her two boys and make ends meet. The only male father figure figuring into their lives was an uncle, Byron. There were lots of other women; Ethel had five sisters, and to varying degrees all but one were an influential presence in my father's early years.

So my dad became a dad without any dad role model in his own life. He had to wing it. He did an admirable job for someone with relatively little to look back upon and imitate or emulate.

For her part, Frankie became a mother after growing up without a mother.

Not literally, I know. Berthe was always around. But Frankie grew up without experiencing the kind of loving, affectionate, nurturing influences most people associate with devoted mothering. Understandably, Frankie was relatively inept at mirroring mothering when the role devolved to her.

For two adults without same-sex models of their own, Frankie and Doug did pretty damn well, I'd say. Relatively speaking.

For most of my adult life, I considered my relationship with my father to be the more sterile, disconnected. I was always a little scared of him. He was a New Englander with a conservative, stern demeanor deep down to his Puritan roots. He was the disciplinarian in the household, and the ultimate authority. He didn't show his love openly in hugs or kisses or words. He worked long hours, and was physically absent from a lot of family life—off doing jobs, or searching for better jobs, or away in advance of the rest of us prior to resettling the family somewhere else after taking a new job. We lived in six different places by the time I entered third grade.

But in remembering my childhood, I've found no shortage of memories of doing meaningful things with my father. He built me a wooden basketball backboard at the edge of our driveway. I remember the whole project. He built me a go-cart with a salvaged Briggs & Stratton lawn-mower engine and a legless aluminum lawn chair for a seat. I remember working with him for months on the project in our basement, excited all the way. He took me out to shopping center parking lots on Sundays to drive the go-cart. Later, he helped me buy a tubular-steel, factory-made go-cart, and I got into competitive racing. My dad loaded the cart into the back of our car weekend after weekend, and drove me all over Maryland for races. I won six trophies in my short carting career. I remember my dad being proud.

He took me camping in the Appalachians. He bought my brother and me a chemistry set and built us a little laboratory room in the basement. He helped me find my first newspaper job and encouraged me to pursue a journalism career. Even the bad memories I have of my father are memories of things being done out of caring for me, viewed from his perspective.

In retrospect, it all looks like caring about me. There was clear connection. If there had been a corresponding amount of connection to my mother, I wonder if I'd ever have dreamed about my parents being employees.

I just don't remember Frankie relating to me much. She took me to the beach quite a bit, summers on Cape Cod. I remember that. She liked to go to the Little Side at Dowses Beach in Osterville, the protected side of the sandy peninsula along East Bay, opposite the larger, more crowded expanse on Nantucket Sound. There were no waves on the Little Side, and the water was shallow, so it was better for little kids. But when I reflect now about Frankie and the Little Side and priorities, the picture I get is of a stimulating stage for her, not a safe bathing area for me. Other mothers, her friends, went there, including her best friend June Curtis. A wrinkled village character and self-appointed mayor of the beach known as Fiskie held court there for all the gathered young mothers. For these women there was more apparent nourishment from the healthy servings of gossip than from all the peanut butter and jelly sandwiches combined. The children could splash around and torment fiddler crabs, eat sand, and collect shells, but more important for Frankie, I think, was that afternoons on the Little Side were times to connect to her friends. In other words, she didn't go there for me. She went there for herself.

It's so hard to know whether this is fair, saying these things. She's entitled to socialize with friends at the beach. I think she kept an eye on me to make sure I didn't drown. She brought PB&Js and root beers and gave me a quarter when the Good Humor truck rang its bell in the Dowses parking lot. But I just don't remember my mother doing things with me. Expressly for and with me. I don't remember her giving me her undivided attention, sitting me down in front of her, staring me in the eyes and saying, "Hey, Nane, I love you. What do you want? What do you need? What's going on inside that freckle-faced, blond-haired head of yours?"

Frankie was emotional. Frankie was frantic, energetic, talkative, scattered, passionate about what she became involved in, or in her causes of the moment. When I was a little kid, I was shy and always kept a safe distance. I didn't engage her and she didn't engage me. But by the time I was in my teens, I would tease her, argue with her, toss outrageous opinions at her. I'd challenge her in ways I never dared use to confront my father. She'd argue right back. She liked the discourse, the banter, the communication. She was opinionated, and liked people to listen to her opinions. I'm not sure that happened a lot when she was a girl.

Because of these talks in my teen years, I came to think of my temperament as much closer to Frankie's than to my father's, and I felt our spirited arguments were evidence of a genuine closeness. I see it differently today. I remember, now, that our lively back-and-forths always happened while Frankie was doing something else—cooking or cleaning, organizing a collection or preparing an exhibit, putting things away or taking things out, writing things down or searching through some publication for something. This wasn't because Frankie was ahead of her time in the modern art of multitasking. It was because Frankie couldn't relate to me, one on one, with direct, undivided attention. I'm not sure she could do that with anyone. She didn't know how.

She needed distractions. She needed to be busy, perpetually busy. She needed things, objects, props—things to prioritize, organize, things hard and fast to physically hold on to. She was uncomfortable directing all her attention onto someone else, and having that person focus solely upon her. Originally I saw this as just part of her hyperkinetic personality. But now I'm convinced Frankie needed routine, mundane activity to run in parallel with times in which my presence took us probing toward personal intimacy. She needed a place to escape to, I guess, if getting too close or becoming too connected raised too much anxiety in her about giving, or receiving, love, raised too much risk of rejection, or generated too much fear of pain.

It isn't supposed to be like that, is it? It's the growing, fragile child who's supposed to struggle with questions of inadequacy, popularity, self-worth. The parent is supposed to provide the safe sounding board and the private intimacy to see a kid through her or his natural insecurities. It's children who are supposed to fidget and play with pencils or roll toy trucks along the broad arm of the sofa, or make believe they're absorbed in some other activity, one foot firmly down in some other place, when sharing intimate time with parents. In childhood, I certainly did my share of fidgeting and playacting at being otherwise occupied while waiting, hoping for intimacy with my mom.

The hope drifted into my adult years. I wasn't especially aware of it, until now. I think I long resented the sense I had that Frankie didn't care much about who I was, what I did, and what I became. She never let on that she cared, at least. And now I wonder. Another box of stuff I found while sorting through Frankie's collections long after her death was a box full of my newspaper clippings. It was the sifting through that box that got me wondering.

I became editor of that Cape Cod newspaper, *The Register,* when I was twenty-eight. I was a young man, and hardly seasoned or secure in my journalistic work. Over the following eighteen years I wrote countless stories and editorials, and each week an irreverent, freewheeling column called "Sensibility Gap." I saved everything at first, assuming that later in life I'd want a complete record of all my brilliant work. As the years passed and those weekly deadlines rolled relentlessly by, and articles, editorials, and column after column were cranked out, I began to think there would never be an end. I figured I'd be writing the "Gap" and community commentary to the end of my days. For this reason, I think, saving my writing eventually became a sporadic discipline. When I finally left the paper in 1990 I realized there were big gaps in the "Gaps" I'd saved.

But Frankie, I found out in this discovered box, had saved virtually everything I wrote. Everything up to the spring of her death in '83. The Brain Book lived! With a week's worth of clippings going into the box for years, suddenly Dana's collected brainy mementos had swollen out of all comparison with brother Doug's.

When I found the box, I felt a swell of pride. I never even knew Frankie read my columns and articles. She never, ever, that I remember, congratulated me on any or spoke of my writing to other people in front of me. Yet here they were, all carefully clipped and piled high in a cardboard carton, sometimes marginally notated in ballpoint pen in Frankie's hand with comments like "good," or "well written." Some said "letter on back" to indicate that on the flip side of the clip with my column was a Letter to the Editor from someone commenting on a previous column of mine. And all other letters to the editor mentioning me were clipped and saved too, along with bylined stories and bylined photos. It was all there.

I'd long ago stopped saving everything. But Frankie hadn't. And she hadn't told me.

She hadn't held me much as a child, rarely kissed me, and never let on that she cared much about what I did. I never heard praise from Frankie. But here, unknown to me, she had collected the complete newspapering works of Dana Hornig. Was it out of obligation? Or out of neurotic obsession with collecting anything related to our family?

Or out of pride?

And if it was out of love and pride, if it was out of caring about me, why couldn't she tell me, show me, share those feelings with me? I needed that attention, that love. I yearned to hear it from her.

Frankie wasn't able to do that for me. She couldn't. Frankie became a mom without a mom ever being that for her.

sunday, march 30

It's Mother's Day in England. They call it Mothering Day. And Mother Earth is shining on all of us again, this day. The sky is radiant blue, cloudless; the sun beats down, and the temperature is very mild. All along my 40-mile drive northeast toward Avebury, I see families responding to the unseasonable warmth—out walking, biking, picnicking, or lined up in front of restaurants waiting to be seated for Mothering Day brunches.

Avebury is mobbed when I finally get there. It seems like the height of summer tourist season. But it's a spring Sunday, Mothering Day, and beautiful weather conspiring to make for perfect family outings. Children are kicking soccer balls. Where neolithic worshipers once held mysterious ceremonies, dads and mums and kids and grandparents are lounging on blankets spread on the grass. A few people are using standing stones as backrests as they munch on crisps or read books.

I stop in at the National Trust office. I'm scheduled to meet Melissa Viney here, tomorrow, now that I'm at the end of my journey. She's the radio freelancer I met in Worth Matravers while returning a rock to Corfe Castle way back at the beginning of this trip. We've kept in contact by e-mail over the past three weeks and she'll be coming out from London to tape an interview. She's been commissioned to do a piece for a show on BBC Radio 4 called *Women's Hour*. We're due to meet at the office of Avebury's site manager, Rob Mimmack. So I decide to say hello to him today, and perhaps talk to him now in case Melissa's efforts tomorrow take up all my time.

Mimmack isn't in on Sundays. But the visitors' services manager, a young man named Richard Henderson, is there. He greets me, and as I introduce myself, he interrupts. "Oh, you're the American returning your mum's rocks. I've been expecting you. You met my colleague, James Parsons, down at Corfe. He asked if you'd been by me yet."

"Word gets around in world heritage circles, eh?" I say.

"I saw James at a National Trust conference we both attended recently," he explains. "Welcome to Avebury. Can I see the rock?" He seems enthusiastic.

"Well, they aren't much," I say, pulling them out. "I've got two." Like the pebbles from Stonehenge, the two pieces my mother removed and marked *Avebury 4000 BC* are small, white, and very unlikely to have actually come off one of the monoliths. Just as on the first stop in my journey, here at my last stop I'm convinced the rocks themselves aren't very interesting.

Each piece is about an inch long. The larger of the two is also about an inch wide, about ¼-inch thick, snow-white, and flecked with yellow. It is chalk. The other piece is only ⅟₁₆-inch thick, slender, and broken on one end, revealing a dark flint core. It is chert. None of Avebury's standing stone is chalk or chert.

Richard Henderson concurs. These aren't pieces of the famous arranged rocks. Avebury's stones are hard sandstone, brought here from nearby Marlborough Downs. There is, however, plenty of both chalk and chert at the site. It was loosened from the ground with red deer antler picks and piled seventeen feet high when the huge circular earthwork was dug here between 2600 and 2100 B.C. The 1,300-foot-diameter earthen bank is the outermost circle at Avebury. Just inside it is a deep ditch, retained by a rough wall of chalk blocks. Inside that is the thousand-foot-diameter Great Circle of ninety-eight standing stones, some as tall as sixteen feet and weighing as much as twenty tons. And inside this are two smaller central and south circles of twenty-seven and twenty-nine stones. It's suspected there may have also once been a small north circle.

After leaving Richard, I walk among the stones, and confirm for myself that Frankie's rocks don't match. The standing stones are quite smooth; millions of tourists have had ample opportunity to pry apart any weak cracks. It seems as if many visitors' hands have stroked the rocks in places, giving them an unnatural smooth shine. Where the grass is worn away at the foot of stones, I find bits of chalk and flint. Frankie probably picked up her pieces from one of these bare spots.

It seems like a lousy place to return them, though.

Despite the crowd at Avebury today, I'm swept with loneliness. I'm surrounded by families with mothers. On this Mothering Day I'm concluding a string of stops connecting me to my mother. It's fitting, I suppose, that this last stop comes on a day devoted to mothers. But it's not especially satisfying. When the last rock is returned here, will this rocky connection end? I feel lonely.

And now I feel the need to be alone.

Across the A361 from Avebury's car park is a path that follows a small stream and leads to Silbury Hill, the largest artificial mound in Europe. It's a stunning sight, a 130-foot-high, conical hill covering a 5½-acre base and surrounded by a lakelike moat of standing water. It's unknown what the hill was ever used for. Shafts sunk into the mound at different recent times have found nothing inside.

Despite the crowd lounging around Avebury, I see the path to Silbury Hill is empty. I strike off, and spend the next hour alone.

As I walk, I notice a moving shadow to my left, and stop and stare at my own shadow, sunglasses, baseball cap, and my family's distinctive nose clear in three-quarter profile, projected on this bit of Salisbury Plain by the late-afternoon sun. A newly planted, furrowed field slopes up a gentle rise behind my shadow to the east. The creek gurgles on the other side of me. It sounds sad. Staring at my dark silhouette, I see a lonely man, concluding this strange pilgrimage, now on the edge of an empty plain echoing with the ghosts of mysterious people, long, long gone. No more gone than Frankie. Just gone longer.

Gone longer where? Wherever. I don't believe in heaven. Neither did Frankie. But I think she believed dead people's spirits go reside somewhere. Her hoarding of rocks was an attempt to gather those spirits of the lost around herself. So whether she'd have admitted it or not, the evidence I've carried back here to England suggests Frankie believed the spirits of deceased reside in rocks. So why not also up there in the pale-blue overhead, or down in the soft earth underfoot? Somewhere, those spirits can be gathered together like stones in a cardboard box, and if you try hard enough, you can converse with them.

As I stare at Silbury Hill, I feel a chill. A wind has come up, and the sun is getting low. The pieces of Avebury are in my pocket. I turn them in my hand. Objects give their collector a sense of permanence in a scary world where mothers can be perpetually mean to sensitive daughters, or beloved fathers can take their own lives. Frankie had rejected the Catholic faith, and rejected its transubstantiation of bread and wine into the body and blood of Christ. She had no use for symbolic Communion either. Yet she embraced the collector's way of life, and its repeated and passionate communing with the mysterious, the magical, the spiritual, the dead. In life, she could hold rocks and feel connection to Roman lighthouse keepers, medieval kings and abbots, or the Beaker people, builders of Avebury's circle behind me and the massive, haunting ceremonial mound in front of me. She could feel connection, yes, and also subconscious assurances there can be life after death.

I turn, zip my wool vest, and begin walking slowly back to the car park. It's ironic, I think. Obsessive collecting so that you can commune with the dead gets in the way of communing with the living. Trying to establish a connection with King Arthur—who, face it, might not have even been real—came at the expense of intimate connection with a very real son. And sons and daughters are a parent's most tangible assurance of life after death. My mother is dead, yet I'm here on the Silbury Hill path, quite alive, dealing with the late-afternoon chill, carrying Frankie's genes and history and influences. And carrying her memory and my love for her. And carrying the last of her rocks.

It's Mothering Day, so I'll keep these last two little rocks until tomorrow. Then I'll give them up. Give up this connection between her and me. It's not the kind I've wanted. It's not enough, for me, to feel close to Frankie through bits of chalk, chert, limestone, or slate. I want more. I always wanted more. But these rocks, in some small way, became pieces in a barricade between my mother and me. I'll feel sad, I'm certain, replacing these last two rocks. Maybe I'll feel more lonely than I feel now. But I don't want the rocks. I want her love and her attention. And for those things, I realize, I'm just going to have to wait until I join her.

That night, following a grand-slam rugby win for England, four inebriated blokes wearing England's colors come into the nearly empty pub in nearby Devizes where I'm having a solitary pint. Despite my repeated objections, and subtle efforts to escape, they buy After Shock shots for me, the bartender, and themselves. After Shock is a sweet, brightly colored, high-octane, inscrutably flavored liqueur that tastes like a mixture of melted lollipops and cheap aftershave lotion and is popular with youthful Brits whose only interest in a pub is in departing pissed.

One of the guys, revealing speech inflections that suggest this is not his first

After Shock shot stop, tells me he has a piece of Pompeii at home. Picked it up in Italy on a trip to watch an international soccer match.

I wonder if he's one of Britain's infamous soccer-fan hooligans. It looks possible. But I don't ask. Instead, I say, "Does it make you feel connected to the ancient Romans?"

"S'wat meck me feel 'nected ta ta Talians?" he asks.

"Your rock. Your piece of Pompeii."

"Naw, mate," he says. "Me only c'nection is me car."

His friend pipes up, "He owns a Fiat, don't he?"

monday, march 31

Avebury this end-of-March, late Monday morning is practically deserted. What a difference a day makes. And completing the record-setting string of days of sunshine for the month, it's yet another cloudless day. Rain might have been a more fitting end, with the melancholy I'm feeling. But in a way, my lonely trip ended yesterday.

Today I'm turning over some of the pacing, serendipity, spontaneity, authenticity—some of the story, really—to someone else. To a BBC reporter. Frankie has been firmly my focus for nearly a month, and I pulled in toward me people from all around the country as I traveled with her rocks and her memory. Today I'll be letting someone pull me into the story's focus. Today will be much more artificial, much more scripted. I know this right from the beginning. But I find the thought doesn't bother me. The trip is over. Returning these two little pieces of chalk, under the watchful microphone of a newsperson, is now little more than a formality.

From her flat on the east side of London, Melissa Viney has traveled three hours by Underground, railroad, and bus to meet me here in Avebury. She's in black pants and black pullover and wearing a green suede coat, and has a scarf of rainbow colors tied around her neck. Two bags with a tape recorder, a microphone, a mike stand, cords, batteries, tapes, and notepads hang from her shoulders.

Although the piece she's doing is for *Women's Hour,* a popular weekday morning show on BBC Radio 4, the mother-son theme fits the format anytime, I suppose. Yet it would have been ideal to have done it in time for Mothering Day. Imagine if it had been known, a month ago, I'd be in Avebury, my last stop, on Mothering Day, leaving the final stone in my journey honoring my mother. That's BBC TV material, I'd think. But I didn't know, nor did anyone else. I made no effort to publicize this journey before embarking on it. No one in England knew I was coming. No site was expecting me. I admire Melissa's instincts. Way back there weeks ago, in Worth Matravers on St. Aldhelm's Head on the Purbeck peninsula, she recognized an odd story when she saw one. She's bird-dogged me by e-mail ever since. And here she is, beaming but nervous, on my final day with Frankie's rocks.

Melissa is sensitive to intruding on what, she understands, is time I'm spending with Frankie. I try to put her at ease. I've weighed that, I tell her. I'm an old newspaper editor. I know that media mars events even as it records them, and that a microphone in my face isn't the most natural way to get in touch with my feelings. But I've decided to return the last rocks with her tape deck running, partly because that's the way it worked out—Melissa came to me, not the other way around—and partly because I've decided getting this small story of my mother's English collection onto a BBC women's show is something Frankie would have found totally exciting.

Melissa crinkles her eyes and smiles. "I wish I could have met her," she says.

I've brought pictures of Frankie with me, and I show them to Melissa: a picture of Frankie from 1961, in her white nurse's uniform; Frankie in dark evening wear inside their London apartment in 1968, standing next to a grandfather clock (that box of rocks, off-camera, swollen somewhere in the apartment by then?); Frankie lying in a fetal position on gravel inside West Kennet Long Barrow, undated, being playful by playing dead; Frankie much later, perhaps around 1980, standing next to one of her life-sized brass rubbings at an exhibition of them at Cape Cod Conservatory of Art; and Frankie posing in front of a huge stone, unidentified and undated. From the looks of it, it's from her time in England. It looks, in fact, like it might be from exactly where we are right now.

Was this last picture taken at Avebury? Call me dense, but not until I pull the picture out and show it to Melissa does it occur to me that it's a picture taken at Avebury—a picture of Frankie in front of one of the big standing stones encircling us today, a picture of her at the scene of the crime.

She's holding a small blue bag. What's in it? The same thing that's now in my pocket, two small rocks?

The first thing I do when Melissa and I get to the administrator's office is pull out the photo of Frankie in front of the big rock. A tall, middle-aged man with a close-cropped beard, Site Manager Rob Mimmack, looks at it.

"Is this one of yours?" I ask.

"Yes, it would be," says Rob. "That's the Devil's Chair. No doubt about that." The stone is at the far southern side of the circle of largest stones, the outer circle. It's a fifty-ton portal stone, placed where one of the four original causeways once entered the great circle complex. There's a small, flat shelf on one side of the rock. Local lore holds that if you sit there, you soon see the devil. The tour guides always relate this story, and usually add, "especially after a long stop at the pub."

"Guess this proves my mother was here," I say. Not that I ever doubted it.

"Must have been in the summer," Melissa says. "She's got on a sleeveless blouse."

"Couldn't be at real summer tourist time," says Rob. "There's nobody else in the picture." He's right. Other stones and a sizable portion of open grass show in the background, and there's not one other person in sight.

"Must have been an early spring day just like today," I say, softly, more to myself than to them.

"Though the trees back here are fuller than today," Rob says, pointing to the treeline at the very rear of the photo. "Must have been April or May."

I ask if anyone has ever brought back a stone before. Rob doesn't know of anyone. "I'm afraid, years ago, the traffic was the other way." At historic sites across the country, he says, there was a time when people guiding trips encouraged tourists to take home rocks as souvenirs.

"We don't do that anymore," he assures me.

Melissa and I walk over to the Devil's Chair. In Frankie's picture, all the ground around the rock is thick grass. Today, millions of visitors later, bare, brown earth surrounds the stone. I notice I could pick up a chalky piece much like the one I'm bringing back. The ground wasn't open to Frankie. Not here, anyway. Somehow, this makes me feel better.

Melissa takes a photo of me standing exactly where Frankie stood over thirty-five years earlier.

Melissa wants to interview me outside, capturing the ambient sounds of the countryside as we talk—sounds of wind, trees rustling, birds chirping, and the occasional bleating of far-off sheep. She doesn't want motor traffic sounds, though, and with the A4361 literally bisecting Avebury's stone circle, this means we need to find a spot off to the far east, upwind side of the circle. I suggest we sit in a grove of trees at the outside bottom of Avebury's encircling earthwork. The high embankment shields us from the roadway and from the center of the tourist flow. We find it is, indeed, very quiet there.

I've made the decision to put Frankie's rocks into the earthwork, which was built by the Beaker people out of chalk rubble excavated from the inside ditch around 2500 B.C. No, Frankie, not 4000 B.C., as you've written on the rocks. Four thousand years ago, very possibly, give or take a few centuries, but not four thousand years before Christ. The earthen circle is composed of chalk. Frankie's two pieces will be in like company there. And they'll return to an actual, and impressive, part of the Avebury monument itself, unobtrusively replaced, and naturally restored. So as we talk, I gaze at the steep bank and think of my mother.

Melissa asks me all the standard questions. What was your relationship like with your mother? Why did your mother collect things? Why did she take these rocks, do you think? Have you come to understand your mother better from taking this trip?

I babble at my interviewer. I'm not sure I'm a good radio interview. They like short answers. I'm used to writing. I drone on. Melissa isn't especially assertive, and she lets me carry on where she probably ought to cut me off, save tape and time, and drive the story in the direction she wants. I suspect she can see that this quiet time in the sun, beside the bank where I'll be leaving my mother's last two rocks, has made me sad, reflective, and emotional. I sense she's afraid to interfere with that. I'm thankful for this, later. She lets me babble.

When I finally come to a stopping place, Melissa is very quiet for a moment.

Then she asks a final question. "Do you think you've become closer to your mother?"

I've asked myself the same thing many, many times over the past month. And I think I am closer. Not close, but closer. A clear answer is what the BBC women's show listenership surely will want to hear. So I say, "Yes, I can say that unequivocally." In fact, I'm less than entirely certain. But I've had strong feelings carrying the rocks, and returning them. I've cried. I am closer to Frankie.

"You've got to remember," I say, "that these rocks, they have my mother in them now. And so for me to part with them, for me to give them up, is a sort of separating from my mother. And yet it's also a connecting with her that didn't happen when I was a child."

The loneliness and sadness in my voice is not an act. Melissa knows it, and knows her audience will hear it. She knows the interview is nearly over.

"Let's go and lay the rocks," she says.

I choose a spot on the slope of Avebury's circular earthwork. I find a small, soft area and with my fingers, burrow about three inches deep into the soil. I brush aside dirt, and then press Frankie's pieces of Avebury chalk and chert into the hole. Before I do, I kiss them both good-bye. Am I doing this for Melissa's radio story? No, it's spontaneous, just as it was when I replaced Stourhead's stone at the Iron Age fort. That was a month ago, quite close to where I am now, just to the southwest of here across this same Salisbury Plain. I'm at an ancient ceremonial circle at the end of a 1,888-mile circumnavigation of Great Britain which began at another stone circle, Stonehenge, even closer to Avebury. I've come full circle, back nearly to where I started.

I feel surprisingly sad, looking at the little rocks lying in the little hole, about to be buried. Frankie's handwriting is staring out at me. It feels a little like I'm burying her. I instantly push that ghoulish thought out of my head. This trip and this ritual itself are quite the opposite. Frankie hasn't had this much attention, this much light shed upon her, this much feeling unearthed about her, since her death twenty years ago. Perhaps even for years before that. At least not by her son. And Frankie basked in attention when she could get it.

I cover the rocks and compress the turf so it's impossible to tell the spot was disturbed. My face feels burned. Too much sun. Imagine that, getting too much sun in England in March.

"How do you feel, replacing this last stone on your journey?" Melissa asks. Her hand microphone is pointed toward me. BBC Radio 4's lady listeners will be wanting to know. How do I feel as I bury the last of the rocks?

I can't think what to say, for a few seconds.

Then I say, "I feel done."

epilogue

A Wee Journey

Perched atop England like a tectonic tam-o'-shanter, Scotland is a land of stones. Standing stones. Stone circles. Roofs of stone. Walls of stone. Monuments of stone, twenty feet tall, to the horrific Scottish losses of life in World War II. Piers, cattle gates, and crofter cottages of stone. Stairs of stone, floors of stone, balconies and balustrades and buttresses of stone. Loch shores of stone. Great metal grids gripping cliff sides beside roads and paths to keep rocks from falling on people's heads. Goats resting their heads against stones, the only available pillows in pastures. Seaweed and mussels at the surf line holding on to stones for dear life. Sea otters knocking open oysters with stones. Stone walls snaking up sheer hillsides like vines up the stone sides of shepherd sheds. Stones tumbling down streambeds, rolling in the tide line, hopping down hillsides in the joyful free fall of gravity. Stones pinging off windscreens. Stones kicked up behind grazing animals. Scotland is a land of green. But the green is framed by stone gray.

I went to Scotland for a hiking trip in August 2002, seven months before my rock-returning visit to England. I had stones on my mind. I still wasn't sure about taking Frankie's rocks back. I was still carrying them around in my head. Gail Caesar, my Tobago friend, had said the rocks were a path back to my mother. She'd said they were jewels, and important. She'd urged me to return them. But skeptical, hard-case guy that I am, I still wasn't sure.

On my Scotland hike, I met John Douglas in Blair Athol in the central highlands. "They call me 'Wee John the Shepherd,' " John told me, a smile that seemed half as wide as he was tall stretched across the little man's face, and permanently stuck there, it seemed. He was a "Black Douglas," he let me know, from the Douglas clan with dark hair, not a "Red Douglas," the redheads. "The Reds tried to kill off all the Blacks back four hundred years ago, they did," he said, grinning expansively. "But they didn't get me."

Wee John had turned eighty that May but was fit and hearty. He attributed this to a lifetime of chasing sheep on slopes, breathing mountain air, drinking Scottish ales and mountain water tinted with peat. He had spent his life as a shepherd and had only recently retired. On the floor of the pub was his sheepdog, Cody. When he spoke to her it was in Gaelic. And when he did, the dog did exactly what he said.

Wee John the Shepherd knew the surrounding hills. When he heard I'd be hiking between Pitlochrie and Alberfeldy, he told me to be on the lookout for a four-thousand-year-old neolithic stone site near the hiking trail, a small circle of four standing stones and several other scattered, fallen stones partially buried, located on a hilltop in conifer forest. Keep a sharp eye, he said, because there would be no sign identifying the site, no gates or fencing, no gatekeeper.

"Good thing my mother isn't with me," I said. "Sounds like the circle would be easy pickings for her." Which got us talking about Frankie and her rocks.

I was embarrassed. I told him I felt badly my mother had taken the English rocks, and I was thinking of trying to take them back. I admitted, though, I wasn't sure this made any sense.

Wee John the Shepherd was much amused by my discomfort and seriousness. Barely suppressing an outburst of laughter, he said something in Gaelic to the dog, which rotated her ears intently listening. I imagined the mountain man said something like, "Do you see, Cody, the silliness of Americans?"

Turning to me, he said, "For the lady," meaning my mother, "the rocks were precious. It was fine to take them, because they were precious. Aye. The past was precious, and she needed to have it. Those stones weren't lost," he said, "they were saved. Aye. The stones were waiting to be picked up and carried off. And they've been waiting for you to return them to their resting places. Aye."

Then he said, "And when you go, your mother will be there, she will. She's been waiting there, aye."

Aye! This was too weird. Within six months, a middle-aged black West Indian female restaurateur and an elderly white Scottish male shepherd, two people from hemispheres and lifestyles that could hardly be more disparate, had declared with simple certainty and clarity the same basic thing: The taking of the rocks was neither disrespectful nor wrong and certainly not pointless. It was positive and poignant and a life point for me to return to my mother.

The warmth of this eighty-year-old's smile was powerful, and his steady eyes were fixed on me. "The stones were always going to come back," he said with blunt certitude, as if he were talking about full moons, or first frosts in the Grampian Mountains, or summer-fattened sheep descending in autumn from high pasture.

"They simply took a wee journey," he said.

"And they're to send you on one," he said. "Aye."

And so they did.

I confess, though, the following spring when I boarded that airliner headed for England and my wee journey, I still wasn't sold on the notion that I was taking an inevitable and important trip that would lead me to my mother. I'd been leading a life in which emotional feelings and matters of the heart had been consistently beaten back by journalism's hard facts and pragmatic life practice. The person I'd become, I guess, had left me incapable of envisioning how returning Frankie's rocks could resurrect my dead mother. I didn't hold much stock in séances. My spiritual side was full of holes.

So I took off for England mostly with a simple, literal goal: the need to right a wrong; the need to make up for something my mother did that she shouldn't have done. That was my opinion: she'd done wrong.

I quickly found during the trip, however, that people didn't much care about the crime. Many felt no wrong had really been done. I was surprised.

What seemed a widely held belief by the people I met in England was the opinion that what's done is done, what's history is history, whether going back to the seventeenth century, when old edifices were smashed up and their stones quarried by farmers for homes or walls, or back only to the mid-twentieth century, when Frankie collected mementos, a time when the environmental preservation movement was just beginning. People seemed to feel what Frankie did thirty-five years ago was less important than what we can all do now. We can honor historic places. We can fund and support efforts to preserve them. We can teach kids about sites and history and about showing respect for stone still standing at these places. What we can't do is stop the inexorable losses and decay of time, or stop history itself. And Frankie was history.

Fairly early on my trip, then, I began to see I wasn't, and couldn't, right a wrong. I couldn't fix anything. I could honor the sites. Replacing the rocks still felt like the honorable thing to be doing. But the stones didn't really fit. Not now. They had changed. The lichens and mosses were gone. In no case could a stone be replaced in the spot from where it was taken. The stones had lost all context. The sites had eroded even more since the 1960s, or had been transformed by tourism control restrictions, or their fabric had been intentionally reinforced or repaired. And Frankie's rocks had Frankie's handwriting on them. The pieces weren't the same. The sites weren't the same either.

As I traveled along, I began to understand that honoring the sites by replacing what was rightfully theirs was a minor and almost pointless exercise. Instead, and much more important, I saw myself honoring my mother. Instead of fixing something at the sites, giving them back small, long-lost pieces of themselves, I began to feel I was giving the sites she held dear small representational relics of my mother, a woman lost to me such a long, long time ago.

The rocks no longer held in themselves the spirit or history of the places. They no longer held what had drawn my mother to them and compelled her to take them. A rock might have been touched by a Roman or a Saxon or an Edwardian. Frankie could never have been sure. I'll never be sure. But I can be sure each rock was touched by Frankie. Not only touched, but spirited away and cherished. Each individual rock got a lot more reverence from Frankie than it ever got from any of the ancient peoples. Now they held only my mother—her spirit, her choice of dislocation, transoceanic travel, and new definition as hand-labeled pieces in a collection's set. I was providing the rocks' newest context, my journey back with them, to be with my mother. But this context was meaningful only for me.

By restoring the rocks to their historic sites, I intermingled Frankie's history and her story with the sites' histories and stories. A tiny bit of my mother, I can say with certainty, now dwells where King Arthur is said to have been born, where he's said to have created Camelot, where he's said to be buried. A totem of my mother is now in walls and earthworks of Beaker people and Roman conquerors and medieval knights. Several stones are now in the hands of curators who have promised to consider ways to use Frankie's rocks to teach children and future visitors lessons about respect for protected sites, illustrated by the story of one mother, one son, and one closed, circular journey.

If that's not honoring my mother, I don't know what is.

Yet honoring isn't repairing, and early in the returning of Frankie's rocks I realized I wasn't fixing anything she did. It took a while longer to comprehend that something, however, was being fixed as I wheeled around the countryside, landmark to landmark.

I began the trip with the attitude it would be a lark. I'd right a wrong, yes, but doing it would be a goof. I'd joke around with people I met and have some high-spirited, Anglo-American blended, ale-assisted fun. As it got under way, though, I was hit with an overpowering feeling of loneliness. I wasn't having fun. I became very lonely. And I stayed lonely.

I always knew I'd be a solitary traveler on this trip. But being alone and being lonely aren't the same thing. Now it seems obvious to me that the journey had to make me lonely. Because figuratively it was always a trip I was taking with Frankie, and being with Frankie in life, literally, had always felt lonely. Of course I would feel the same way traveling with her now. It couldn't be otherwise. I realize this now. But before the trip I had never connected Frankie with my deep, internal loneliness.

As I sat in the sun at Tintern, a memory came to me. I remembered Frankie participated enthusiastically in a "child-study group" when I was a child. A bunch of neighborhood mothers met every month or so to discuss common kid problems and share thoughts about solutions. Nothing, that I could see, ever came back to me from that activity. I don't believe Frankie ever brought anything home with her, any connection to me made at the group. The child-study group was all about Frankie interacting with her friends, and not about study of her child. I remember, after some of the child-study group sessions, overhearing Frankie's concern for other mothers' kids. But I never had the slightest sense that I was a cause for concern. I was quiet and reasonably well behaved. I think I was considered normal but not too bright or gifted, and well adjusted, if a bit shy. No school office notes were sent back to my parents warning them that Dana was being disruptive in the classroom. Neither were academic awards coming home. I was ordinary. So leave Dana alone. Let him be. I think she felt this. There are more pressing places to invest attention, in some cases more worthy children. And these got Frankie's attention. My emotional needs were not my mother's priority. I was alone with those.

And so I was left alone. Alone with my Dinky Toys, books, plastic customized car models; with early TV friends Buster Brown, Rin Tin Tin, Sky King, and Howdy Doody, and later with episodes of *Gunsmoke*, *The Rifleman*, and *The Untouchables*. Dana's okay, he's upstairs by himself watching *Maverick*. Leave him alone.

And so I was. And I've felt alone ever since.

Circumnavigating England with Frankie's rocks and with her memory brought the feeling of lifelong loneliness out of me, deposited it squarely in front of me, and fixed it firmly in thoughts of my childhood relationship with my mother. That had never happened before.

And so it was very emotional to be in England again with her. I often cried. In revisiting Frankie's memory, I revisited my lifelong loneliness, and what stunned me was that this felt like being with my mother. Returning Frankie's rocks took me back to feeling her presence by evoking my loneliness.

Thus the sad, lonely trip became long overdue personal repair work. It began the fixing of something inside me. And that felt very good.

Nobel Prize–winning physicist Erwin Schrödinger once said, "The present is the only thing that has no end." Another word for the present is the moment. And it's in the present—the moment someone is in, not the past, not the future—where life's splendor and meaning are revealed, and lived.

Frankie didn't understand this at all. She couldn't be in the moment and accept a moment's endless, deep beauty. She used her moments to take rocks (or photos or souvenirs), hoping physical specimens from places would connect her to their magic. She postponed the moments, trying to possess them in physical forms, hoping to relive the present later on. She squandered genuine appreciation for the sites she visited because their magnificence and very existence are only in that moment, the moments of the visits, not in rocks brought home in a box.

Returning Frankie's rocks, my time-machine journey back, underscored for me the impermanence and temporal nature of things, and in turn the importance of living in the moment.

Frankie came, Frankie left, Frankie died. So, too, all the historic sites—they were created, now they're departing and dying. We think of rock as rock-solid, permanent, forever. It isn't, of course. Except in the moment. Beyond that it's quite soft and fragile. All the sites I visited are decaying away. What Frankie did the wind does daily to the abbeys and castles. The sea scours Tintagel. Stonemason John David relentlessly replaces York Minster's fabric with new limestone pieces. Lichens worm their way through cracks in the rocks of old walls. Wind and frost and acid rain erode stone. All sorts of destruction is taking away these wonderful places. Their time will come to an end.

Frankie's effort seems to me now so futile, and so long-lost. Frankie's imperative carried nothing forward, not science, culture, or history, or her family's benefit or well-being. What drove her, what motivated her to take rocks, has come and gone like the fat, bright yellow-and-red tour buses that crunch the crushed stone of historic sites' car parks under their massive tires, disgorge scores of eager tourists, idle awhile, then scoop up their passengers, pull away, and disappear.

If only Frankie had understood that it was being at these places at the moment she was there that was important, not what could be dislodged and taken away. If only she'd had insight into this idea: Only the moment is without end, so enjoy each moment at Avebury, Tintern Abbey, Hadrian's Wall, and all the others. Truly reside in the moment, not the past, not the future. If you do, then it's possible to forever become a part of the historic sites. That's something Frankie wanted. Taking a rock home won't do it. Neither will taking a photograph. Accept no substitutes. Being there, in the moment there, is what gets you there.

I wish Frankie could have known this for a very selfish reason. She could have been with me, and would still be today, if she'd understood at the time we were together in life that only that present, those moments with me, were what mattered.

Throughout my journey returning rocks, this realization—of what never happened, of what was lost forever by Frankie's failure to reside in living moments—made me very, very sad.

So it came to this: Because her eye and attention fell instead upon English rocks, or upon all those other collections and activities, what connections of intimacy Frankie was incapable of making with me during her lifetime were instead artificially made for her, by me, on this trip. In an odd way, taking the rocks looped us together, back upon something I'm sure was truly much dearer to Frankie than pieces of stone: her son. Me. She didn't know how to show it, I guess. Or she was too distracted to show it, or in too much personal pain. Yet I'm certain it was inside her. She loved me, I've no doubt about that.

So I find myself now thankful at least for this. Frankie's taking of the rocks was pointless except in the sole way Gail Caesar and Wee John the Shepherd said it was significant: The stones represented calling cards for reintroducing me to memories of my mother. They were collected specimens that Frankie left behind from life moments lost, which motivated and enabled me to experience new and meaningful moments with her. They were tickets to travel with her, authorization tokens to spend lots of time together. They were jewels, Gail had said. Fourteen golden philosopher's stones.

It bothered me at first, as I traveled, that specific memories of my mother and me were so hard to bring to the surface. I found no broad body of memory, no sweeping recollection of the shape of days or time spent with her. I recalled little things, one here, one there, disjointed and disconnected. It seemed abnormal, to have so few memories. What, I wondered, was wrong with me?

Eventually, I realized there's nothing wrong with me. Not so far as memories are concerned. Vivid memories just don't matter. Those feelings I found traveling with Frankie's rocks, they matter. But to be concerned with memories—or the lack of them—began to look more and more like my mother's concern for her objects, her stamps or stones, unicorns or antique fans. They weren't the moment. They were items from the past. They weren't what was important.

When you rummage around in your head and unearth old memories, you're digging into a collection. That's what memories are, lifelong accumulations of miscellaneous stuff, placed in our cranial collections by mysterious synaptical file clerks who make judgments on our behalf—always arbitrary, it seems, often bizarre—of what's urgent or important enough to store away. Experience is collected. Impressions are collected. So are six facts from one fifth-grade history lesson, and not one fact from a full year of eleventh-grade social studies. Go figure.

A fair share of faces are remembered, fewer names, even fewer feelings. Taken all together, a life collection of personal memories is always unique, never the full set, full of mundane and weird things both, and frustratingly subject to loss as the years pass and memory fades. And for me, frankly, now at age fifty-eight and counting, memory is getting as foggy as what hugs the heath on a cool Dartmoor dawn.

All together, though, fading as it might be, a life's collection of memories amounts to a self-definition of a life. What we see in that assemblage of brain-bound stuff is what allows us to decide who we are. We all amount to walking *wunderkammern*. Until the day we drop dead. Then all that collecting just vaporizes.

No loss. The collection never had any significance anyway. It represented the accumulation of a lifetime. But it wasn't the life. Or the time.

It was just a collection.

I read something crucial into what both Wee John and Gail had said. I understood them to imply that by following the rock-littered path back to Frankie I would rediscover her as a person. I'm not sure now, in retrospect, that either Gail or John actually said this. Both had said the rocks would lead me back to her, but that's not saying I should expect to find her standing at the ancient English sites. In the early stages of my trip, though, being such a literal kind of guy, I kept waiting for Frankie to pop up in front of me, if not in three-dimensional, high-contrast living color, then at least as an ethereal, ghostlike apparition.

When she just wasn't showing up in human form all on her own, I tried to help her. I'd shut my eyes and squeeze my temples and think hard of Frankie. Sometimes I was able to force a shadowy image of her to appear for me. Having photos of her helped. I could imagine Frankie at some of the rock places, in a wispy way. The images didn't seem very authentic, though. I would see her in the same pose as one of the photographs in my suitcase or one of my photos of her at home. I realized I was just cutting and pasting her face and form into wherever I happened to be. Straining to see my mother at the Dover pharos where she'd been thirty-six years earlier and where I was at that moment was like trying to see the Roman lighthouse firekeeper two thousand years ago come back again. The Roman I imagine ends up looking an awful lot like the drawing of the Roman in the mural at the visitors' center.

Memory is an odd thing. Memory isn't history. It isn't accurate. It's quite selective, not one thing objective or impartial about it. In remembering a mother, then, the best you can expect is a hazy, distorted visage of Mum filtered by powerful past preconceptions, hurts, experiences, and biases. She doesn't come up freshly formed at York Minster or Corfe or Bodiam Castle. She'd once been at these places. But she'd left. She wasn't preserved in their moments. I never found the face or body or spirit of Frankie at any of the fourteen sites I visited.

But Wee John and Gail Caesar, I think, hadn't meant that I would. The path back to Frankie wasn't the route to a ghost. It was a way back to her, yes, they were right. But what I think they both understood, which I didn't, is that the person I'd rediscover on this journey would be myself.

I made contact with my deep-seated loneliness in Dover, along the crag at Hadrian's Wall, on the bluff above the sea at Tintagel, and all along my trip. I rediscovered and examined my lifelong sadness, sitting with Frankie's rocks and her memory at site after site. As the trip progressed, out of the loneliness and sadness emerged the love I had for Frankie. I realized how strong it was, how bottled inside me it had been, and how much I had yearned both to feel her love for me and express my love to her.

Taking the rocks back brought me back to my mother because it took me back to my love for her and to all the feelings about her I'd spent a lifetime holding inside.

She came alive not because of the rocks replaced or because of a ghost who appeared. She came alive for me because the journey brought to life feelings inside me.

Not memories.

Feelings.

Feelings from deep inside me, disconnected from Frankie for nearly a lifetime, reconnected for me on this odd road, returning Frankie's rocks.

acknowledgments

The most vital person to me in preparing this book was my father. At age ninety-two, his memory isn't as sharp as it once was, for sure. But over the course of several years at work on this, the many sessions spent with pen and notebook, sitting with my dad—reflecting on and recollecting Frankie, his life with her, and our shared lives together—were a truly great help. His guidance was clear, his honesty striking, his insights invaluable. And just as doing this book reconnected me emotionally to my mother, so too, I think, the introspective time spent with my father brought us much closer together. At any point in life, there can be no greater gift.

Both my brother, Doug, and cousin Nancy Crisona also contributed valuable thoughts and impressions, as did a variety of Frankie's close friends. Thank you all.

Geologist and friend Jon Nickerson put his loupe and trained eye upon Frankie's rocks before I returned them, and Dr. Abraham Dietz, another friend, carefully considered my mother's migraine records and treatments. Their professional comments were very helpful. Thanks, guys.

On the road in England, I met many preservationists at the sites I visited. Many of them are named in this book. As a group, I was consistently struck by the passion these folks possess for their jobs, the caring they show for their country's antiquities, and by the open, friendly interest they showed in my mission and the help they gave me. Britain's treasures are in good hands, and its citizens are fortunate to have such men and women holding the nation's heritage so close to their hearts.

Few books make it to print unless people beyond the writer believe in it. I was fortunate to find an agent, Stacey Glick, and an editor, Terri Hennessy, who both believed in *Returning Frankie's Rocks* and provided me professional guidance in crafting it. Thank you both.

And finally, I want to thank Egila Lex and her wonderful children, Léonie and Aristide, for their years-long support, encouragement, patience, and belief in my book. Thank you. This is a book about closeness and love, and our closeness and love has meant everything to me.

sources and recommended reading

Blom, Philipp. *To Have and to Hold: An Intimate History of Collectors and Collecting.* Woodstock and New York: The Overlook Press, 2003.

Bragg, Rick. *All Over but the Shoutin'.* New York: Vintage Books, 1997.

Brown, Bill. "The Collecting Mania." *University of Chicago Magazine* online, October 2001.

Bryson, Bill. *Notes from a Small Island.* New York: Perennial, 2001.

Elsner, John, and Roger Cardinal. *The Cultures of Collecting.* Cambridge, Mass.: Harvard University Press, 1994.

Lowenthal, David. *The Past Is a Foreign Country.* Cambridge: Cambridge University Press, 1985.

Lynch, Bohun. *Collecting: An Essay.* New York: Harper & Brothers, 1928.

Mann, Nicholas R. *The Isle of Avalon.* St. Paul, Minn.: Llewellyn Publications, 1996.

Meyer, Karl E. *The Plundered Past.* New York: Atheneum, 1973.

Muensterberger, Werner. *Collecting: An Unruly Passion.* New York: Harcourt Brace, 1994.

Muensterberger, Werner. "The Quest for Possessions." In *Pictures, Patents, Monkeys, and More . . . On Collecting.* New York: Independent Curators International, 2001.

Nicholson, Geoff. *Hunters and Gatherers.* Woodstock and New York: The Overlook Press, 1994.

Orlean, Susan. *The Orchid Thief.* New York: Ballantine Books, 2000.

Pearce, Susan M. *Museums, Objects, and Collections: A Cultural Study.* Leicester: Leicester University Press, 1992.

Rheims, Maurice. *The Strange Life of Objects.* New York: Abrams, 1977.

Schaffner, Ingrid. "On Collecting." In *Pictures, Patents, Monkeys, and More . . . On Collecting.* New York: Independent Curators International, 2001.

Thorson, Robert M. *Stone by Stone: The Magnificent History of New England's Stone Walls*. New York: Walker, 2004.

Treasures of Britain. London: Drive Publications Ltd., for Automobile Association, 1968.

Wainwright, Clive. *The Romantic Interior: The British Collector at Home, 1750–1850*. New Haven, CT: Yale University Press, 1989.

Weschler, Lawrence. *Mr. Wilson's Cabinet of Wonder: Pronged Ants, Horned Humans, Mice on Toast, and Other Marvels of Jurassic Technology*. New York: Vintage Books, 1995.

Winchester, Simon. *The Map That Changed the World: William Smith and the Birth of Modern Geology*. New York: HarperCollins, 2001.

about the author

Dana Hornig has been a print journalist for over thirty years, including twenty years as editor and co-owner of *The Register,* a weekly Cape Cod newspaper. Recently he has been freelance writing and editing, producing videos for environmental groups, and working on his second book. His passions include Caribbean islands and culture, sailing a twenty-eight-foot Cape Dory sloop on Nantucket Sound, and remaining a leading hitter on the softball team he founded in 1968, The Radish. He is single, and lives with his cat, Bishop, on Cape Cod.